he Autobiography of
MICHAEL PAUL STERLING
tional Bestseller

705.3

MAN
CHILD
IN THE NOT SO PROMISED LAND

ARPress

MAN
CHILD

IN THE NOT SO PROMISED LAND

Apostle Michael P. Sterling

ARPress
ILLUMINATING IDEAS
EMPOWERING VOICES

ARPress
45 Dan Road Suite 5
Canton MA 02021
Hotline: 1(888) 821-0229
Fax: 1(508) 545-7580

Ordering Information:
Quantity sales. Special discounts are available on quantity purchases by corporations, associations, and others. For details, contact the publisher at the address above.

Printed in the United States of America.

ISBN-13: Softcover   979-8-89330-939-3
          eBook   979-8-89330-938-6

Library of Congress Control Number: 2024902449

CONTENTS

DEDICATION

I, Michael Paul Sterling, dedicate my life story to the poor widow Bessie Parthenia McDowell who adopted this man child into her Christian family. She was the chief intercessor and prayer warrior for me her wayward son. I knew if it had not been for effectual, ferverent prayers, and the moaning and groanings that I heard in the midnight hours I would not be here to write this book. Mama Bessie I love and miss you so much. It would have been wonderful if you could have seen me preach just one day before going to heaven, thirty-eight years and counting.

This book is also dedicated to Chaplain Gregory Payson who visited me often in the county jail during the year I was there on my way to prison. He helped to turn my life around. Upon my release from prison he triained me at the San Bernardino County Hospital as a Chaplain.

To Pastor Raul Genera, my pastor and mentor, who I served as an armorbearer for several years. A special shout out to Pastor Fabie Genera who made sure I had everything I needed when I opened the first men and women's home under their ministry.

And, to my big sister Claudia Marshall, now a bishop, who stood by me every step of the way and is still standing. Words can not express the love and gratitude I have for you.

Last, but not least, to all my children who loved me as I walked out Matthew 6:33 "Seek first the Kingdom of God and its righteous."

Jakuma Yashen Sterling

Leoshie Mims

Rascheed Sterling

Brandon Sterling*, who as a grown man said, I owe him 20 years.*

Desirea Sterling

Kai Alexander Sterling

Chrystal Vaugh

TO ALL MY GRANDCHILDREN…

Alexia Sterling

Malcolm Mims, Jr.

Rascheed Sterling, Jr.

Tasia Sterling

Oshieana Mims

Malia Mims

Ziona Sterling

Zeila Sterling

Savanagh Sterling

Michael Justice Sterling (name sake)

Damon Sterling Amina Yasen Sterling

Amanirena Nicole Sterling

ACKNOWLEDGEMENT

Special thank you to Dr. John and Janice Bowden who allowed me to stay in their mansion, in the upper room, for over two months where I wrote over a third of this book. Their kindness will never be forgotten. Without their love and support this project would still be in the archives of my mind.

FOREWORD

This is a redemptive story filled with truth, and historical accounts of social injustice, racial conflicts, childhood histories and miraculous events that shaped the life of the author. The significance of prophetic people such as Mama Bessie and Reverend Moss, who pray and influenced the destiny of children is a familiar story to many who have experienced a challenging childhood and lived to express it. The writer, in his own style, tells his story and recalls the significant events and times that shaped and delivered him and ultimately brought him into the ministry. This story is told without the anger or personal indictments that so often accompany such accounts. Apostle Sterling brings us into his journey and allows us to experience the challenges, disappointments, surprises and the victories. From the beginning to the end of this work there is a tone of redemption and thanksgiving. I was privileged to be a brief part of this journey and I recommend this work because of the fruit of the author.

Dr. Kirby Clements
Presiding Archbishop of The International
Communion of Charismatic Churches

TESTIMONIES

I've observed my spiritual father reign triumphant despite the hardships that once threatened to dismantle the man that God created him to be. His authoring of this book has been the amalgamation of all of his victories, eloquently written in servitude of our Lord and Savior. May this book serve as a looking glass into the totality of who he is as a spiritual father, leader and man of God.

Your Spiritual Daughter,
Dr. Antwainett the Prophetess Richmond
Prelate East Coast Division KOGAPMI

I met Apostle Sterling in a Founder's Day service over ten years ago, and he said to me "Come let's talk", not knowing that I was praying and seeking a spiritual father. When he began to speak I heard the Spirit of the Lord say, "This is your father, humble yourself unto him.", and I did.

Its been a blessing being under his leadership as a son. I've traveled many places with him and gleaned many things. I was ordained a Bishop over the Southern region of California under his leadership, and received the gift of prophecy from an impartation according to Romans 1:11, received my Bachelor's degree in Chritian Counscling, a Master's in Theology and I'm working on a Doctorate through the Kingdom of God Bible College foundcd by Apostle Sterling.

His Voice Christian Ministries is honored to be part of KOGAPMI. I thank God for Apostle Sterling because of the fathering spirit he walks in, and his true anointing of an Apostle, of which I am proud to be one of his spiritual sons.

Bishop T. Redmond
Founder His Voice Christian Ministries

Bishop, Southern California District KOGAPMI

Man Child In The Not So Promised Land is a provocative and compelling Autobiography of a young man experiencing life through the eyes of a child, while watching history unfold. Truly riveting Sterling describes his early years, which ultimately prepared him for a life of humility and the clery, which also led him down a path of misconceptions as to what and who he was. The inference of racial injustice is skillfully presented. The occurrences of the story are emphatically sobering. Sterling's encounters in black versus white and black on black clashes climax instinctively in scenes of violence followed by a retreat both literally and figuaratively. Expletives of similar experiences have been told previously but never with such transparency, sincerity or power. This is Sterling's second novel as he demonstrates complete control of his story in his style, the first was "Upon This Rock." Absolutely a must read!

Dr. René Pryor

International Evangelist

Ambassador KOGAPMI

NOTE FROM THE CO-EDITOR

In the autumn of 2018, I was asked to edit Apostle Sterling's life story. His life journey is beyond anything I ever expected to read – much less edit! I am a white woman who was reared by a loving, wonderful mother who was my best friend. I had many opportunities and advantages. I had difficult times that I have written about, but nothing I have ever read can begin to compare with this man's life story. It is a mighty story about poverty, hatred, self-reliance, resourcefulness, and the grace and mercy of our Lord to watch over a wayward man and the prayers of his "adopted" Mama Bessie that kept him alive.

I knew practically nothing about Watts, California, except that it was south of where I lived as a teenager in Westwood – next to Beverly Hills. A world away from Watts.

We are all "products" of our family and environment. As children that is all we know. Watts was Michael's world. A world of hardship, violence, crime and the struggle to stay alive. He learned to be tough in order to survive. And he was as tough as they come. By the grace and mercy of God, he survived to become a man after God's own heart and a blessing to all who are fortunate to know him and be part of his ministry.

For those readers who are older, we read in the newspaper about the Black Panther's and crime, but how could we relate to it – if we are white middle class Americans. We don't know about what it feels like to be hated and mistreated, just because we are born of a different race.

As you read his incredible story, put yourself in that position and what you would have to do to survive in a vastly different culture. I lived in Montgomery, AL when the Selma March came there. Dr. Martin Luther King's church was across the street from the Alabama Supreme Court where my husband was the law clerk to the Chief

Justice. I was Vice President of the PTA when our school was the first desegregated school in the U.S. As a Christian, I had great compassion and always showed kindness to the black people of our city, but never struggled for survival as they had to do. When the river flooded, the women of our church were the first ones to collect clothes, supplies and record the names of those who lost their homes and we helped in these tangible ways. Compassion and concern is something all of us should have. But that is far removed from having any idea what life is like for them. May Apostle Michael Sterling's book cause you to look deeply into your own heart and stir within you a greater love and compassion for those who are different from you. Your city is your mission field to show the love of our Savior.

Diane M Blacker,

Author *The Spiritual Roots of Abusive Relationships*

INTRODUCTION

The *Man Child In The Not So Promised Land* is a riveting indictment of a nations failure to provide equal justice, equal protection, or equal opportunities to a young black male population. Surely the words of life, liberty and the pursuit of happiness seem as foreign as Tiananmen Square in China. The etchings seen throughout the halls of justice and the bedrock of our civilization are mere imprints of hypocrisy. We find that this dream, the American dream, is as bleak as the Valley of Death, or the Mohave desert, whose lack of water or vegetation, provides no hope or life for a thriving young black populous. The tears of humanity are crying out for justice much like Abel's blood was, after he was slain by Cain, his brother.

There are many that have languished, suffered, and perished along Liberty's path only to find road blocks of hatred, racism and white supremacy. These names are just a drop in the bucket of those that America has failed to serve or to protect from racism, hatred and even fear. These famous and infamous heroes of our struggle are a small sampling of America's history, whose real story is yet unfolding, on the very streets of our cities, no longer to be hidden or left unchecked.

Give me liberty or give me death shall once again be the battle cry of a people whose reparations are long overdue. The name of a few that have paid with their lives, while reaching for the sun, are people such as James Byrd, Jr., Medgar Evers, Little Bobby Hutton, Tyesha Miller, Elmer Pratt, the Scottsboro Boys, Fred Hampton, Mark Clark, Alprentice (Bunchy) Carter, John Higgins, the Rev. Nathaniel Turner, Martin Luther King, Jr., Trevon Martin, Michael Brown, Tookie Williams, Marcus Garvey, Huey P. Newton, Elderidge Cleaver, H. Rap Brown, Sandra Blan, Malcolm X, and the list goes on and on. Their blood cries out from the ground along with the millions of slaves, that were emasculated, torn from their families, raped by their slave masters, mutilated, beat with whips, conspired against, thrown off slave ships, drowned, castrated, hung, tarred and feathered, dragged behind cars, sodomized, injected with syphilis, falsely imprisoned and shot down while unarmed.

This is the handwritten account and true life story of Michael Paul Sterling whose embryonic stage of growth and development was hidden by Sister Bessie MacDowell (Mama Bessie). Through her prayers and intercession, in the city of Riverside California. Yes Bessie Parthenia Mac Dowell adopted this man child while doing maid work for Judge Rex Escondido. As you read the polarizing and shocking events of this man child's life, and how he was protected along life's hazardous roads, you must figure out for yourselves, was this luck, coincident, or the divine hand of God, that choose to protect one sperm cell, out of millions, that were swimming for life. Many of the true accounts, are so fascinating and almost unbelievable. As you read, this story of survival, in the asphalt jungles called America, remember...STILL I RISE! Now, where should I start?

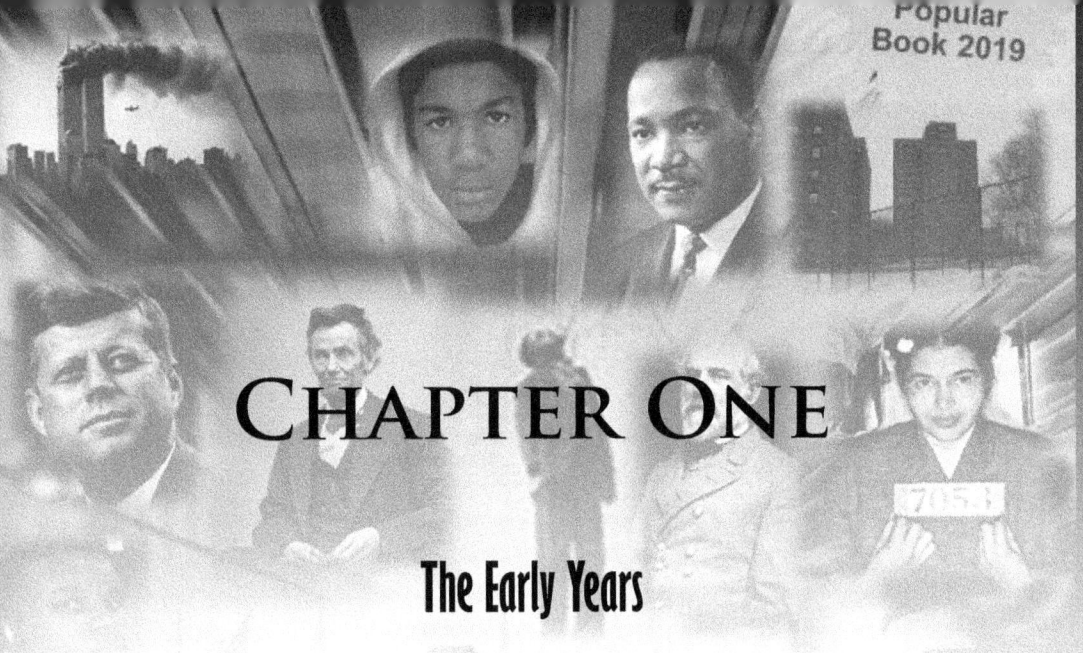

CHAPTER ONE

The Early Years

I t was a bright and sunny day as this skinny little 5-year-old boy attended his first day of class at Ritter Elementary School in the heart of Watts, California. They had the biggest cookies I had ever seen! My time at Ritter was short lived as you will see when I tell you what happened next. One day this classmate of mine, and his older brother, tried to Baby Bully me saying they were going to get me after school. I stood in the regular spot where my mother picked me up every day, and here they came. My mother was running late. The older one grabbed me and my classmate hit me once and started to hit me again. Boom, bam, the older kid fell to the ground and my classmate ran away crying. As I looked up, to my amazement, there stood Leonard Edward Sterling, my big brother. It was good having a big brother for a short time. I was born in East L.A. Eliso Village, but grew up in the Inland Empire, Riverside and San Bernardino counties. I would come back to Watts, California at 113th & Grape where we had a Black Panther chapter some twelve years later.

My real mother, Gloria Hilton, now deceased, drove up in a white 1955 Chevy, with a 3-speed stick in the floor. You could hear her coming a mile away. She picked me up and we drove to our house. The police were standing in the front with the landlord. Our front door was wide open and they were throwing our belongings on the grass. In wonderment, I watched my mother beg and plead with that "old cracker" to no avail. She dragged the couch to the curb and sat me on it. She told me not to move and that my older brother, Leonard, would be there soon. My mother gave me a bottle of Mother Pride strawberry soda, jumped in that Chevy and drove off.

It was about 45 minutes before my brother, Leonard, showed up. These days they would have locked her up for child abandonment. Life was so much simpler back then. Leonard was only 7, and I was glad to see him. I told him what had happened and gave him the envelope that Mama left in my care. We just sat there until my 9-year-old sister, Gwen, arrived. I called her "Gwenie." She was my favorite throughout my formative years. A couple hours later, Sandy arrived from practice and took the envelope with the money. The three of us proceeded to the taco stand on the corner. Can you believe that on Fridays a person could get 5 tacos for a dollar? We ate well that evening as we hurried back to find Leonard, who had fallen asleep on the couch.

It started to get dark and I was cold and began to cry as we sat on the couch. The night became eerie as four little children crouched together on a dark and lonely street. Gwen became so agitated she began to scream "I'm not staying here all night." We needed to walk to "big mama's" house a few blocks away. Our family still has that house. Sandy began to shout that "we're not going anywhere - it's too far" and I began to cry again. Leonard grabbed my hand as the two girls began to argue back and forth. The moon began its journey into the midnight sky and the night wind began to howl as it whistled through the trees of despair. As four little children sat alone in a lost and dying world. I had fallen asleep and was awakened by the sound of that old '55 Chevy. I didn't know if it was a bad muffler, but it sure was good to hear it coming. Mama Gloria drove up and there seemed to be a strange car following behind her.

What happened next would change my life and I would not see any of my brothers or sisters for several years. Suddenly, my mom, Gloria, jumped out of the car, grabbed a paper bag and threw some of my belongings in it. She placed me in the back seat of that white Riveria with a strange looking man that I would later call Daddy Moss. He was the Rev. L.B. Moss of Park Avenue Baptist Church. As we drove off, I started to sob and his soft gentle voice began to comfort me. I fell fast asleep only to awaken in Riverside, California at 2791 9th Street where Mama Bessie lived. She raised this *Man Child In The Not So Promised Land*. Mama Bessie was no relation to us and Mama Gloria had never met her. Several years had passed when Mama Bessie and I were awakened by a telephone call from my oldest Sister, Claudia. She called to tell us that Mama Gloria had a nervous breakdown.

One day I was playing on the porch when Rev. Moss drove up in his white Riveria, The door swung open and out jumped Gwenie. It was one of the happiest days of my life. Life was good with Mama Bessie. I remember that she worked as a maid for several years for a Judge. Later on, she opened a babysitting agency at our house. There was one boy I remember distinctly, Joseph Jamerson. He was my age and he and his mother, Mrs. Lee, went to the same church as we did. We grew up together. He was also one of the kids who would be bussed to Pachappa Elementary School.

Joseph went on to U.S.C. and I went on to the University of the Streets. We would not see each other again until the age of 60. The details of that story will unfold throughout this book. There was also a friend named Donnie, who I saw again once in Juvenile Hall. And Michael McKnight, now deceased, who would become my armor bearer later in life. We traveled across the country through many states and counties including Niagara Falls, by way of Lookout Mountain in Tennessee, the ATL, and I surely cannot forget The Klan Cemetery in South Carolina. Yes! Michael McKnight was my dedicated son to the ministry.

The Assassination of Martin Luther King, Jr.

It was April 4, 1968 - right before my 14th birthday. I was playing in the front yard of the house in Riverside, which is about 54 miles south east of Los Angeles. The loud cry from the living room area is a sound that I would long remember. The sound seemed to be full of anguish, despair, horror and unbelief. It caused me to literally freeze in my tracks. Sobs of pain echoed from my house.

Suddenly, old lady Turner, who was an Eastern Star, was screaming at the top of her lungs. She was a deaconess at the Second Baptist

Church and among the social elite. She prophesied to me when I was 12, that I would be a preacher. Now, she was screaming so loud I thought the world was coming to an end.

Simultaneously, Miss Frenchie, our next-door neighbor, began to scream "They shot him. I can't believe they shot him." As I ran up the porch steps, inside the living room, I saw my mom on her knees sobbing. She was saying, "Oh God, please no! Oh God, not him."

On the Black and white TV Walter Cronkite was saying, "News Flash! In Memphis, Tennessee the Rev. Martin Luther King, Jr. has been assassinated. I repeat, the Rev. Martin Luther King, Jr. has been assassinated." As I sat looking at the TV, scenes were flashing from the Lorraine Motel and excerpts from Dr. King's various speeches. Right then and there my mind was made up. The prophecy from old lady, Turner would be nullified. I thought to myself, "And you want me to be a preacher? I think not!" That day will be forever etched in the memory bank of my soul. On April 4th, 1968, they killed the King – Martin Luther King, Jr., a Prophet of God.

When Dr. King, the Civil Rights leader was assassinated, America began to burn. In over 100 cities they was rioting and looting. Throughout Chicago, the slogan, "Burn Baby Burn", rang. (It was initiated by Hunter Hancock of Los Angeles). In Washington D.C., which seemed to be hit worse, there were 28 blocks of looting and rioting. It was 6 days of unrest following Dr. King's assassination. Next was Baltimore, followed by Louisville, Kentucky. America was on fire.

Now remember, I was 13, about to turn 14 years old and the epitome of the Man-Child by this time of my life. I had been bused to Pachappa Elementary School in Riverside. Yes, I was bussed to the all-white school across the tracks with Jeffery Norris and Joseph Jamerson. This was one of the worst programs that was initiated by all the white liberals. We had rocks thrown at the bus, we were pushed and shoved, and they made us go to the back of the line. This was not Birmingham, Alabama nor Georgia. It was Riverside, California where we were harassed, called "niggers" and "chocolate drops."

The term "Nigger" was familiar because of something that happened several years prior. I will come back to Pachappa after I explain my first encounter with the word "Nigger", after a short sidebar.
NOW WHAT HAPPENED WAS...

My Hispanic friend, David Albetres and I were invited over to a little blonde hair, blue eyed, white girl's house for milk and cookies. It was just a few blocks from Longfellow Elementary School in the neighborhood. I must have been about 8 years old. It was a beautiful day in America and all seemed right with the world. On Donna's big porch there was a swing and chairs. Donna went into the house as David and I laughed like two children without a care in the world. I could hear Donna tell her mother, "I have some friends here. Can I bring out some milk and cookies?" The smell of the ginger coming through the front door was wonderful.

Donna came running out and she flopped on the porch swing right next to me. We assumed that her mom was coming out right behind her with the milk and cookies. The front door opened and Donna's mother appeared with a tray in her hand and her expression went from sweet and beautiful to rage and anger. She shouted, "Get that nigger off my porch." I had never heard the term nigger, nor did I understand its meaning, and I started looking around for the "nigger." It became one of the worst days of my life as she threw the tray at me. I had just missed the kick of her foot as I scurried off the porch and ran home with tears running down my cheeks.

Now let's go back to Pachappa Elementary School, where about 25 Black kids were forced to attend because of the new integration policy. I understand that the schools in the south were deprived, lacked books, and materials, but Longfellow was a good school. It was not poor or dilapidated. There were white kids, Black kids, Mexican-American kids, and blue eyed Donna less I forget. By the way, she never ate lunch with me again.

My cousin, Jeffery Norris, was bused that year with me to Pachappa and there was this kid named Brian Bayliss. Brian was the worst one when it came to giving us hell. If we were playing kick ball, he would take the ball. If we played tether ball, he would stand in the way. He would always talk about this was his school. When we would tell the teachers, they would say to simply wait our turn.

One day Brian pushed my cousin Jeffery down and Jeffery started to cry. That was the day I whipped my first Baby Bully. He was the toughest on the playground. After the fight, to my surprise, they left us alone for the rest of the year. Hum! I learned a valuable lesson. Cut off the head and the snake will die. This is not an absolute, but it is definitely plausible in some situations.

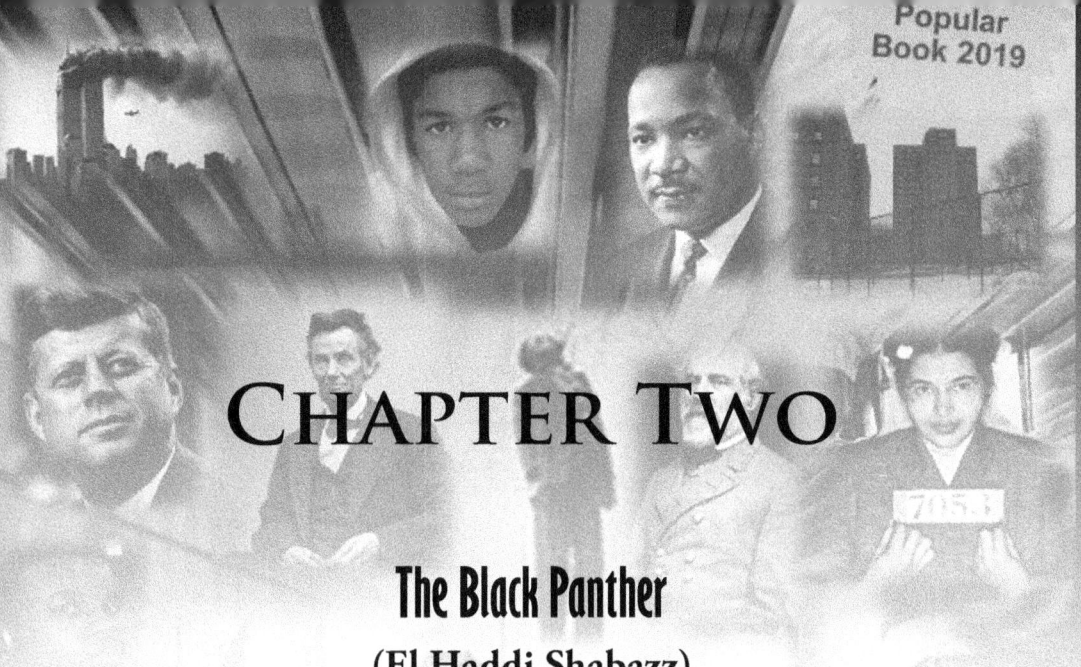

CHAPTER TWO

The Black Panther

(El Haddi Shabazz)

On a cool summer night one of my best friends, Ronnie Butts (aka Poor Little Corpse) and I were strolling up Park Ave. smoking on some Acapulco Gold. It was in the middle of the week and the pool hall and gambling shack were close. All of a sudden, a red Volvo drove up and a big-headed man, with a Black tam, and a Black leather jacket jumped out the car. I thought it was strange to wear a Black Leather Jacket on a summer night. He put a poster on the pool hall door. What it said was fascinating, and the pictured showed a light skinned brother with the same tam on, who also sported a leather jacket, sitting in a huge bamboo chair, holding a riot pump shot gun. The poster read "Free Huey." As I was staring at the picture, I heard Ronnie shout to the big-headed man, "Who in the hell is Huey?"

His reply was, "He is the Minister of Defense of the Black Panther Party." They were trying to kill him along with Bobby Seals, the Chairman. As I ran up to the gambling shack steps and approached the door, the poster had a brother sitting in the electric chair. I shouted, "Who is he and what did he do?" Then the big-headed man turned around and said with a big smile, "I am El Haddi Shabazz" the Captain of the New Riverside Chapter of the Black Panther Party. They are having a meeting on Dwight Street on Wednesday of next week." Ronnie and I assumed the man would be there. I came to find out later it was a P.E. meeting. The first of many I would attend. Yes, Political Education meeting to help a brother understand the degradation, murder, incarceration and the ultimate demise of the Black man.

By this time in my life I was beginning to hate white people even though the Black Panthers did not aspire to that philosophy. It was my upbringing and all that had happened in my life which was causing the erosion of any human concept of equality that I did not see. I was excited about the upcoming meeting. I can vividly remember that night as we walked into the meeting. Incense was burning and "Love Theme" from Spartacus, by Yusef Lateef, was playing on the record player. Everyone was sitting around with an expectation as if something great was about to take place. Brother Shabazz came from behind the beaded doorway. His infectious smile lit up the entire room as he eagerly welcomed all the attendees. "All power to the people" was his cry as he began to repeat it, again and again. "All power to the people." Those words became infectious.

The whole room started shouting, "All power to the people." The first lesson taught was on excerpts from Malcolm X. Then, Frantz Fanon quotations from MAO, commonly known as the "Red Book." After several weeks of classes, Ronnie and I joined the Black Panther National Committee to combat Fascism. I was soon sporting a Black leather jacket, blue shirt, Black pants and a Black beret. I started feeling really good about myself at 6 feet, 190 lbs., facial hair and now 16 years old, but looked every bit of 19.

There was just one problem. In class, they would ask everyone to read. When it came to my turn, I would refuse and they never pushed me until after I joined. Ronnie and I began to spend more and more time there and sometimes even days. El Haddi Shabazz had us spellbound with the revolutionary rhetoric. He served it as if he was Rembrandt himself. I was the canvas upon which these ideological prose had begun to develop a freedom fighter that would stand against injustice for all eternity. The Black Panther has been born. It wasn't long before I stopped going home altogether. Mama Bessie and I had a big blow out over a blue-eyed Jesus. **WELL, WHAT HAPPENED WAS...**

One Sunday morning while Mama Bessie was gone to church, I slipped into the house after having been away a couple of weeks. I went to the house to pick up some clothes and money, which she always left for me on top of the dresser. She always made sure I had some money. Anyway, I walked in the living room only to see the blue-eyed Jesus still hanging on the wall. I immediately took Him down, threw Him under the bed and put up a poster of Huey P. Newton sitting in that famous wicker chair with the shot gun. I had gathered some belongings, placed them at the door, and went into the kitchen only to find some of Mama Bessie's famous hot water cornbread and some chili beans and rice. It wasn't that I was hungry because we ate well at the headquarters. If you ever had the chance to taste Mama Bessie's hot water corn bread, chili-beans and rice, you would understand!

As I finished my plate of food, I heard a loud scream at the door. I've stayed too long I said to myself. Mama Bessie was home from church and yelled, "Michael Paul where is my Jesus?" I could hear her screaming "Where is my Jesus"! I said, "Probably still in heaven according to you." She replied, "If you do not get my Jesus and put him back on my wall and take that Black nigger down!" I said, "Mama, I thought you said Black folks were not niggers." And then she hit me with a broom." She screamed "Give me my Jesus." I stood my ground shouting some of the new revolutionary jargon I had learned until she began to cry. "Where is my Jesus?" Well that did it! I did not mean to make Mama cry. I immediately took Huey down and reluctantly put Jesus back up and walked out the door. I would not come home or see Mama Bessie again for a couple of years. I don't even remember Christmas coming during that time...*Man Child In The Not So Promised Land*.

The Riverside Chapter began to grow rapidly and one day this beautiful brown skinned sister, with blonde hair about an ½ inch long pulled me to the side. She said, "Young Blood, it's going to be me and you every day for the next 6 months at 4 a.m. every morning, to meet here in the kitchen." This young lady was the epitome of "Sister Soldier." Her name was Primo as she would become a great influence in my life. She must have been about 24 years old at the time and she was a "looker." At the very first 4 a.m. meeting she said, "Young Blood you are a genius. The white man has denied you of your heritage

9

that created dynasties, kingdoms, and empires. Your ancestors built the Great Pyramids of Africa. I see the bloodline of a great African Prince in your future!"

Then, she shoved a 6th grade book in my hand and told me to read the first page. I stumbled over every word at 16 years old and could not read "Run. See spot run." But something rose up in me that day, it was that genius gene. I believe that in every human being there is a genius gene just waiting to be activated. Once I started to learn how to read I rapidly began to devour literature. My comprehension became outstanding. I read books like Franz Fanon's, "Wretched of the Earth", "Black Skin White Mask", Eldridge Cleaver's "Soul on Ice", Malcolm X's Autobiography, Che- Guevara, MaoTse-tung, The Red book, and Karl Marx Dialectical Materialism.

In 6 months, I could read on a high school level, memorizing and quoting speeches. It was like a whole new world had opened for me. I also learned how to shoot. We would go to Perris, California where we had set up our own gun range. I could take a 9 millimeter apart in the dark and put it back together. I was very proficient in weapon training but there was this one young lady that could out shoot us all. Her name was Tyra Scott and she was the finest woman I had ever seen. Oh, my goodness! There was Taki, Margo and my girl, "Asheka." Her husband, John, "a-wanna-be" also became one of my tutors, but he made one mistake. He took me to his house. **AND, WHAT HAPPENED WAS…**

Loretta Newman, A.K.A. "Asheka"

Now listen closely! I was a big 16-year-old "man-child" and had developed into a hard core revolutionary. My proficiency in the Red Book got so strong they later changed my name from "Young Blood" to… well, I'll save that for a later chapter. First, let's talk about "Asheka", who was my first love. She was about 20 or 21 years old and they had a one bedroom apartment behind U.C.R. College off University Ave, in the city of Riverside. John, her husband, tutored me in English literature and grammar. He started leaving me at his house and I began my "MACK-caroni" and swept her off her feet. She didn't have a chance. I was in full effect. She was young and impressionable. I was tall, dark and well, a light skinned, handsome dude with an afro flowing or blowing in the wind.

John was a nerd who I soon sent packing out of his apartment. I had found my first real woman. This ebony queen and I made passionate love throughout the summer. Surely, this "man-child" had become more man than child. As I caressed her ebony thighs while raising her butt cheeks in my hands and ravishing her with the love and passion of a Mandingo warrior. We danced throughout the night as rhythm and poetry captured our momentum while the ecstasy of love dripped from the sweat of our bodies. I pounded the drum beat of an ancient land. She sighed and mooned her approval and later confessed that was the first time she climaxed. Moving right along…

On the next few pages, I am making a serious effort to tell the whole truth and nothing but the truth without opening old wounds or getting someone in trouble. Most of the collaborators are dead and gone. This is the very reason it took so long to write this Autobiography. Asheka is already shaking in her boots because she became a professional with the school district. She has now retired. I saw her at a 50-year class reunion at the Radisson Hotel in Ontario, CA. She had the audacity to apologize to me for having an affair with a 16-year-old boy. She must have forgotten that I was the "man-child" that swept her off her feet. How could she resist.

She was not the only grown woman that Young Blood had mesmerized back in the day. There was Mickey, who was 23 years old. She gave birth to one of my sons on the QT. I thought you knew, now you do… the bitter sweet life in the depths of the Hood had caused me to grow up way too fast. It seems I missed the socially acceptable adolescent years. I was learning a lot about life, women, racism, crime and the revolution. In reflecting, the Black Panther Party had a profound impact on my life.

The Police Raid

It was an early morning raid on the Dwight Street headquarters of the Black Panther Party National Committee to combat fascism. I was around the corner at Taka Bare house on Douglas Street. It was our safe house. The Black Panther youth were there. Each one of us was assigned to babysit one night out of the week. It was simply my turn.

In some kind of way, I was protected, by the prayer of an intercessor; Mama Bessie McDowell. I remember coming out of the safe house about 10 a.m., as two police cars passed along 12th Street. They paid little to no attention in my direction. I later found out this was the round up crew and the last to leave the raid that had taken place. I went back inside and began to cleanup for the day as I had a strange feeling.

My mind wondered where was my replacement. We were supposed to change shifts between 10 and 11a.m. every day. I strolled back outside and a neighbor shouted, "They didn't get you?" I replied, "Didn't get me what?" The neighbor continued with, "They took everybody to jail about 6 a.m. this morning." I started running towards the headquarters. As I approached the house in the middle of the block, I could feel the sun blistering over my head and the heartbeat of an uncertain fear. I could plainly see the front door had been broken down and the place was a mess. Tears filled my eyes as I quickly shook my head and squared my shoulders. I told myself that I will not have one more tear fall this day. ***Man Child In The Not SoPromised Land.***

The next thing I did was grab the record player with an extension cord and placed it on the porch. I turned it on and played Elaine Brown's record "Seize the Time – Black Panther Party." I can still remember the words even to this day. At the age of 60 years old, the "man-child" is now a grandfather with 10 grandchildren; Alexia the oldest and Michael Justice Sterling the youngest. Who would have thought it was Elaine Brown's

"Seize the Time" recording that began to echo throughout the neighborhood?

The climate changed from fear and despair to rage and strength. These are the words I can faintly remember, "*Have you ever stood in the darkestof night screaming silently, you're a man. Have you ever thought the day would come that you must stand up in the noon day sun? Now believe it, myfriend, that the silence must end, we just got to get guns and be men.*" Now, at the age of 60, I understand that "the weapons of my warfare

are not carnal but mighty through God, through the pulling down of strong holds and casting down imagination and every high thing that will exalt itself against the knowledge of God." I say this now and not because I'm old, but because it is a precept by which I live and breathe. "When I was a child, I thought as a child." I understood as a child but now that I became a man, I put away childish things. It is the mentality of a child that would fight the devil with a physical weapon.

As the words of the song "Seize the Time" played and permeated the atmosphere, I took a broom in hand and began to clean up and declare the Black Panther Party is open for business. Now, 17 years old, Mao Young Blood is large and in charge. I called the Stockwell Headquarters and Elaine Brown herself answered the phone. I told her what had happened. When I was transferred to the 113th Grape Street center several months later I had the privilege of meeting her. People began to come from everywhere, bringing food and "posting up." Revolutionary Rudy appeared. He was a character and one of the most out-spoken members of the party. He wore full regalia. Rudy was a motor mouth, but I was glad to see him.

A few hours later, two cars pulled up. About 30 to 40 people had gathered. I just kept Elaine Brown playing while I handed out the latest edition of the Black Panther newspaper. I knew it was the L.A. Chapter when all of a sudden Key-Bo (Virgil Smith) jumped out and began to take charge. Now Key-Bo's girl was Tommy Lewis who had gotten shot during the raid at the old Central Headquarters in Los Angeles. Seeing him was a sight for sore eyes. As the other 7 Panthers began to secure the perimeter, Key-Bo called out, "Where is Young Blood? I stepped forward. He put his arm around me and said, "Well done." Several weeks later all those who had been arrested were released. Key-Bo was put in charge and Cheryl Curtis and I were shipped off to the L.A. Chapter.

Elmer Pratt (Geronimo), this General, who later died in Tanzania, Africa, was one of the most dynamic men I would ever meet. Tears filled my eyes as I write about this noble man who was a hero to me and a prince to others. He was on J. Edgar Hoover's hit list and for 27 years, he was falsely imprisoned. I say to you, the reader, "What type of society do we live in where the FBI had Elmer Pratt under 24-hour surveillance and they knew exactly where he was during the robbery and murder. They sat by and let him be framed by the LAPD, the District Attorney's Office and to rot in prison for 27 years. Elmer Pratt was an army veteran who served two tours in Vietnam for America, "the land of the free and not so brave." A mere 4.5 million dollars did not make up for this atrocity by John Edgar Hoover.

The first day I came to Stockwell, I met Elaine Brown. She came in and sat down right next to me and asked about El Haddi Shabazz and Primo. They left the Center after Key-Bo had arrived and were reassigned. This was one of the most confident women I had ever met. She would save me and James Spencer from disaster. **NOW, WHAT HAPPENED WAS…**

I had teamed up with James Spencer at the 113 Grape Street, Center in the middle of the Jordan Downs, projects. Big Craig was in charge and they called him "Bougie." James Spencer and I had strolled up to Will Rogers Park to sell Black Panther papers, as we supported the party line. Suddenly, a van pulled up with some hippie looking white boys with Che Guevara buttons on military vests that read "White Panthers." I had never heard that term, so James Spencer stepped up and asked, "What do you want"? They opened the door and said, "this is a donation." I looked in total amazement. It was a crate full of M-16's.

James Spencer found a phone booth and called our headquarters . There were no cell phones in those days and we were not allowed to get in strange vehicles. James Spencer gave them the address and told them to wait for us four houses away from the Stockwell Headquarter. They were to await our arrival and instructions. They proceeded on and we double timed to the Center taking a secure route. As we approached, James told me to stay with the White Panthers as he ran to the Center. I listened to their Marxist Communist dogma and never could really feel their philosophy. It seemed like some kind of Socialist structure. James came running back and a disagreement ensued. As James was talking, a car pulled up and several Panthers unloaded those M-16 rifles and placed them in the trunk. The car sped off and James motioned to me as we crossed the street and posted up.

In about an hour, the White Panthers drove away in disgust. James later told me they were not allowed to come inside the Center and we were all put on Red Alert. Divide and conquer.

Watts Festival Confrontation
US Organization … Karenga Tangs

Later that summer, the Watts Festival began. James woke me up and said "Young Blood" hurry up! We're going down to the Watts Festival. Bring the 9-millimeter. We might run into someone from the "Karenga Tangs" (Black Nationalist).

The Panthers policy was not to take any guns out of the center because they were only for self-defense in case of attack. James said, "We're not going to be caught naked." By that time the US Organization had become the mortal enemies of the Black Panther Party after killing the founder Alprentice Bunchy Carter of the Los Angeles Chapter, another hero of mine. I remembered a poem he wrote titled, "Nigger Town."

John Higgins was also killed on the campus of UCLA over some crumbs off the Master's table. It was later said that J. Edgar Hoover initiated the drama and recruited the Stiner Brothers to assassinate Bunchy and John. The Stiner brothers were sent to prison for life and escaped. One was never recaptured and the other stayed out for over 20 years. Hell, Yes! I believe that the FBI arranged the assassination and the escape. It was a conspiracy. The actual shooter, Chuchessa was never found.

When we got to the Watts Festival, it was in full effect. They were playing African drums, people were dancing, and the celebration was joyful. The reconstruction of that community was finished. After the Watts riot of August 11th, 1965, which lasted 6 days, and 34 citizens were left dead. Over a thousand people were arrested.

This began the collapse of the social structure of America. There is still frequent rioting and protesting today. When you look back at our history, from 1965 to 2018, we have not collaborated effectively to end this tyranny. We must do better – from the killing of Trevon Martin by ruthless Zimmerman to the killing of young Michael Brown for being

Black in Ferguson, Missouri. The city will never be the same. Truly justice has fallen in the street. And the brother, Eric Gardener, who was choked to death by police. In each case, there were no indictment. It was because of the beating of Black men that the Watt's revolt began. I cry as we commit fratricide in our own neighborhoods.

Even back in the Black Panther days, it was the Panthers against a Black Nationalist Organization. As we were enjoying the festival, we were confronted by several Keranga-Tangs. They seemed to come from everywhere, about 12 in total. We put the few papers we had left on the ground, so we could free our hands. I could feel the surge run through my body as I took the stance for self-defense. Remember, we were "packing", but I was following James Spencer's lead. He said to me, "Be cool Young Blood." Now, that was right on time, you see, because I was ready to start "popping caps."

All of a sudden, I heard the squeak of trucks, several cars pulled up, and Robert Ryan, and Stanley P. jumped out with a cadre of Panthers. They were in full effect and you should have seen those US boys scatter. We must have been 60 strong in a matter of seconds as Panthers began to arrive. I felt like a million bucks. As James said, "Don't let anyone know we're packing." I understood and kept it to myself even to this day as we did the "Panther stroll" all the way to Stockwell. What a day! I was proud to be a Panther, but looking back it was the same old story of Black on Black crime. Blood against the Crips. Booker T. Washington against W.E.B Dubois. The Willie Lynch syndrome is still in full effect.

Angela Davis

The climate was electric as things began to move real fast. We were to serve as security for Angela Davis, when she come to town. She spoke at a rally and we went in full effect. Huey had gotten out of prison and was supposed to come to the Los Angeles Chapter. He was on his way but then canceled. Johnathan Jackson attempted an escape plan for his brother George Jackson and he was killed in Marin County.

I saw Johnathan once at the Stockwell Center. It just goes to show, you can never judge a book by its cover. He did not look like the type to try something so bold. The truth is those who know, don't tell, and those who tell, don't know. Now let's move on.

When Huey was released from prison everyone was happy and excited, but something was terribly wrong. I was a youngster and had been involved since 1969. I will say this very plainly that the Huey P. Newton that went to prison was not the Huey P. Newton that came out. I remember watching "The Mission Impossible" series on TV. "The Beast", the true enemy is very powerful and I do not put anything past them. They could have cloned a fake Huey, faked his death and everything else. The real Huey P. Newton could be languishing away in some special unit. If you ever watched the TV show called "Scandal" with a unit called B-16, need I say more.

After this fake Huey got out of prison he started to dismantle the Black Panther party. He initiated the split with the expulsion of Geronimo and other key leaders. The next thing he did was to systematically shut down most of the headquarters and centers across the country. It does not take a rocket scientist to realize "Houston we've got a problem!" Right after that, Jim Zan appeared. He was a Vietnam Veteran and appointed Captain over the Louisiana chapter. We became really good friends as I stood up for him one day.

We were at the Riverside chapter and had a conflict of interest. They wanted to discipline him, but he wasn't going for that. He flashed his 9- millimeter along with his gold tooth and I grabbed the shot gun and cradled it in my arms. I let them know that no one was going to do Jimmy Zan like that. They backed off as I was Young Blood and had juice even at my age. We talked and he went on to LA. I caught back up with him about 18 months later as the party was being scattered. We went to a little town called Monrovia and went underground. We separated from the Huey factor and sided with Eldridge Cleaver. I look back on it now and it was really "6 in one hand, ½ a dozen in the other." The movement was in trouble because of "J. Edgar Hoover, and the F.B.I Klan."

"Now It Can Be Told"

"I heard that boy Geraldo say...That the truth could be told the otherday... Now if he can, I can too... now in my heart this is the truth... So, if you listen and listen well...you will believe the truth I tell... Once upon a time, in a great, great land. There were principles of right that ruled over man. Where equal protection under the law, wasa great moral strength. Yes! Freedom for all. There was even aclause called "due process of law", it backed up the first. Yes! Freedom for all. The right to assemble was part of the plan, even freedom of speech for every man.

But then came a wind of demagoguery, fascism in America...the F.B.I head beast. J. Edgar Hoover was this man's name, a self-*righteous giant who killed and tamed. He controlled a government with the wave of his hand, had presidents killed...the Texas plan. No holds barred was the order of the day, he was the boss of the U.S.A. Now hear this story and hear it well, because there in Tennessee... Dr. King fell. Same old story, same old man...J Edgar Hoover... FBI Klan. Now there are many things, that I could tell...like the way he framed (Geronimo) Elmer Pratt and locked him in a cell. What about Fred Hampton? When he was asleep...bang-bang baby. Have a sweet dream or what about L.A. election campaign...Bobby Kennedy killed... bang-bang again. Now Hoover is dead, but his spirit lives on... it's the mark of the beast... 3...666...song. Well now it is time for this poet to go, but listen to this...for you all will know...Power corrupts but absolute power... corrupts absolutely."*

By The Poet Laureate – Michael Paul Sterling, aka Mao Young Blood, Written February 1992.

Monrovia California Shoot Out
(1971 Underground)

Monrovia, is a beautiful little city nestled in the foothills of the San Gabriel Mountains. My sister, Gwen, lived there and I hadn't seen her in a while. She had that sharp little Volkswagen with Bold Soul Sister written in the window. She swooped me up during one of those in between months and took me to a party in Pasadena, near the Rose

Bowl. I told Jimmy Zan that we would go to Riverside to see Mama Bessie for a while to stack up some dollars and get ghost. We stayed in Riverside for a couple of months. I bought a 1966 canary yellow Chevy Impala with true spokes.

Back in the day-day I really believed that the white man imperialist system of racism and capitalism owed me something. I was determined to get my forty acres and my mule, with interest. I felt I was justified to take it by force and that's exactly what we did. We called it "liberating capital funds." I must have liberated over 100 places in my younger years back in the day-day. I'm glad the statute of limitation is up. That's another reason why it took so long to write this book.

One thing is for sure, no one ever got hurt during our jobs. I tried to make sure of that by being the first one in and the last one out. My favorite slogan was "This is a robbery. Do not make it a murder." I could not see myself shooting someone for money. You see, somewhere in my moral being, I realized that no money, no matter how much, can't be worth more than a human life. That's real talk, I did get arrested one time for a Coors Beer Corporation robbery, because Leon snitched. I went all the way to a jury trial and something curiously happened. Let me stop because I'm getting ahead of myself.

I called my sister Gwen, and told her that a friend and I needed to come up for a couple of weeks. She was happy to hear from me as I had not seen her since her husband, Big Gerald Bush, and the family tried to pull what we call now days as an intervention. Yeah, they tried to kidnap me from the Black Panther Party. My eldest sister Claudia, now a Bishop, was a part of this conspiracy along with her husband L.C. Neal. They called the Panther Center and told me they were at Mama Bessie's and needed to discuss some family business. I had no idea that I would be the family business.

They told me their feelings and after expressing them, Big Gerald Bush told me it was time to forget and leave all that Panther madness and come with them. I told them "no way", but Big Gerald grabbed me by the arm and insisted. I was not about to fight with Big Gerald Bush who weighed in at 300 lbs. or better. I said okay and he let me go. I politely sat down for a few minutes and then requested the restroom. I jumped out the bathroom window and that was that.

This would be the first time I would see them again in almost 2 years. When I called Gwen and told her I was on my way she told me that she was no longer with Gerald Bush. When we got to Monrovia, all the family was there. My older brother, Leonard, and my three younger brothers, Jimmy, Robert and Rick. They stayed in an adjacent apartment. I had never been close to any of them, except Gwen. This felt strangely good.

Gwen was in her partying years and we were underground. The last command that we received was to blend back into society. Boy! When we partied, we party hardy and we partied all night long. We partied for days while smoking weed and drinking heavily. Now understand this "Young Blood" was in full swing and felt like the epitome of a Mandingo Warrior. I had just passed the ancient test of manhood. There was no one my age that I could relate to. I was a child that had been transformed into a man without the full natural process of fatherhood.

I would snatch up pretty girls like Romeo, and Casanova rolled into one. I had moves and was known to be "triple cool." At parties I would tap a dude on the shoulder like Humphrey Bogart, I saw in the movies or on television, and the next thing you know I was gone with your girl like Jodie. I was so full of myself.

I was the cat's meow and "Mukey" was my main squeeze. One day I got my head bumped as I pulled that canary yellow, '66 Impala super sport into the Huntington Liquor store. I was by myself lighting up a Kool cigarette when the finest tenderonie I had ever seen looked over at me. She shook her head in approval or acknowledgment and while my head was spinning, 'she stepped out the car with those ebony "Taj Mahal" legs, sporting a mini skirt like "peek-a-boo baby." She had style and grace while strolling toward me like Cleopatra herself and grabbed the door handle of my car. She sat down, looked at me and said, "Young Blood, I'm Mavis Montgomery and as long as you are in this town, you belong to me, understand?" Like a puppy, I nodded okay. She kissed me "real good" and got out the car. My reputation was spreading like wild fire. I came to find out that Mavis was a few years older than me and came from an upper middle class family and she was sophisticated to the bone. This is when I learned that most ladies, during the day, could become a freak at night. **Moving right along ...**

El Monte Nazi Party

We stayed underground maintaining our livelihood while having a few P.E. (Political Education) classes with the new recruits. Tabby, Quince and my older brother, Leonard was in their twenties and I was only 17 years old. We were underground for several months, doing things that certain subcultures consider normal. Some things you cannot let slide, like when the American Nazi party came to Monrovia High School in full array. There were German Shepard dogs, full uniform, flags and swastikas. One of our groupies, Ms. Mary Ray, informed us of what was going on. We pulled out our Black Panther uniforms, grabbed some newspapers and met them on campus. Jimmy Zan was our spokesman and began to read them the riot act. I was little more aggressive and began to physically persuade them it's time to go. One of them was persuaded to hit the ground. He jumped up and yelled at his companions, "Let's get out of here." As I rolled up on the Nazi who had the German Shepard, another one of them hit the ground. Yes, Tabby was following my lead, they ran out of there and never came back. We traced them all the way back to their headquarters in El Monte, California and began to monitor their activities.

We continued having P.E classes with a select few. There was Isenell, Mukey, Mary Ray, Tabby, Quincy, Leonard and a young girl I slipped off with every now and again named, "Suckey." Now Isenell was Jimmy Zan's "Queen" and one year they brought forth a beautiful child. It was in the summer of 1971 when we had the shootout. It started with some of the Durante boys and ended with one man, Murry, being shot. The police showed up as the Duarte boys got away. But we were now surrounded by the Monrovia police. The shooting had been going on for several hours and our ammunition was low. The police were now on the loud speaker saying, "Come out with your hands up." I was 17 years old at the time but in the exchange of fire, I heard one man scream. It was Murry who was with Dwight Hayes. A shot caller who had a rep. He fired the first shot. He had called my name. I yelled back and they shot at me and the fragments from the stucco hit my face. Baby Bullets began being fired everywhere. My reputation had gotten unwanted attention. **AND WHAT HAPPENED WAS...**

About a week prior, I went to a party in Duarte, California and this dude was walking with this fine "Philly." I swooped my arm under her arm as I caught her looking. They were locked and she was in my arms smiling. She said, "Who are you?" as I complimented her eyes. I replied, "You know exactly who I am?" "You must be Young Blood", she replied. As her dude stepped up, I told him to go play. I stepped up to him and he bowed down as he met my steely gaze and then he scurried off. I didn't know he came from a big family and Dwight was his uncle. I took his girl with me and we partied for two days.

Now, the repercussion was they were out to get me, but acted like they wanted to talk. They had already assaulted my brother Leonard at a party earlier that night as they thought he was me. One thing about "Young Blood" - he never got caught slipping. I paid attention to everything moving and I still do even to this day. I found out later that I had several charismatic gifts working throughout my life and one was the gift of discernment. Discernment is a prophetic insight that would signal me when danger was near and most of the time I would "shake the spot."

My Mama Gloria, Sister Gwen, Brothers, Robbie, Ricky and Leonard were all in the front house. While we were, all posted in the back. Until this day I don't know how many shots the police fired. I heard a 22 shooting and nothing heavier than a 38 towards the end. I was pumping that 12 gage like there was no tomorrow boom, boom, boom. I know that Zan was letting that 30 odd 6 ring every now and again. I could hear it thunder. I came in from the back-bedroom window and was looking down the hallway. Tabby and Quincy were in the adjacent bedroom, while Zan was in the living room. I yelled to Zan, "What's up." He said he was out of ammo and I only had two shells left. I thank God to this day, but then I was fuming mad when I turned back toward the room. I heard a voice say, "Drop it!" In the window was an officer and he had me, "Put the gun down," he said. I remember yelling, "The only reason I quit is because I am out of Baby Bullets."

I was charged with attempted murder. Jimmy Zan was charged with criminal anarchy. Tabby, Quincy, and Lee Elzie were each given a gun charge. They took us right up the street to Monrovia City Jail and did not feed us. It had been several days, so I inquired about food. One of the cops stated, "Doesn't it say in Ho Chi Minh's rules that you Panthers are supposed to be able to go without food for several days." I laughed to myself and said, "everybody stay down."

When I awoke I heard the police laugh about this real nice car that had gotten torched. It was my '66 Chevy Impala Super Sport. I was sent to L.A. Juvenile Hall where I awaited trial for attempted murder. I remained there for several months. I beat the case because too many Baby Bullets were flying! After I was released my mom drove me back to the spot in Monrovia. It wasn't until a year later that I saw Jimmy Zan.

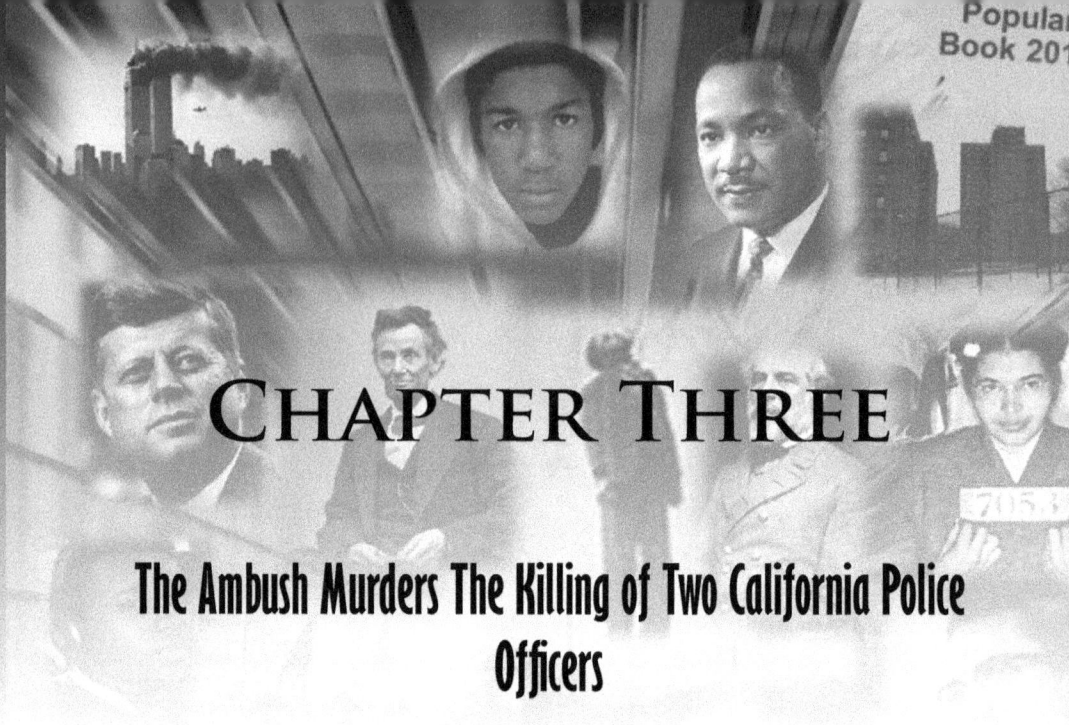

CHAPTER THREE

The Ambush Murders The Killing of Two California Police Officers

(For further reference see "Ambush Murders", by Ben Bradley Jr.)

I had been out of jail for a day and was awakened by 10 police cars. There was a loud knock on the door and the announcement, "Open up, it's the Monrovia police." I went to the door dressed in my boxer shorts and a T- shirt. "What do you want now," I asked. There were about 5 officers in the front and 2 of them were plain clothed detectives, as they motioned me to One of them grabbed me and pushed me up against the fence and asked, "Where were you last night?" I replied, "I was here, they threw a party for me since I had just gotten out of jail yesterday morning." They harassed me for several hours and asked if they could look around. I said no, not without a search warrant. They seemed to be confused as they were communicating back and forth trying to figure out something. All of a sudden, they took the handcuffs off and let me go while saying do not leave town.

As soon as they were gone, I grabbed a duffel bag, put some things in it, and disappeared. I had no transportation because they had burned up my car, no guns due to police confiscation, and no money.

I headed down Foothill Blvd. and hitchhiked to our safe house in San Bernardino, California, about 50 miles away. I had gotten out of the "skillet" and had no idea that I was headed to the "frying pan"!

As soon as I got to the safe house on Darby Street, it was manned by one of Eldridge Cleaver's groupies, a white woman named Patrice. From time- to-time she would run paper for us. She was a senior executive at the bank where she worked for over 20 years. She was an older lady who had an adopted son. When I arrived I was welcomed with great admiration. I had been working for that center for a couple of years before being sent to the Los Angeles Chapter.

Every other week I was sent from the Riverside Chapter to the San Bernardino Chapter to teach P.E. classes. Yes, "man-child" had learned to read on a phenomenal level and was teaching grown-ups out of the Red Book. When I saw Patrice, she said "MAO", I see ya got vengeance for the unlawful killing of comrade brother, Palmer. It's all on the news but you're safe here for as long as necessary." I did not know what she was talking about but I learned early in life to keep my mouth shut and access the facts.

As I sat down they showed me my room and prepared a special meal. After I got settled, I sat in front of the TV and immediately saw a news flash... two police officers had been ambushed in Riverside, California. Officer Paul Teel and Leonard Christiansen were killed on the night of April 2, 1971. I was in shock as I remembered there were several special meetings that they wanted me to attend.

They wanted to discuss the cowardly murder of comrade brother, Palmer, but I was unable to comply. Brother Palmer was shot in the back by a Riverside Police officer for being Black. Our slogan back then was "an attack against one, is an attack against all." Well, I said to myself "out of the skillet and into the frying pan." I now understand perfectly well, why the police officers showed up at my apartment in Monrovia.

They had been going back and forth for hours trying to figure out how I could have gotten out of Juvenile Hall in L.A. County on the morning of April 1st, make it to Riverside to help with the Ambush murders, and get back to Monrovia on April 3rd. It was possible but highly improbable and that little witch, Holly Gavin, didn't help matters with her lying statements. I stayed at the safe house for a couple of weeks knowing I would have to eventually return to Riverside. I told Patrice a little bit of what happened in Monrovia and that I was strapped. She put a couple of hundreds in my pocket out of the defense fund and then led me to the gun room where I picked up a 380 automatic. She supplied me with some bogus papers and told me to come to her bank, to her window, where I would use the phony check and retrieve $700 dollars in cash. That would be the last time I saw Patrice. She was a kind woman, I hope she eventually got saved. She is now deceased.

I slipped into Riverside under the cover of darkness and made my way to Mama Bessie's house at 2791 9th street. It was the only stable place in my life. I can still remember her phone number OV-40598, wow! We don't have numbers like that anymore… just a little nostalgia. It's hard to remember some of the people and events. As I reflect, the question is; how am I still alive? I often wonder about this. Most of the people who were my friends, comrades, homeboys and relatives are dead or in prison for life.

Some of them have lost their minds, but I know it was Mama Bessie's prayers and intercession that saved me from myself.

As I knocked on Mama Bessie's door, she came to the screen door, saw me and began to cry. She grabbed me and I thought she was never going to let go. I dropped one of the last tears that I ever allowed to fall from my eyes for many years. It was quickly retrieved and during the next few years I would become as hard as nails.

As I settled in at Mama Bessie's, back in my old room, I became disillusioned. It seemed that everything and everyone I believed in crumbled right before my eyes. The very ideology that I had been taught was dashed against the wall of nothingness. While truth became obscure from view, the one thing that I understood is that we underestimate the enemy and really do not have a clue to his evil working power.

The enemy appears in many forms, shapes, and disguises whether covert or overt. It was the same evil force of darkness whose intent is the total destruction of mankind. It seemed many years passed before I correctly identified the Devil, Satan, Beelzebub, Lucifer, and the fall. It took 12 more years in the darkness before I awoke. In the next chapter, I would sink into a subculture that would almost cost me my life on several occasions. The loss of my mind and a life of imprisonment.

CHAPTER FOUR

The Gangster Life

I stayed close for about a month and became stir crazy as I decided to hit Park Ave. This was home, but it had been awhile since I had been in the hood. I was a changed man and the city had also changed. Two police officers had been killed, ambush style and the city demanded blood.

Tension filled the air as this "man-child" proceeded down the boulevard. I had been strolling down Park Avenue for about two blocks and right before I got to the pool hall, a police unit saw me. They called for backup and the next thing I knew, I was looking down the barrels of at least 10 guns.

It's bad to experience guns being pointed at your head by the so-called law enforcement deputies, who many are undercover Klu Klux Klan members, that have been given the authority to act on behalf of the city. These scary white boys have never been taught protocol. Or, schooled on how to behave themselves in the inner-city. You're lucky if there is one real police officer in the bunch who truly, in his heart, wants to protect and serve. John Birch was a Nazi, and all their constituents were just plain racist.

They picked me up and took me down to the police station for interrogation. They came in one after another, good cop, bad cop questioning me about April 2nd and the Black Power meeting we had after the killing of Brother Palmer. For hours, I replied, "My name is Michael P. Sterling. I live at 2791 9th Street," and that was all I said. Then detective Tenell came in and he would be my nemesis for many years. He threatened, Baby Bullied, slammed the table, and threw a cup across the room. He told me that every police officer was angry and they all would be told that I failed to cooperate.

As I was released, he walked me to the door and said, "There's a target on your back." The walk home seemed haunting, but I knew this was not the end. Once again, I was "out of the skillet and tossed into the frying pan" of life. The short cut through the overpass, across the railroad track and through the Sunkist Orange Company seemed a little forbidding, so I opted to travel the long lighted path down University Ave. I made my way home and stayed in close for several months. The tension was very high as arrests were made. Soon Gary Lawton and Larry Gardner were put on trial for the murders, along with Nehemiah Jackson. Everyone knew they had the wrong people.

One day my childhood friend showed up, named Big Hank, Irvell Morgan, who became one of my best friends. I was completely different than the 14-year-old boy he knew. I was dangerous and everyone knew it. I fought at the drop of a hat. I never smiled nor did I laugh, as there was nothing to laugh about. A lot of good people gave their life for the struggle.

As time went on, I was introduced to a Red Devil pill, and I enjoyed it because it knocked me out. It helped me to forget the pain and the demise of the Panther Party and its disillusionment. We soon hooked up with Drack and Jerry Davis who was a natural athlete and a ping pong champion. The three of us did everything together for the next few years.

Assault On Police Officer Roy Rogers

It was right before my eighteenth birthday, about April 25th, 1972, and we had been drinking White Port wine with lemon juice. I had dropped a couple of yellow jacks and was feeling real good. We had been shooting dice on the corner stoop next to the gambling shack as the police passed by. The game came to a halt as the police made a U-turn, stopped the car and jumped out. He told me to stand still even though I was tipsy I complied. The officer began questioning and searching me at the same time. Big Hank and Drack moseyed on down the block and I asked the officer why he was harassing me. He replied, "Oh, I'll harass you alright, you're under arrest." I said, "For what?" He pushed me against the car and I laid him out with a right cross "good night Irene" as he hit the curb. I was so high. I stood there yelling, "Get up! I thought you were going to take me to jail."

My birthday was in 3 days and I could not see myself in jail on my 18th birthday. As Police Officer Rogers laid there on the ground I could hear Irvell yelling, "Come on Young Blood let's go." I stood there yelling at Roy Rogers who was in dream land saying, "Get up." Soon there were several other police cars that drove up. They immediately jacked me up, threw me in the police car and took me to the County Jail.

Once I got there and met a sheriff named Gonzales and I would later have many encounters with him. My life became a revolving door in and out of jail. I must have been arrested over 50 times in those days. One day I was arrested three times. Eventually I became sophisticated in the laws of the jungle, had a bail bonds man, named Phillips, on speed dial. I was dealing with huge quantities of drugs and my money supply had gotten real large. But, let me not get ahead of myself.

When we got to Riverside County Jail, as the officer was escorting me to the elevator, there stood, Officer Roy Rogers. He was fuming mad yelling, "You F***-Nigger. You hit me while I wasn't looking." The elevator soon opened at the booking desk and he was ranting and raving like a mad man. His jaw was swollen big time and his eye had turned black and blue. I did not know that he was head of the police boxing gym and they considered him quite a pugilist.

Officer Gonzales, who seemed to be in charge, quickly said," What do we have here?" Officer Roy Rogers immediately said, "This little punk hit me when I wasn't looking and do you have a quiet place where I can personally question him?" By that time my high had come down and I knew what that meant. I may have been born at night but not last night!

Officer Gonzales immediately stepped around the desk, unhand cuffed me, and pushed me to his right side. He told the other deputy to put me in the cage. He said to Officer Roy Rogers and the rest of R.P.D that "This young man is now in our custody and if you want to question him you're going to have to go through the proper channels." They left there, "smoking mad" and I learned a couple of things that day. I learned to respect Officer Gonzales as he was a standup guy. I never gave him any trouble and addressed him with "No, sir. And yes, sir." The other officers weren't so lucky.

I had a lot of hatred in my heart as I remember the Metro Squad of Los Angeles. They would drive up on us in a plain car and draw down on us. They said, "If we shoot you down, nobody is going to miss you." This type of behavior was common amongst the police department and it caused me to hate the police.

They found out I was a juvenile and called over to R.P.D stating, "You can't leave a juvenile here." They began to clown officer Roy Rogers. He was embarrassed and furious to say the least. I was now on his hit list. I stayed in Juvenile Hall for a few days and spent my 18th birthday counting bricks on the wall. They released me and gave me probation. I know it was the prayers of Mama Bessie and Judge Roy Escondido. A few years later, I was framed for a robbery I did not commit. This new centurion generation practice would happen when there was a badass, they couldn't convict. **NOW WHAT HAPPENED WAS…**

It was a familiar sound that awakened me out of my sleep that morning. I heard bang-bang. "It's the Riverside Police open up." Mama Bessie made it to the door first as I quickly grabbed my pants. "Mrs. McDowell, where is Michael Paul?" Before she could reply, I came out. I shouted, "What do you want now?" Then detective Tenell pushed his way forward. He was polite with Mama Bessie saying, "excuse me", as he said "Michael is under arrest for armed robbery."

I was locked up and awaiting arraignment as my bail was $100,000.00. By the time the preliminary hearing came, I was convinced I was in deep trouble. You see, when we gangsters come up before a judge, we already have our alibis intact. The problem was I didn't have anything to do with this incident so I could not come up with an alibi.

On the morning of my preliminary hearing something strange happened. Unknown to me officer Tenell, the devil's finest, was peering through the little window outside the courtroom door. He was standing with the victim and pointing me out. The witness was telling him I did not look like the same man who robbed his business, but officer Tenell insisted. As they were going back and forth, Lawyer Finn was coming down the hallway and heard the exchange of words.

Dennis Finn had become a friend of mine a couple of years earlier. I helped him with an important case when I was in my twenties. I was calling long shots and regulating on the Eastside and my juice card was full. I ran a cold protection racket and nothing was moving unless we got a piece of it. It was Big Hank, Drack and me,. My name was ringing like the Catholic Church bells that could be heard throughout the city; "Big Mike, OG (**O**riginal **G**angster) Michael Sterling."

We did not mess with the Old Timers or real O.G.'s due to respect for the game. Lawyer Finn's client had told him that he was innocent of the robbery and felony assault that carried big time back then. Well, we thought it was big time until the sentencing guidelines changed. It seemed to be specifically aimed at young Black America. Laws such as the "Little Bitch" and 5 to Life. A mandatory five years and an appearance at the board every year for the next 15 years. They could keep you in limbo. This was hard on a man's psyche and some Con's started refusing to go before the parole board as they thought it was a farce. A guy would program himself to be really good, do everything he was supposed to, stay out of trouble, get good reports from the prison staff, only to get to the board and be dehumanized. So, guys jumped off the top tier after this type of rejection and others slit their wrist. It was the definition of cruel and unusual punishment.

Then came the California enhancement laws. The Big Bitch! These enhancement laws have become one of the most outrageous legislations that I've ever read about. We must understand that every law ever written must in no way infringe on one's constitutional rights. Let's keep it simple so everyone can understand this. There is a provision in law called the Double Jeopardy Clause, which is the moral standard of Due Process. It outlines, that if a man commits a crime, went to jail, sentenced to five years in custody, completed and paid for his crime, finished any probation or parole, he was then free from all legal entanglements.

If three years have passed by and he commits a first-degree burglary, this may carry a 16 month, 2 years, or 4 year sentence. A Black man is sentenced to the max of 4 years. They look back at his record and give him an additional 3 years for a crime he has already paid for. When he did five years, they call it an enhancement. It's really a flat out double jeopardy. America shame on you. This is why years ago the Indians said, "White man speak with a fork tongue." Moving right along …

Dennis Finn, Attorney at Law, went into the Judge's chamber and told him what he observed. Then he walked over to me with his jolly cheerful self and said, "You are going to be released in a little while." He told me the whole story and then walked away. The judge came out and took the bench. Officer Tenell and the victim were sitting in the front row. They called my name on the docket and my Public Defender was not even there. The D.A. was called up to the bench, shook his head in disgust, walked away, and called the victim outside. Officer Tenell started to get up, but the District Attorney motioned for him to stay seated. They went out for about 15 minutes and walked back in with my Public Defender.

My Public Defender came over to me and said, "Good Morning." Next, the District Attorney motioned for him to stay seated. He told me, "I'm going to try to get your bail reduced." I said to him, "Man I'm going home today. I do not know where your dump truck ass has been. But you do not have a clue." He said, "Mr. Sterling, this is a very serious case. They have an eyewitness, so maybe I can get you a good deal." I said to him, "Man, if you don't get out of my face, I'm going to catch a real case."

The judge called my name again and then called my attorney. He acknowledged his presence and the D.A. did the same. The D.A. then said, "Your Honor, we would like to dismiss this case in the interest of justice." I was released and my "dump truck" attorney started scratching his head. While Officer Tenell jumped up from his seat in disbelief.

The Judge called Officer Tenell and the DA into his chambers. Lawyer Finn peaked in and looked at me. I shook my head, he smiled and walked away.

Throughout this book you are going to read about some unbelievable and shocking events of how I narrowly escaped with my life, my freedom and my sanity. I think about the brothers sitting in prison for crimes they did not commit. The next time you see those "Scales of Justice" understand they are not tilted in our favor. There are some Black men being released after many years only because of the new technology that has been developed called DNA, which was developed by Alex Jeffrey in 1984, which deals with Y-DNA testing. Deoxyribonucleic Acid, DNA, is found in the hereditary material in humans and almost all other organisms.

Street life

As my reputation started to spread I developed my own unique swagger. You could see me coming a "mile away." The walk I developed was like this. I would kick my left foot out heavily with a long drag in my right foot. I could stop, pivot or L-up at any time which is a defense posture. L-up, in some school of thought, would be called standing on the square with your heels together in a L shape.

Now I needed cash and began to plan and pull off some very successful heist. One of the heists was the Baby Bullock's Department Store truck in LA. Our plan was to lay and wait for the next arrival of goods. We looted the truck and it was easy money. Then we headed over to my cousin, LaVenia Dudley's house in Lambert Park, off Garth Way and Stocker, where we set up shop.

My sister Gwen worked right there on the West side at the telephone company on Crenshaw Boulevard. On Friday night when the "eagle would fly", she would bring the chicks over to the spot and when they walked in, we would be sitting there in the latest apparel. It was a fashion show and we were the models. We had on full length jumpsuits, double knit sweaters, with iridescent pants and original blue suede shoes.

We had a plate made of the finest China with real 10 carat gold overlay with at least 50 of the finest marijuana sticks sitting there finely rolled to perfection for the customers. It was Acapulco Gold, the finest weed in the land. The table next to it had several glasses of champagne with a bottle on ice, and one of those sterling silver chalet vases with K.J.L.H. radio blowing in the background.

The Player, hustler was in full effect and as we socialized. We kicked back and watched those garments sell themselves. Our inventory included fur coats, miniskirts, and the latest evening attire. We made money hand over fist. I liked the smooth player life. It was distinctively different from the usual gangster Motif I was accustomed to.

I was still hard, but now I was a little more smooth, suave, and debonair. Jerry Colley, an O.G. Player had laced me up good and took me under his wing. It was a good life. We would party at Maverick Flats on Crenshaw Boulevard and frequent Lighthouse by the Sea on Hermosa Beach. But it only lasted about six months. **AND WHAT HAPPENED WAS...**

It was a cool winter day in early November. I had come into my own. I was sitting "maxen and relaxing", awaiting the usual crowd that had become quite large. We were the "talk of the town." Well, the inner circle of the elite, which was a closed mouth set and you needed a special invitation just to get in the door.

Jerry Cooley ran a smooth operation. The girls could come, have a sip of champagne and fire up one of those joints. For the very sophisticated, they could get a couple of lines of coke on the house. Things were going fine and we were about to close shop for the night as the crowd had thinned out. When I saw those two brother's walk-in, they were playing the role real well, but my antennas went off. I eased myself out of the crowd, got my back up against the wall by the front door and posted up.

Suddenly one of them pulled a gun on Jerry and slapped LaVenia across the face. Before they could react, I sprung like a cat. I hit the one that was going for the money across the face with the nine and shot in the floor with the 380 auto. I planted it in number two's back and told him to drop it. He dropped the gun and I hit him in the head as blood splattered all over my brand-new gold double knit sweater. I sent them scurrying out the front door. They were in shock. LaVenia became hysterical and Jerry looked at me bewildered. He did not realize that his young protégé was really a gangster. They shut up shop for good that day. I caught the bus back to Riverside.

On the east side, I was being educated in the "University of the Streets." I now had a cooler demeanor and had changed my style of dress. When I stepped on the Boulevard, even my swag changed from the hard-killer demeanor to a smooth player look. Everyone stopped when I walked into the pool hall. Red Runnie said, "Is that Michael Sterling? Well look at you all grown up." I slapped him a high five and placed a $50 bet on the table. Pimping Lee Cole was shooting dice and I bet on him to hit. He rolled a seven, I let it ride, he hit 11, and again I let it ride. He hit an eight on his next shot and I picked up $400. I dropped the customary $20 for Red, the house man. He shook his head in approval while I found a table and ordered some food and set up shop.

I posted up at the pool hall for the next couple of years and made a nice score. Blackbird, Lonnie Graham, Junior and I went to LA. He was a gangster for real and had a big rep. I was about 17 years old at the time and bought a jar of Red Devils, Lilly F – 40 Baby Bullet head which was top- of-the-line and a key of Acapolco Gold marijuana - 2.2 pounds. That was the equivalent to an average brick back in the day.

Now with the first payment I moved into a duplex on Cridge and Park. I had Billy Paul blowing in the evening and West Montgomery bumping on Sunset in the early morning hours. My young life was good. I allowed Ed McKinley to move in and we had it going on. I had Johnnie Simpson and another Philly whose name I will not mention as it's called being "good to the game."

One day early in the morning, I woke up, then fired up a joint, did a couple lines of Peruvian Flake and had a cup of coffee. I put on Grant Green's jazz album and opened the front door and Wow! Look what was coming across the street. It was a vision of loveliness coming from the bus stop that only can be described through this poetic license.

As I gaze upon this tapestry of loveliness
I became mesmerized like a deer caught in headlights
I'm frozen in time as the essence of this ebony goddess strolls into my
enchanted moment.

I began to see the very curves of an excellent body through the canvas of silk which has been properly designed to meet hip and thigh as they caressed her behind which danced for me in a rhythm of an African drum that began pounding on the very heart strings of my love.

As she turned the two towers that graced her chest, seemed to be standing at attention.

While she smiled as if making a commercial for Colgate. She was indeed Venus, Halle Berry, and Cleopatra all rolled into one.

This was Miss Edith Craig. The most beautiful woman that I ever saw. I was determined then and there that I had to have her. But, to capture this feline, Youngblood would have to step up his game. She never saw me as I hid from her view. You see first impressions are truly lasting. Miss Edith Craig the wow factor. **AND WHAT HAPPENED WAS...**

A couple of months passed and Jonie and I were hitting it off well. She asked me to go to a house party with her and her big brother, Alex and his date. I said yes. They picked me up about 10 o'clock that evening. I was sharp as a tack and on full. I left my heat at the house. They pulled up and I cocked my Stetson brim ace 2 to the side and jumped in the back seat of that black on black Lincoln town car.

To my surprise, low and behold Alex's date was none other than Miss Edith Craig in full effect. Alex introduced me and I was grinning like a Cheshire cat. I requested that we stop at Carlos liquor store, and I asked the ladies what they wanted to drink as I did the Popeye stroll into the store. I looked over my shoulder and caught Miss Edith Craig checking me out. It was on and popping as we arrived at the party. I had everybody laughing and we were having a good time.

Alex was playing me and Mrs. Jones. I had my arms around Jonie who was real cute, but understand this, my mind was on Miss Edith Craig. We got to the party and I kicked it with Jonie for a while, got her situated, and began to make my rounds. It was about midnight when I noticed Miss Edith Craig stroll up the stairs by herself and she paused for a moment. She looked at me and I followed.

When I got to the top of the stairs, she was in the bedroom sitting on the bed. I said, "What's going on sweetie pie?" And she replied, "I'm bored." That was all I needed to hear. I grabbed her by the hand, wrapped my arms around her like I would never let her go and kissed her lightly on her honey lips. I looked deep into her eyes as my tongue went dancing a fandango after a long sensual kiss. I looked her in her eyes and said, "Let's shake the spot", and she said "okay."

We maneuvered through the crowd and out the front door. There was just one problem. Neither one of us had a car. I got outside and realized what we had done. She said, "We're about to be in big trouble. Our dates are inside holding hands. Alex and Jonie were brother and sister. We both busted out laughing, knowing this move could be problematic. The heart wants what the heart wants. I said, "Don't worry baby girl, big daddy got you." Then I attempted to flag down a car.

Roy Parchea pulled up in a truck and I told him I would give him some bread if he took us to the Eastside. He said get in. I grabbed Edith and as we got in the truck and busted out laughing like there was no tomorrow. I kissed her real good and she melted into my arms. We made our way through traffic. The evening scene was enchanted and yours truly, Young Blood, began to reflect on the nights event.

I really did not want to fight Alex. He was about 260 pounds, stood about 6'5" and he was twice as big as me. I was about 18 and he was 25. His sister, Jonie, was 22, and Edith seemed to be between 22 and 24.

Yes, I had made the conquests of my life. We arrived at my flat and I put on "Me and Mrs. Jones." It was number one on the hit parade and soared over K.J.L.H where it stayed number one for about 4 to 6 weeks. I asked if she would like to make herself comfortable and she asked for a big shirt as I poured a second glass of Margarita. I was in seventh heaven as I romanced her throughout the night. We awoke early the next morning around 6:30

a.m. and I walked her home. She lived about a block and a half away. We arrived at her door and she said she had to talk to me about something important later that day.

My sister Gwen came by and I got caught up for the next two days in Pomona, CA. When I came home, Ed McKinley a.k.a. "The Spinner", asked me where I had been. He mentioned that this fine girl had come by a couple of times looking for me. She left a letter and as I read it she described the beautiful night we had a couple days prior. She wrote, "I came by and I guess it was just a one night stand. I must leave town by no choice of my own. I wanted to speak to you before I left. Love always, Edith Craig."

I went down to her house and an old man answered, saying very rudely, she does not live here anymore and she won't be back. I never saw Miss Edith Craig to this day. I had regrets and more regrets for the next few years. I would hear the Chi-Lites playing "Tell Me Have You Seen Her?" That song haunted me for the rest of my life. I think I'll go to Google Play and download it.

It is October 7, 2014, 8:43a.m. and I'm at the Twin Pond Estates in Philadelphia, where I am writing this book. My host Dr. John and Janice Bowden (a.k.a. Shepherd Mother), two wonderful Apostles have graciously opened their home. I think I'll pause for the cause and reminisce for a moment.

I met "El Dorado Butch" during that time. He was a protégé of Tootie Reese and the magnificent seven. They were gangster players and real O.G.'s from out of Los Angeles. Now Uncle Butch, that's what I called him, took me under his wing and I loved him so much. My emotions are even running now. He's been long gone due to an overdose of heroin. He was a professional burglar and part-time bank robber. Yes, I knew a few bank robbers.

My cousin, Clem, now deceased, big Jack Daniels, an inmate at Cochran Penitentiary, where he has been for 34 years, Orie-love, who had robbed banks and Western Union's from Anchorage, Alaska to San Diego. They would come by to drop some "paper" and tried to recruit me from time to time, but my antennas went up and I wanted no part of that crew. Once you were in they would not let you out. "Stormin Norman" tried and that's a story we will not tell.

One of the craziest moves I've ever made was to rob "Tom Tom" a Mexican Mafia dope dealer. I would regret that move for years. It was me and Floyd Avery, now deceased. He was shot in the back with a double barrel shotgun in front of his kids. They tried to hit me several times, but Mama Bessie's intercessory prayers were invincible. I remember after the robbery, we went straight to Cici's Supper Club. It was a swanky little spot that later became Riverside Faith Temple where I would speak at many conferences for ETM Apostle, Joseph Sims, my Spiritual Father, who also is now deceased. What a difference a day makes. Faith Temple purchased the whole shopping center and they are still going strong today under Apostle Beatrice Sims.

Big Floyd was about four years my senior, but I was always the young mastermind. Big Floyd had driven his '58 Chevy convertible that night. It was sharp and I would love to have one myself as my "Sunday go to meeting" car. It was a real classic. We made about $2,500 cash and about 3 g's in heroin. It wasn't a big heist, but it was good money back in the day. It is about 20 g's in today's market.

El Dorado Butch showed up in that big golden El-dog. I kicked him down with a few balloons of H. He disappeared for a while and came back and was the life of the party. That night I left with him and we went out to Johnson Ranch in Perris, California. I had the time of my life. El Dorado Butch had class and I enjoyed "kicking it" with him. He took me to Irv Silver's Clothing Store and they tailored me up with a double-breasted powder blue suit. I was "styling and profiling." He told me to trade that nine-millimeter that I was carrying, for a snub-nosed 38 and shoulder holster. I kept the nine and paid cash for the snub-nosed 38 and shoulder holster. It felt really good under my new blue suit and was very accessible.

We wined and dined at Cask and Cleaver steakhouse. Eldorado Butch taught me how to eat and which fork was for what. Yes, even gangsters gave classes in etiquette. He knew everything and told me stories of Street life along with the O.G. codes. It was fascinating and I learned quickly. The "man-child" was coming into his own. I kicked it with him for a few days on the other side of town.

As I was leaving his house, I turned the corner and Lonnie G drove up. He said, "Young Blood what have you done?" They kicked the pool hall door down last night with shotguns, looking for you. Lee Cole and my dad drew down on them and told them they were out of bounds. They left but you are in big trouble." Trinidad passed by and saw us and made a U-turn and sped down the street. I jumped in the car with "Bird" and told him the story. He said that Tom Tom was a runner for the Mexican Mafia. People knew not to mess with him because he was hooked up, everyone except Young Blood. Me. Yours truly...

I had to lay low and stay off the East side for over a year. Lonnie G (a.k.a. Blackbird) was an old friend of Tom Tom. He went and told him to lay off and he would owe him a gangster favor. Tom Tom assured him that if they came up with the money in cash for the drugs he would tell the locals to lay off. Lonnie G went to Jesse James Jackson, Junior (b.k.a 4J's). He was a Golden Gloves champion and had an original A-number and had been violated 6 times. His "juice card" was the heaviest on the east side.

He always wore a three-piece suit and gangster hat. Molly Taylor was his grandmother and he lived with her for most of his life. She and Mama Bessie were real close and they both attended Park Avenue Baptist Church, three blocks from the pool hall and gambling shack. The way I heard it was like this, Jesse's grandmother ran the local gossip line and always had her "ear to the ground". She evidently told Jesse, "I heard what Michael, Miss Bessie's boy did and you better fix it. Don't let nothing happen to Mrs. McDowell's boy. You know that's all she has."

Jesse was dealing big dope for Dumbo at the time. It was said that he went down to Tom Tom's house and gave him a couple of ounces and told him it was over. And, it was over for a while, until Flex Barron got out of the pen. He was mean and followed me home one night about two years later and almost had me. Yet again my antenna went off, that charisma gift of spiritual discernment was working. I fell backwards as the Baby Bullets went over my head. A car pulled up two doors from my mom's house. I saw the shotgun and the saw the face of the man.

I would find out later that it was Flex Barron, a hitter and shot caller for the Mexican Mafia. They thought I was dead as the car paused for a moment. I laid perfectly still and could hear them arguing as porch lights began to come on. They sped off in the stillness of the night. It was like the Matrix movie. I could literally see the shots passing my face as I was falling backwards. Mama Bessie's prayer saved me again. She was a warrior. The Bible says, "The effectual fervent prayers of a righteous man avail much" (James 5:16).

I never told anyone except Big Hank, Drack and Butch Mimms who had joined our crew what happened. Jesse James was back in the joint on a parole violation, along with El Dorado Butch. Lonnie G. had run off to LA with the drug lady, so I was on my own. We posted up at Mama Bessie's house while setting up a slight security without "putting any alarm clocks in the graveyard."

I started hanging out at Boardwell Park where all the brothers and sisters would come. They would come from Casablanca on the Westside and as far as Perris, California on the Eastside. It was somewhat of a natural spot where we could come and "graze in the grass" on Friday and Saturday night. The parties at the Rec. Center were off the hook. Dale Roberts ran the place.

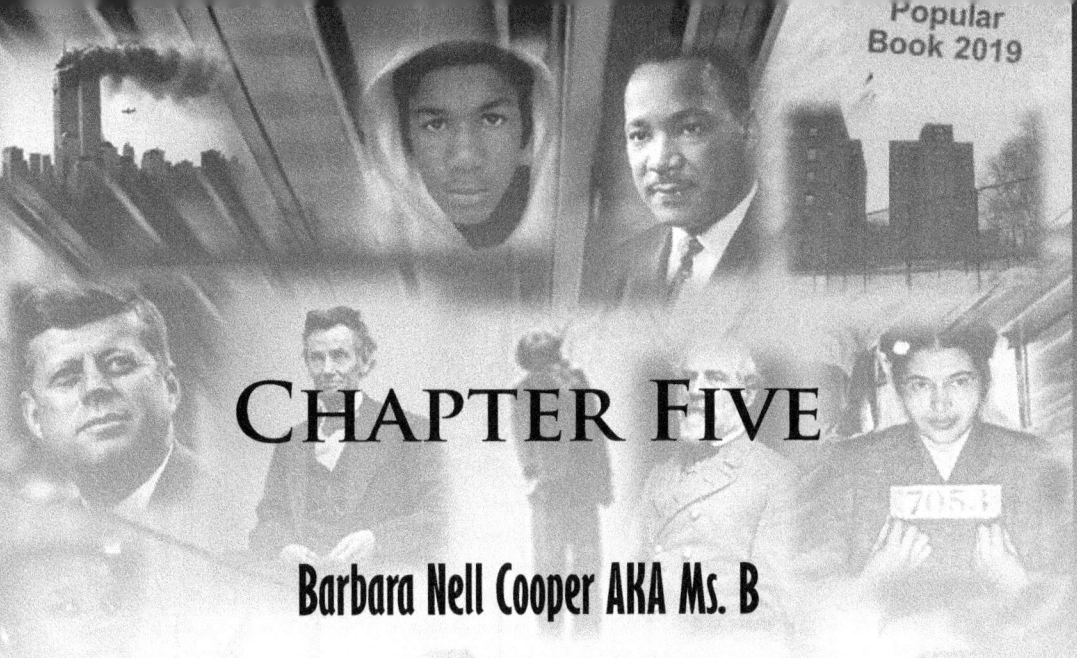

CHAPTER FIVE

Barbara Nell Cooper AKA Ms. B

(My first wife)

It was the summer of 1974 when I met Barbara Cooper at Boardwell Park. I had gotten into a scrap with some San Bernardino boys behind Drack. I knocked one out and then he got up and ran. My antenna went off and I knew he was going for a gun. I was in hot pursuit. I saw him put his keys in the trunk of his car but I was two steps behind him and was ready to pounce on him, when I was grabbed by Dale Roberts, O.G. from Parks and Recreation. He said, "Michael you're always causing trouble." Now when Dale grabs you there is no getting away. He was only about 5'7", but had a massive frame. He had won many muscleman trophies and kept himself in good shape. I yelled, "Dale he's going for a gun", as we both looked back. He was coming up with a shotgun.

Dale let go and turned towards the assailant and I pushed him with all my might into the man with the gun. I could hear the shot as it rang, but I was in the wind. I came back later, circling around the park and saw Barbara Cooper. She said that some man had pulled a gun and Dale grabbed him and made them leave the park. She said that Drack took the gun that fell and when it hit the ground, it fired and people started hollering and running everywhere. I put the Mac down on her, got her digits, and told her I would be back. I found Drack walking around like James Cagney. He had the shotgun and I took it from him saying, "This is my trophy. Spoils of war." I reminded him that I almost got killed tonight helping him.

The next day I called Barbara. She became my main squeeze. The next thing I knew, we were out one night and I was on "triple full." When I woke up I was in Las Vegas, Nevada standing before the Chapel of the Bells saying, "I do." Don't get me wrong, I had already fallen head over heels for Barbara. She was also a couple years older than me. Barbara did not know for several years how much I was involved in street life. I played it close to the vest and began to live two totally separate lives.

She worked at a place called, "Taro" for many years and always kept a job. We got a nice apartment over on Chicago Avenue. I was husband by night and gangster player in the day time, but I never brought my work home. She would drop me off at Mama Bessie's about 7 a.m. each morning and I would meet her at home later that evening. I had a 1965 mint condition Riviera town car and it was sharp. In those days I never let anyone know where I lived.

My son, Jakuma was born June 29, 1974. It was great to be a father. His name means "warrior prophet" and I sure was glad when he was born. I was so proud. I just wish that he had not seen me in those days. Children try to emulate their father and he's been in prison over 12 years. He almost died early when I had funk with the Eastside Mexican Cartel. **AND WHAT HAPPENED WAS...**

There was a dope drought every once in a while. The supply of Heroin would not be sufficient for the demand. Marcelleno and Trinidad must have come up short on their re-up and sold us a half ounce of some straight bunk powder sugar. I caught up with them on Sedgwick and 10th and pulled my car in front of them and jackknifed in the middle of the street. My car went up on two wheels by the time it landed. I was almost instantly out of the car and at their car door. "Get out, put your hands up." I hit Trinidad across the head with the nine and fired at the same time. He fell to his knees and began to holler like a little B***. I made them empty their pockets and took everything they had. It was only a couple of hundred dollars cash and a few 30 bag packages. I guess they had just picked it up.

This move started a war. I had two cars, a 1975 Firebird and a Coco Brown 1969 Riviera. I jumped in the Riviera and dropped Mrs. B off at Mama Bessie's house and took off for Pomona, and landed at Mama Gloria's. Our relationship had gotten better as I got older. They came by Mama Bessie's where my wife Barbara was and shot up the Firebird and also fired into my bedroom.

For a few days, I did not know what happened. Three-year-old, Jakuma, was asleep in my bed and the Baby Bullet holes in the wall indicated it missed his head by about 6 inches. Oh, by the way, I never called the police back in the day. Real gangsters never called the police; we just handled our business. When I got the news, I made a few calls and collected a few gangsters' favors.

I was out of town with an alibi when Trinidad's house went up in smoke and so did Fat Jack's. I never knew who or what. I just sent the word up the pipeline that they had almost killed my son. When I hit Broadway they were out of the "life" and in retirement. He never sold drugs again and signed a peace treaty after Marcelleno had gotten shot up over by Tony's market. There were good rules back in the day-day. The code was in full effect. It was before that gang banger element came in. We were Original Gangsters not Gang-Bangers who fought over the color of a rag.

Over the next couple of years I kept my eyes open and stayed in close. Then one night something strange happened. It was about 11p.m. on a hot July night. I was laying across the bed listening to Lee Morgan and this bad 47 Chevy truck drove up. It was nice. I grabbed my roscoe and jumped out the side window and duckwalked down the driveway. I watched as this Hispanic brother, all suited up, jumped out of the truck while the driver stayed motionless. I had made my way up behind the bush in the driveway as he yelled, "Spotty, it's Jerry."

Now there were only a few people in the world that knew me by that Moniker and they were all Mexican and we were tight. I had this beautiful patch of white hair about two inches on my head. It was my birthmark, so in some real circles they would call me "Spotty." I eased up a bit but remained cautious as I recognized gangster, Jerry, from Juvenile Hall. I politely asked, "What's up, are you filling contracts these days?" He replied, "Aw man come on Mike, I came to talk business."

I told him to have a seat on the porch and carefully took a safe position. He threw me a bag with three packets in it, "That's for you from the big man." He explained how Trinidad, Fat Jack and Marcelleno all worked for this guy. His turf stretched from Corona to Riverside. I took Jerry inside, busted open the package, took a single bag and tossed it to him. He said "O.G. Michael Sterling you don't trust me?" As he rolled up his sleeve I gave him a brand-new syringe and a cooker. After it was ready, he drew up and let it ride and I did the same following his lead.

I became hooked on heroin in those days and it was the best I ever had. I found out when Trinidad and the others got the packets they would step on it at least three times. My God, I would step on it once and still double the money. I walked out with Jerry and met the man. Well, let me change his name.

He became a very good friend to me and Mrs. B. I'll call him "Little Jesse." We talked for a while and he explained to me that they had a sit down after the three amigos closed shop. They were afraid of some big black cat on the East side that had knocked out a cop. This guy seemed to have had nine lives. Yes, they were talking about me.

They tried to hit me twice. Once they thought I was dead but then I re- appeared a year later cracking heads and taking names. My reputation was really growing. During a sit-down, the Cartel planned a hit on me. As they were going through a high school album trying to find my picture Gangster Jerry recognized one of the photos. He said he knew me and mentioned I had helped him out one time. They usually did not deal with Blacks but I became the exception. I dealt drugs for them for over 10 years. They bailed me out of jail twice, sent me a lawyer once, and gave me an old mint condition Cadillac one year. I made them really good money and I opened up three spots once I got my feet wet.

Papa Religh, on the East side, Baby Baby Bull out of Hillside, and myself, after 10 p.m. to 5a.m. sold to hookers and top-flight clients. The minimum to spend was $150 just to get in the door. Then there was Lily May and Robert Earl on Ninth Street. I would do a lot of cutting preparation there. I told everyone that I had working for me, that they could never tell anyone. This was my stuff and to keep everything "on the one." I would cut some of the heroin with milk sugar and the other with procaine. This way no one would know that drugs on Hillside came from the same supplier as the East side, because it was totally different. Sometimes I came down on the avenues to buy my own stuff. I pretended not to have enough money for the drug I needed. This would keep the cheat off. It worked for a while. I even put a package in Lily and Robert Earl's possession right down the street.

Shoot Out At Park Ave

Now I was making money hand over fist and this international pimp robbed one of my spots. His name was Allen Walker. I was in bed with the flu and this negro went to Lily and Robert Earl's spot after I had just given them a fresh packet and he "gangstered" them without a gun and took their stash. I was smokin' hot! I stayed in bed for a couple more weeks. As soon as I was well, I went looking for Allen Walker, the pimp. I ran into him early one morning on the Avenue.

It must have been about 9 a.m.. He was sitting in that Black Cadillac of his. I pulled up alongside in the river dog (Riviera) and asked Big Al: "Why did you take off, Lily May and Rob? You know that was my stuff and I need my money." He looked straight into my eyes, started up that Cadillac, and then told me, "Go F yourself." As he drove off, I made a U-turn, grabbed my pistol and went after him. He was cruising like nothing was wrong. I pulled alongside and that's when the shooting started as Baby Bullets began to fly by me. I made a right turn on ninth Street and jumped out of the car. He made a crazy U-turn and was coming my way and all of a sudden, the police came from out of nowhere.

We both went to jail - me in one car - him in another. The officer asked, "Mr. Sterling what happened out there and I said "I do not know. I was just standing here and you arrested me. Go ask him." We got to County jail, and they placed us in the back end. I was sitting talking to Jesse James a.k.a. 4- J's and took my eyes off him. He stole on me, knocking me to the floor. I got up dizzy and started to swing. I still, to this day, do not know why Jesse James did not warn me. The police had rushed in and broke it up. We both bailed out that same day. We both said nothing to the police and the charges were dropped.

When I got out, the first thing I did was to retrieve my pistol which I had handed off to David. He was a handyman who lived at the second house down the street and our children played together. By the way, everyone understood. If you did me a favor, I really would look out for you from that day forward.

David was square and a straight working man. A John Doe citizen. He knew it was smart to be in the good graces from a shot caller like myself. I got word from the penitentiary to back off Pimpin' Al and he was told to do the same. I told Stormin' Norman what his brother had done and hoped that it didn't interfere with our relationship. It did not as the O.G. squashed it and we stayed out of each other's way. That was the O.G. code in full effect. It was a greater respect back then. I'm 60 now and I keep my eyes open, but nothing else became of it. Big Al left the City and became an infamous pimp in the San Diego area. Last I heard he was driving a Stutz- Bearcat and slamming doors - more power to him. I hope he got saved.

It was 1980 and this date is still a little fuzzy in my mind. My son, Rascheed, must have been about one year old. Big Hank was in Soledad prison. Miss B and I were living down on 10th in one of Sheriff McWaters properties. It was a little two-bedroom apartment. It was the worst place we had ever lived. I was making money hand over fist showing up on the Avenue in overalls and blue jeans acting like I was down and out. It was one of the greatest fronts of my life. I was stacking dollars and buying clothes from the street boosters.

Big Hank was scheduled to get out of prison soon. I had planned when he got out we would go down to Tate Cadillac in the PO (Pomona, CA). The two of us would buy Cadillacs as we begin to run and regulate the Eastside. When he got out, I bought a steel gray with burgundy interior, half vinyl burgundy top, 30,000 miles, 1978 four door sedan Deville. He got a cocoa brown coop and was dissatisfied with it. One day it caught on fire and the next week he copped a 1979 coop Black on Black in Black. We were rolling hard.

He and Shirley had copped a spot in Pomona. We celebrated but there was something a little different about Irvell Morgan a.k.a. big Hank b.k.a Makeynie. I could not quite put my finger on it, but I guess five years at the Gladiator school; to wit; Soledad Prison, would take its toll on the best of men. Oh, by the way, it was where Cleveland Edwards was killed and the retaliation spun the Soledad brothers.

The Soledad brothers along with George Jackson, Fletta Drumgo and John Clutchette were charged with the killing of John V. Mills, a prison guard. This all started as W.L. Nolan and Alvin Miller retaliated for the murder of Cleveland Edwards, who died on the prison yard, January 13, 1970. They were released from Solitary onto a yard with white inmates, as these men were set up for execution. This manipulation was created by these new Centurion guards whose mindset is to control and demolish at their own request.

The fact of the matter is that they killed one of the OG home boys from Riverside. I played football with his younger brother, Oscar Edwards. He was a running back on our team. We called him crazy legs. He could be running in one direction and switch directions midstream. He had a stutter step that was awesome and amazing to watch. All three young men meant a lot.

In the annals of our struggles against the racist demi-gods and profiteers that had caused slavery, slaughter, and injustice to a nation of kings… that never asked to come to America. We have been degraded, castrated, hung and boiled in oil. Black men in America have been systematically put in prison, unjustified, just to clear up unsolved crimes. We have been sentenced by Judges who wore Black robes in the day time and Klansman hoods at night.

Whether we are Christians, Muslims, Jews, or atheists, we, as Black people in America, are involved in the same struggles. I personally serve Jesus Christ, my Lord and Savior, who said in His Word, "the last shall be first and the first shall be last and that the wealth of the wicked is stored up for the righteous." I declare and decree as a prophet of God, "It is our time!" The wealth transfer has begun… Just a reminder, Pres. Barack Obama was never the answer. He was just a sign of things to come, it's unstoppable… Let us remember, we must bring justice to all mankind.

One day I was "Maxen" and relaxing. It was a beautiful sunlit day. Smokey Robinson was playing on the radio and all of the sudden, I saw him as he saw me. Yes! Policeman Tenell past me as I was cruising down

14th St. about a week later. He made a U-turn hitting the pedal. By the time, I got to the Boardwell Park, I jumped out of the car and sat down on the bench as they drove by doing about 60 mph. They saw me and hit the brakes doing another U-turn. They jumped out of the car as I lit up a Kool cigarette and believe me I was cooler than the Kool. I had on a two-piece suit with a pair of brand-new "Bisquicks" on my feet, with a matching godfather hat. Yeah! Your boy was sporting.

Now they had been watching me on the skid row for the last year. So, they really thought I had robbed a bank or something because after about three hours of dispatching and questioning they finally let me go. "Michael Paul", they said, "We know you're up to something and were going to get you." I smiled with a smile of confidence knowing I had gotten better in my craft. I chilled out for a while and enrolled in an O.I.C. program where I was getting paid to learn solar installation and conversion. Mrs. B was still working at Toro doing a swing shift. I had stopped using at that time and things were going well. We had moved from the Eastside to North Maine into a beautiful townhouse. One night while I was at the pool hall, a.k.a "The bucket of blood", I went in and ordered some food and walked outside as the jukebox was blowing a Marvin Gaye tune. I was clean and sober and focused on the legitimacy of life. **AND WHAT HAPPENED WAS...**

CHAPTER SIX

Barbeque Bar Melee

(Felony Assault On 3 Police Officers)

While Mrs. B was at work, I drove over to Mama Bessie's and decided to stroll down to the Barbeque Bar. After the sun, had set on the horizon, the night became still and the summer heat was still blistering about 90°. It was a very hot summer night. The temperatures had been in the hundreds for weeks. I decided not to cook and told my kids to sit quietly as I strolled down to the Avenue. They were in good care with Mama Bessie who loved my kids, especially Jakuma, our firstborn son.

As I arrived at the Barbecue Bar, (the best barbecue on the east side), Diamond Jim ran the place and had turned the other side into a small nightspot. The gambling shack was next door on the second level and there was a small patio that led to the actual gambling shack. It was where all the high rollers would meet. They would come from all over Southern California. "Pimping" Bobby Walker, who caught the wrong chick - this girl ran away from her husband and began turning tricks on Holt Boulevard at Bobby's request. One day that jealous husband caught up with him and shot him six times. Now, that was Street life for real.

He'rye was there and my man, Robert Bratton, now retired, who has one of the finest restaurants downtown behind the Mission Inn. It's called Graham's Place and it had the best soul food in the city.

His children now run the place. Lucky for him, he was one out of 1,000 who made it out of the street life. He pimped with the best, sold narcotics to high rollers and dealt with big money cliental only. He was one of the sharpest dressers in the hood, losing and winning fortunes at the gambling shack. We had a little something over Kathy Crawford back in the day-day. She was his girl and one night I snatched her up for half a minute. He didn't like that, you see I was just a youngster, fresh in the game and he was the big "Homie", an O.G. for real. Kathy was one of his main girls, but that did not stop him from helping me beat an attempted murder one year, and still looks out for me today, as a Christian minister. He donated about $1,000 worth of free barbecue for a function I was doing for the church. Big thumbs up to Robert Bratton, the big Homie; who has also embraced our Lord and Savior Jesus Christ. His sister, Daretta, who was a stepper in the life and is now pastoring a church in Victorville, CA along with her husband. I'll see you in heaven! Matter of fact, I saw Robert recently. He had pictures of young Mike back in the day-day. **Moving right along...**

While I was standing out in front of the Barbecue Bar all of a sudden two police cars drove up. It was officer Canale, who was now the new Gestapo on the Eastside. He passed by after giving me the once over, but I was clean as the Board of Health. They proceeded inside and all of a sudden I heard this shrill scream of a woman. It broke the very silence of the night. I immediately ran inside and the picture that I saw will forever remind me of the degradation of our people. I had not seen, "Jango", but I was told, that if you do not stand up for something you will fall for anything, and this is what I saw.

A young Black girl about 20 years old being held by two police officers who were acting like pigs or plantation slave owners. This young girl was crying as her halter top was down, her breast was showing and pig Canale was standing in front of her. All three police officers were smiling and the patrons in the joint seemed to be frozen in time. I had taken Tae Kwon Do from Master Terry Pue. I kicked Canale first in the head and he went down. I moved in and double clutched the one on the left with two wicked punches to his face. I heard a crack as he went down. The other officer dropped his grip and went for his weapon. I pushed the young lady, who was never identified by the officers, towards the back door and told her to run. I knew her well, so let's call her D.A.

I grabbed the last officer by picking him up in the air. Surely he was most definitely the biggest. You see, when I came in, I quickly assessed the situation and knew he was the slowest. His body slammed into the brass foot rail that ran along the bottom of the bar and blood went everywhere. He became blind and grabbed Earl's leg holding on to him and swore in court that Earl had slammed him. What a laugh. Earl got arrested and snitched on me. He was scared to death. It's funny how people miss identify people all the time, when I say "funny", I'm laughing and crying at the same time. I'm laughing at people who swear on a stack of Bibles and are as wrong as two left shoes. And I'm crying tears for all the brothers who have been falsely accused and sentenced to long prison terms. There really needs to be Justice and Court reform because our penal system is broken and we, as Black American men, have become an endangered species.

Meanwhile back at the bar, after I body slammed the last officer, Bruce Love, a.k.a. Omar Cliff Hasen, now deceased, yelled out, "They're coming in with dogs." It happened so fast. I was the last man standing as more officers entered the bar. History told me to drop to my knees and put my hands on top of my head and said, "I can do a year in the county jail. I surrender."

Standing up as a man is something I will never regret. Still today you cannot come into my community and behave any kind of way. The new officers beat me unconscious and when I woke up I was in a pool of blood in a small cell. The next day the newspaper said that the Cinderella girl was still missing, as she lost her shoe making a quick exit. A captain was yelling at the police officers who evidently brought me there. He was standing over me, but his voice seemed so far away as he said, "Why in the hell did you bring him here. Take him to the hospital", as I passed out again. When my eyes opened, next I was in the ambulance and kept going in and out of consciousness.

Months later, they tried to say in court that I broke both my hands punching the officers, and they even brought in a doctor who said I had a "boxer's fracture." In open court I said, "Stop lying." I want you, the readers, to know, for the record, that nothing was wrong with my hands. They broke both my hands while I was on my knees surrendering. I had to have pins and two surgeries on the right hand. The grey patch that was in the top of my head, they beat it out. The doctors put over 50 stitches in my head and I went into a coma for a few weeks. Once I woke up and heard the doctor tell the police he was not releasing me to the jail. The officers went away furious. When I finally woke up, I looked like a mummy. My head was all bandaged up and I could not see one hand because it was totally enclosed by the cast. The right-hand had a metal rod going up holding my thumb and pointer together. On my right hand, I could only see three fingers for months and could not button my own clothes, nor zip up my pants. I also stuttered for over a year during that time. In hindsight maybe surrendering, getting on my knees, and putting my hands on my head was not a good idea. It was a slow agonizing recovery but I now realize that if I had not suffered, I most likely would not be alive today to write this account of my own life. "*Man Child In The Not So Promised Land*."

Barbara Neil, my wife at that time, and my friend today, ran like a Kentucky thoroughbred. She had flyers made up and got the support of a local Rabbi who helped her. She also received the support of the NAACP, The Park Ave. Baptist Church, Rev. L.B. Moss, now deceased, The Second Baptist Church, along with several leaders around the community. They were tired of the wanton murder and disrespect of our people. They would come in like a foreign Gestapo, who harassed and beat people unmercifully. The community was weary and when the two police were killed several years earlier, they forced Rev. Moss to go into a building where they thought the killers were hiding. This was total disrespect and no regards for his safety.

There was even a rally and marched around the jail house, saying: "Free Michael Paul." We went to jury trial and were called "The Riverside Three", Bruce Love, Earl and me. Bruce was the only one that stood up with me that day. He was a real warrior and his entire family was Muslim, except his sister Betty Chocolate Hale. She was a Christian and we went to church together years later as we transitioned from street life to eternal life in Christ Jesus. A "shout out" to my sister, Betty Love. I'm still on the battlefield here on the earth. Save a place for me. I miss you, my sister and my brother, Bruce.

We had some exciting episodes along life's road, back in the day-day. We filed a class action lawsuit during that time. It was for 2.5 million and the attorney that came forth was Andy Roth. I believe that he dumped us and made a side deal with the powers that be. The jury came back with a not guilty on all felony charges and a guilty on one misdemeanor charge of interfering with a police officer. The sentence was time served and no probation.

PC 187 Attempt

James Lang

During the next several months my recovery was very slow. My speech was now slurred and I was frustrated to say the least after stuttering for over a year because of a head injury. I had a pin in my right hand and was lucky to be alive. I know men that have done a lot less than this and they wind up on a slab in some dark and lonely morgue, like Michael Brown.

I'm lucky to be alive and can hear some of the new Centurion conversations, saying, "You should have killed him when you had the chance." Believe me they tried, but it was not luck, it was the effectual fervent prayers of a righteous woman, Mama Bessie McDowell, that availed much according to the latter part of James 5:16. Her prayers were invincible and all you intercessors and prayer warriors, know this.

Mama Bessie never saw me preach one day, but she saw it far off. Her faith became the substance of things hoped for and the evidence of things not yet seen. Her faith is manifested in the writer of this book who has preached around the world for over 25 years. I have preached the gospel of Jesus Christ in India to over 40,000 people, ministered in the Netherlands and several nations in Africa. We went throughout Mexico and all over. My testimony is that our Heavenly Father and His son, our Savior, has been good to me! **Moving right along....**

It was a beautiful summer night. I was now back in the Hood living with Mama Bessie who stayed about two blocks from The Bucket of Blood Barbecue Bar. There was a cast on one hand but the cast on the other hand had been removed. The functioning of my right hand was coming back slowly and I was starting to get stir crazy having been confined to the house for several months.

One night I decided to walk down the avenue and it felt good as I strolled towards the Boulevard. Several cars stopped and congratulated me on my recovery offering me a ride but I was enjoying the slow methodical walk. I reached the pool hall and several young men were shooting unofficial dice out in front of the joint. This was frowned upon by the establishment because the house could not get a cut. The game always got broken up once it became too big.

Young Anthony Lang was on a roll and I knew that his luck would run out soon, so I decided to fade his play. He won the next few rolls of the dice as I continued to fade him. Then one dice fell into a crack - it was a crap and he lost. The other side said he won and he picked up his winnings as I yelled "crack dice no play." He began to protest as I demanded he reshoot. He reluctantly dropped the money and prepared to reshoot. All of a sudden a foot stepped in the game covering the money, as a voice yelled, "Don't let this jive turkey cheat you son. I'm tired of his shit anyway."

I looked up from the kneeling position and I saw the disdaining eyes of his father, Gangster James Lang, an O.G. gambler, hustler, and drug dealer. He began to read me the riot act as his son gathered up the winnings. I was completely shocked at his dialogue of hatred; threats and his degradation of my character was humiliating. You see I had known him and his family for a long time, as I was the next generation under him.

He was the O.G. and my wife, Barbara, and his eldest daughter, Shirley, were best friends. Her husband was Big Hank, Irvell Morgan, my ace boom-coom. His son and my younger brother, "Bad Habit Rabbit" were tight. At that very moment I saw his whole card. He was a punk and a coward with his hands on his pistol. James had a shit eaten grin on his face. I said, "Mr. Lane why?" And before I could say another word, he said he was glad the police had taught me a lesson and that I needed to get on down the ramp before I receive a final one.

As tears gathered in my eyes I began to walk back towards the house while he continued to belittle me as more onlookers began to gather. You see there are several factors that you, the reader, must realize so you understand this episode in its entirety.

#1: He could not whip me in a fight on his best day.

#2: I was crippled in one hand and had a cast on the other.

#3: I never knew until that day that he did not like me. He waited until I was wounded and less than 50% to make his move that would ultimately almost cost him his life. It was by the grace of God.

#4: You see almost a year to that date he laid on the operating table and died twice and was resurrected as I languished in the County Jail between a P.C. 187 or 187 attempt. He was revived a second time and I will not talk about what actually happened, but I will elaborate on the trial and the conclusion of the matter.

While he was recooperating our families almost went to war. My brother Rob aka "Bad Habit Rabbit" had a similar character as "Sonny", in the movie "The Godfather." He was hotheaded and ready to strike first. At the "Lang Clan", he began gathering and recruiting soldiers, but Big Hank was not having it. He knew his father-in-law was an undercover punk. He continued to defuse the situation. Rabbit had gathered Big Blue, G Boyd and Butch Mims. These young men were Homie's that had big reps and the Lang clan was no match for these soldiers who were dedicated to me. These were Eastside Gangsters, I did not say Gang Bangers. There is a stark difference in the two. When the homies heard about my trouble and began to gather at the spot, Big Hank, James Lang's son-in-law, and my best friend, got with Barbara, Mrs. B, and they began to defuse the situation between both houses.

One night my brother, Rob, and "Big Blue" decided to ride, and they got a surprise visit from one of my Panther brothers from New Orleans. He came to visit me in the county jail. I had not seen him for almost 4 years but he heard about what was going on through the Grapevine and helped me hit Broadway once again as he assisted Mrs.

B in my case. The war was called off. I was back and forth in the court for the next year as James Lane took the stand and sang like, "The Temptations"!

I never understood those fake gangsters like James Lane. He was known for selling crack cocaine and heroin. He had a couple of drug houses around the neighborhood and was known for kicking down doors. One time he pistol whipped some dudes that owed him money. He ran numbers and gambled profusely. Now I've been in some scraps and they even tried to hit me a couple of times, but I would never call the police.

As gangsters in the Street Life, we do not call the police. We handle our business come what may. We never snitched on anyone in the street life because there is a certain code with rules and regulations that we follow which governs over Street life. "Beretta" said, "if you can't do the time don't do the crime." If you get busted then be willing to do the time and do not try to lighten your load by telling on someone else. I had settled down in the County Jail with an understanding that it was going to be a long fight.

After about eight months in Stoop, Mrs. B, my wife, came to visit. She came on a regular basis and my books were always fat with money. Mama Bessie would walk downtown every month and leave $100 on my books. They had placed me in the back-end, which was a high powered 6 to 8 men cell. It was two Latinos cells, two Caucasians cells, and two cells of African Americans. There was always tension in the back-end and when I first arrived, there was some nut calling himself "Big Black." He was overbearing, one of those "big fish" that was in a small pond. He was about 6'6", 290 pounds, and all muscle. Big Black was a trustee who regulated the day-to-day transactions from cell one throughout the back end.

When I got to Cell 1, it was old homie week: "Steady Teddy" was there. He was a cold hustler originally out of St. Louis and "Buzz Saw", a high yellow pimp off the West side. Now "Steady Teddy's" girl worked as a librarian and would come in once a week and drop off a pack of narcotics. She was a good girl but a little squeamish. I had been over to their house a few times and knew she worked at the library downtown, but never would have guessed that she had the jail run. She was the "mule" and to look at her you never would have expected it.

There was only one problem, "Big Black" was charging the homies a 40% surcharge of everything that came in. He was something else. He intimidated them. Oh, I forgot, Terry Lewis, was there also. He was a couple of years older than me. He and big Hank were boys. Neither one of these three were riders, so when they saw me their face lit up. This is how it went or **WHAT HAPPENED WAS...**

After I was booked in, I was immediately escorted to high power and assigned to block two, cell one. It was late at night and everyone was asleep as the big cell gates opened. I walked in and the cell doors thundered with an applause, as if it was the finale at the end of a movie. For some it was the final call in that they would never be on the other side again.

Everyone took heed that a newcomer had entered their domain as they peaked from their bunk. I grabbed the top bunk and stayed up most of the night assessing the situation due to being thrown into a tankful of hard-core criminals. You better keep your eyes open. I sat up smoking a cigarette that I had gotten from one of the guards who was working in the night laundry. I was stripped and was given a jumpsuit. **Moving right along...**

It was about 4 a.m. as I saw a small figure of a man get up off the bottom bunk and headed to the back of the cell. As he finished his business, the dimness of the cell light exposed his face and I saw him as he saw me. He must've been grinning like a Cheshire cat, saying "well, well, well, look what the cat drug in. If it isn't O.G. Michael Sterling." He shouted as if I was Denzel Washington or somebody. "Teddy Teddy", wake up Michael Sterling's here." "What?," replied steady Teddy as he jumped out of his bunk." Terry wake up your homeboy is here." "Man!" Terry said, as he got up, "Young Mike, I'm sad they caught up with you. We gotta talk", as they were slapping me on the back and giving high five.

Then all of a sudden that thing that happens when there's something wrong and a certain feeling comes over me. It's like an alarm, a warrior's premonition, and I've had it all my life. I heard a loud deep voice say, "y'all better shut up all that noise, you don't want Big Black to get up." Humm! I said to myself, as I motioned for quiet, then gave a signal and everyone retreated to their bunk as silence stilled the night.

The main light came on around 6 a.m. everyone seemed to awaken and begin readying for the day. I heard the food cart clamoring for entrance and I still hadn't gone to sleep, especially after I heard that "voice." I watched as that voice arose. He was as Black as the ace of spades and was sporting some 19 inch arms, about 6'6 and looked fierce. He gave me the once over and grunted "hum" in a very cynical manner. This "tree" was not going to be easy to chop down I thought. The gate open and he walked out sporting a blue jumpsuit.

He was a trustee getting ready for his morning rounds. As soon as he walked out "Buzz Saw" jumped up and handed me a cigarette. You could smoke in the County Jail back in the day-day, but not now! Things have changed. Now that I have retired from the game, I said, "I'm glad the Nigger is gone. He's just too much," and I took the Camel cigarette, my brand at the time. I had switched from Kool's, and now smoked a non- filtered man's cigarette.

Terry Lewis and Steady Teddy stood in front of Big Black's bunk facing me and Buzz Saw, who was seated on his own bunk. I said, "man sit down, let's talk." Teddy replied, "Man, the big old nigger will go off if he sees someone on his bunk." I said, "What! Oh, man what's going on?" They began to pitch in and tell me about this Baby Bully terrorizing the whole block and taxing everyone's commissary. In addition to the drug trade at 40%. I replied, "Man you got to be kidding." They said, "Naw man, this dude is a trip." My next response was, "Why haven't you all jumped him?" It was obvious, Terry Lewis was really a coward. I learned that in high school, but that's another story for another time.

Now Steady Teddy had a medical condition, he would stick a knife in you if you pushed hard enough!! Buzz Saw would fight, but was not a fighter, if you know what I mean. "It's okay", I said after a second thought. "Tell me more", I replied as they began to explain the situation more vigorously; my blood began to boil. I hated Baby Bullies and have fought them all my life. I knew I had to go at Big Black, but I needed to see him again. They said he'll be back.

After a while he appeared with his jumpsuit tied down around his waist. I stood at the cell door and watched his every move as I figured out my game plan. He had already worked out because those 19's had swollen up to 20 and his chest was massive. "Very impressive", I said to myself, as I stared intently towards him. He saw me looking and began to strut around like a rooster. He put on a show as he yelled to the next cell, "Where is my money? Man, you better get my money. If you have to call your mama and have her put it on my books because we don't want no more broken arms up in here."

I turned to Buzz Saw and asked if he broke somebody's arms. He replied, "Black whipped two of them youngsters and knocked one out cold while standing on the other one's shoulder as he lay on his stomach. He twisted his arm backwards. We all heard the bone break, it echoed throughout the block.

The next day he raised taxes on the block. "What!", I replied. Now I was angry and I could feel the adrenaline rise up the back of my neck into my brain. Okay, okay, okay. I began to take deep breaths confirming to myself my action plan. All of a sudden before I could think, I heard myself address Mr. Black, "Can I have a word with you?" "What the hell do you want?", he replied? "I just want to talk."

He walked towards me and I removed my arms from between the bars. I stated, "I heard you have been taxing the Homeboys." He replied, "What business is it of yours?" I replied, "I'm making it my business" as I probed his soul staring deep into his eyes with a steady gaze. He stared back at me with anger and his eyes became enraged, but I did not break my gaze. I said "As soon as this gate opens, I'm coming at you Mr. Black. I'm gonna whip that ass up and down this tier like you stole a government mule. When I get through with you, you're gonna be my bitch and I'm going to have you wash my draws."

I did not take my eyes off him as they began to yell up and down the tiers saying, "Oh shit, who is that down there talking to Big Black like that?" Steady Teddy replied, "It's O.G. Michael Sterling. He drove up last night." I kept my eyes fixed on Big Black and continued to read him the riot act. I heard someone down the tier yell: "Big Black you are in trouble, that's Michael Sterling -- he is a fool." They began to whistle and holler, "Get him for me, young Mike." Then all of a sudden Big Black blinked and dropped his gaze. I knew I had broken him mentally. He turned and went to the gate and checked out of the unit.

Later on that day two Sheriff deputies came to the cell. One of them retorted, "Mr. Sterling when did you get in? I haven't seen you for a while. I'm walking out this 187." They had informed me that Gangster Lang had died. I did not want him to die, for many reasons. So, for the next several months I began to work out furiously. I had gotten up to 500 push-ups and was on my way to 1,000.

I watched Buzz Saw go home, then Terry Lewis caught the chain back to the Joint. Steady Teddy took a year deal and was sent to Banning Road Camp. Junior Keithley drove up on a 187 homicide. He was one of my undercover Homie's who still owed me a gangster favor. He is still doing time some 30 years later. He may never hit Broadway again. My case looked bad as I settled into jail house rock and over that year I watched them come and go.

While I was there a riot broke out where they tear gassed the whole tier. I have learned how to handle it from my experience in the Black Panther Party. Little JJ drove up with a strange man, Mr. Terry Pugh. We later came to find out he was a 3rd   degree Black belt in Taekwondo. He would receive strange letters from the White House and really didn't look like much physically.

They moved us all into cell number four as the Black population dropped on that unit. We looked up and there were 24 white boys, about 16 Hispanics and 7 Blacks. I wasn't sure if this was intentional or not. But from time-to-time these Neo-Nazi guards would set us up for whippings and beatings by other inmates so we had to always be on our "p's & q's".

The Race War

As the white population increased, tension became very hostile, with the present movement. This exchange dictated the agitation and mindset of the inmates. In the penal system it was easy to transfer from a high level prison to a county jail environment for a few months. All one person had to do was to find someone that had a high-powered case from their city of incarceration. They could talk or pressure the inmates that were going back for a re-trial or another charge, then claim to be an important witness in the matter. He could have his lawyer subpoena you and you're off to Disneyland, the county jail. You are a big fish in a small pond and in most cases, you're able to dictate policy in that environment. Case in point **AND WHAT HAPPENED WAS...**

On Thursday, the chain went out and came in. We were always on alert at this time because most of the hard-core inmates would be sent to the back- end. This particular Thursday, I watched as the Rebel, Doc Savage and Tank, all neo-Nazis were together. Rebel had gotten huge and I had not seen him for a few years. He looked as hard and mean as ever. Yes! It is the same rebel I had to fight three times before I defeated him. He was back, but he was nothing compared to Doc Savage and Tank.

Tank was about the same size as Baby Bull. He and Junior Keithley both sported 21 inch arms and were lifting 400 pounds on the bench. Doc Savage was a whole different story. He had steel blue eyes, and his hair was golden blonde. He stood 6'4", and weighed in at about 290 lbs., all muscle. He had an air of superiority that only a seasoned champion would have after 30 victories and no defeats. We were in trouble to say the least on a roll of 48 inmates. While only seven were Black, 24 where white and 16 Hispanic. There was going to be trouble. I looked at Baby Bull and said, "Awe what part of the game is this?" He smiled and said, "I guess it's time for you to finally earn your stripes." Baby Baby Bull as we called him, was raised in the penal system. He went from the Youth Authority, on to Soledad, which was the "gladiator" school.

Terry and JJ had both gone to San Quentin had made the rounds twice in the Youth Authority. While Baby Bull had been to Soledad and San Quentin at least three different times. He was only 27 years old and was incarcerated most of his life. He had just driven up with a hot 187 homicide and as of the date, November 2014, he was still locked up.

I had never been to any institution and only had done one year in Banning Road Camp. Now do not get it twisted, I had been arrested about 30 to 40 times but always fought my case with vengeance and never took a deal no matter how threatening it was.

The first night I heard them talking next door saying, "The first thing we're going to do is get them 'spear chuckers' off this row." Then another one replied, "I can't stand the smell of them niggers next door. They gotta go." "Hey Nigger, I killed Martin Luther King", one replied, as another began to say, "Those jungle bunnies gotta go." Then Little JJ started talking back with his own barrage of hatred from a Black perspective. He was a two-time loser. I sat there quietly reflecting over man's inhumanity to man and did not say a word. It was in those moments I became very stoic.

Three days later, at the visiting Hall, several brothers from the general population were stabbed and beaten during the visit and several more were attacked coming from court. You see! The edict came from our unit. It said, "attack all niggers." If any Arian white boys did not comply they would face hard and serious consequences. They made one white boy cut his wrist and he died right next door that same month. The edict was a directive sent from our unit. I knew two of the youngsters that got stabbed from my hood. One was in critical condition. We went on "Red Alert", knowing we were outgunned and overmatched.

As Baby Bull, JJ, and I began to strategize, we knew the attack on us would probably come on Saturday during visitation. As Saturday arrived, we ate breakfast and everyone on the row was quiet. It was too quiet - the silence was almost deafening, as the tension began to build. Our weapon tree consisted of a couple of socks with three bars of soap tied together and it would cause serious damage if it caught you upside your head. We also had the razor blade tooth brushes and one metal shank, and that was about it.

I did not use a weapon as I was on an assignment. I was to keep Doc Savage busy while Baby Baby Bull took out as many as he could. Little JJ was given the sock soap sling. As the morning progressed we noticed Doc Savage and Tank had volunteered to clean the tier. Now as I saw it, they would already be on the tier cleaning when they would call for visit. Dog training Jerry's visit came first like clockwork. The little white girl he had would be the first at the window like Secretariat at Hollywood Park.

The plan was that they would call Jerry's name for a visit and as soon as he stepped out, the gate would close. The white boys from Cell 1 would be on the wall, maybe about 3 to 5 on the average, then the Mexicans, 2 to 5+, Doc Savage and Tank. Once again Cell 1 had eight white boys; Cell 2, eight Hispanics; Cell 3, eight white boys; Cell 4 us, with seven Blacks; Cell 5, eight white boys; and Cell 6, eight Hispanics.

Dog trainer Jerry stalled in the middle of the gate while JJ tied the gate with a sheet so it could not close. Once it was tied he went out to the left and I came out second, right towards Doc Savage. Baby Bull came out fast and by the time I reached Doc Savage he had already knocked out two white boys, as he was fierce. I engaged Doc Savage and still today, I do not know what kind of punch he hit me with, all I know is I saw stars. My last thought was "I cannot go down. They need me."

I awoke with Sgt. Gomez tapping me on the shoulder saying, "Mr. Sterling, let him go." To my amazement, I had Doc Savage in a full nelson. Baby Bull and JJ were back in the cell laughing. There were white boys knocked out, bleeding and bloodied up and down the hallway. I threw Doc Savage up against the opposite wall and he slid down and his face was a bloodied mess. As I went back into the cell all the Homie's there patted me on the back saying, "young Mike has earned his stripes." Baby Bull looked at me with that smile and said, "We did it "Homie", we did it!" Oh, I ate it up and began "high siding" and talking smack, as no one ever knew I was knocked out on my feet. I know and you the reader should know by now that Mama Bessie's prayers were invincible. **Let's fast-forward...**

REFLECTION: I am on a U.S. Airways International flight #750 writing this book; in route to Brussels reflecting on what seems to be a nostalgic moment. It is November 29, 2014, some 35 years later. Apostle Evelyn S. Kuwoe invited me to speak in the Netherlands for her anniversary service. What a difference a day makes!

Moving right along...

The war was over and we had "cut off the head." The brothers rallied in one of the dorms as 15 white boys were hospitalized and the jail was segregated for over a year. I had been down about a year fighting my case and was called out to visit on this particular Saturday. Mrs. B was there and she seemed very excited for some reason. We talked for a few minutes as she began to unfold a piece of paper she retrieved from her purse. She placed it up against the window so I could read it. It said, "James approached me and said if we paid him $5,000 he will not testify".

I was floored, the nerve of that snake. Now, this was the break I was looking for so I told her to take the information to my lawyer, and have him record the conversation from his office. She was to call James Lang crying and tell him we could only come up with $2,800 and could he take that and he would get the rest later. It worked perfectly, she arranged to meet him. She was also wired and they took the recording to the D.A.

The next day on a Friday morning, I was called to a special hearing along with James Lang. I sat there in the jury box as the DA, my lawyer and James Lang went in the Judge's chamber. A few minutes later James Lang came storming out and left the court room as the DA came out with the Judge. They called the court into session and the District Attorney said, "Your Honor, I reluctantly must ask that this case be dismissed in the interest of justice."

Now remember no one knew I was getting out. I went straight to Mama Bessie's. It was a surprise to her and she quoted from the Bible, when she saw me and said, that "In the book of James, it says 'that the effectual fervent prayers of a righteous man availeth much." Again, her prayers were invincible.

I now realize the covenant relationship that she had with our Lord and Savior Christ Jesus. She was my Abrahamic Intercessor. Her relationship with God guaranteed her that her household would be saved. We may go through trials and temptations but Satan can only do so much. Satan was hot on my heels, but I'm here today in the Netherlands. This morning Monday, November 31, 2014. I'm reminiscing over Dr. Evelyn Kuwoe's anniversary celebration service last night where I preached heaven down.

REFLECTION: I am on my way to Germany by way of Paris, France. To you the reader I want you to understand that even though Mama Bessie is long gone, her prayers are still being answered. To all prayer warriors and Intercessors, I want you to be confident of this one thing that as you are praying for our children and loved ones, "He that began a good work in you will complete it" – just as he did for Mama Bessie, through me.

On Friday night about 11 p.m., I tasted freedom and went straight to Mama Bessie, only to find out that Barbara had lost my Cadillac. She had moved over to a little apartment on Sixth Street and Mama Bessie gave me the directions. I knocked on the door about 1:30 a.m. and no one answered. I tried the door handle and it opened. As I walked in Jakuma and Leoshia were found asleep on the living room sofa. It was 1:30 a.m and my kids had been left alone. I was hot, yes livid to say the least. How long has this been going on I said to myself? I sat there on the sofa wondering what I was going to do, especially if she had some "nigga" with her.

They came in about 2:30 a.m.. No! Just Barbara and Freda, one of her close friends. When they saw me sitting there, they were both shocked and surprised. "Oh my God", Barbara cried as she ran into my arms. I could see that she and Freda were a little tipsy. I was always afraid that they would be out partying and leave my children home alone.

Jakuma was now about 11 or 12 years old. We talked for a while and went to sleep. The next morning, she explained to me what had happened to my Cadillac. Not to my satisfaction I must say, but I couldn't trip because she was the main reason I was on Broadway. I guess you must take the bitter with the sweet, the sunshine and rain, the joy and pain. It's all just a part of life. I chilled out for a couple of days, but like a race horse I was eager to hear the gun go off.

It was Tuesday evening when I left the house. All was well, but I still had to keep my eyes opened. The James Lang clan could be my last nightmare. My brother Rob had moved back to Pomona (B.N.A.), sin town. I stopped by Mama Bessie's to talk for a while and went to my stash in the bedroom which was under the baseboard beneath the window. It held my 9 mm and a small 380 auto. I left the nine there, placed the 380 Ruger on my waist, and grabbed a roll of Bills I had stashed in a plastic bag. There must have been about $1,200 left. I took $400 and left $800. It wasn't much but it beats zero.

Barbara didn't know about it. In life one must prepare for the unexpected twists and turns. You see nothing is guaranteed no matter how permanent it looks. I remember when Kaiser Steel closed in Fontana. They must have laid off about 5,000 Black workers not including all the Caucasians. Some of those brothers had been receiving a good check for over 20 years. They had bought nice homes that were not paid for and some bought a second car that was not paid for either. Some had little or no retirement and it was brutal. They began to assimilate back into life as best they could, having lost all the swagger that a steady paycheck gives a man. Over the next few years many of them even lost their homes, cars and swagger as others joined Street life and became drug dealers, gamblers, pimps and hustlers (falling through the cracks).

As I reached the Avenue, the first person I saw was, "Black Bird", Lonnie Graham. He was about 12 years my senior and an O.G. Hustler. He still had a little juice left on his card. I did not realize it but when I hit Broadway all my associates, friends, and homies knew that my "juice" card had risen about 50% in stock. It took me years to realize my street value which was increased by the way I carried myself. I was just being me.

I was Youngblood, a cold gangster. Me and Bird strolled down to Carlos liquor store and retrieved a bottle of Jamie 08 and some beer. Yes, it's called a poor man's boilermaker. When we got back to the block, I was on celebrity status. The O.G.'s were lacing me up with drugs and cash. The custom was when infamous gangsters, pimps or hustlers hit Broadway, everyone that was down with the life, would laced them up with drugs or cash. Knowing that at any time the clock could stop and if your name was called you had to pay the piper.

As the evening tide fell, "Blackbird" said, "Man what are you going to do about that fake Home Boy Terry?" I replied, "What are you talking about?"

He repeated, "Awe man I thought you knew", he stated. Then said, "Let me leave it alone. I do not want to be the one to start this shit." I insisted he tell me what he was talking about.

I was good and toasted by now and then suddenly Terry from the East Coast drove up. He got out the car and said, "Man, I'm so glad you made it", as he placed a couple of bills in my hand and a few bags of heroin. I thanked him and went to give him a high five and Blackburn slapped his hand down. He said, "Nigger don't come up here faking the funk. He's going to find out sooner or later. I'm just not going to tell him."

Then all of a sudden that thing began to rise up in the back of my neck warning me when something was wrong. I am not going to go into any details you see, because Barbara and I are good friends and I'll still kill a roach behind her. Bless her and keep her safe. But for the sake of the truth and the authenticity of the book, I will say this. That's the day I walked away from my family for good. I had too much pride and was hurt beyond compare. I dealt harshly with East Coast Terry later in that week. I sent him to the hospital, took all his money, jewels, and his car. Little Pee Wee stopped me from driving off with his car. East Coast Terry, laid in the street, knocked out in a bloodied mess.

Needless to say, I found myself back in jail. I had not been out 10 days and was charged with felony assault and robbery, ain't that a Bitch! Barbara, my friend still today, went to work and she called East Coast Terry and told him he better drop the charges or she would turn him in for something he had recently done. He dropped the charges and then Barbara went to the D.A.'s office and told him something and I was released a week later.

Oh, by the way I caught up with Terry again in San Bernardino on Mount Vernon Ave. There was a club there and I saw him in the parking lot. He was made to give me his wallet and Jewels, while I slapped him around a little and told him he was now my bitch every time I saw him. He needed to break himself or suffer the consequences. He must have had about $500 cash and a packet of heroin. I took it as Marcy Girl and I walked into the Velvet Lounge. Yes, Marcy Girl was my new squeeze.

CHAPTER SEVEN

Marcy Girl

Today when I think about Marcy girl, I become very emotional. She died about 10 years ago, I have two beautiful children by her, Brandon and Desiree. They both are grown and live on the East Coast. I hoped one day I could be a better father to them.

It was a beautiful summer evening. I had separated from Barbara and my kids about a couple of weeks prior. Getting high was my new pastime and it was happening at an alarming rate. I had been on heroin with Lonnie Graham. Yeah, my man, Black Bird but he was only *"chirpen"*, so I thought. Because of the pain and the hurt, I was spiraling out of control. My temperament was about zero.

As I placed the needle in my arm, the euphoria was toxic and I felt like Superman and Iceberg Slim all rolled into one. I placed my godfather hat on my head, cocked it acey/deucey to the side, grabbed my waistline leather jacket and began to stroll. The night was hot with a summer breeze blowing through the recesses of my mind. I lit a Camel cigarette as I examined the terrain, left to right. Methodically, I identified every cranny on the street. Then assured myself that I was ready as I checked the 380 Ruger inside my waistband.

There were enemies who still wanted me dead so I was not going to be caught slipping. Things looked good on the block. Everything was in place and it was about 11:30 at night. I began my stroll examining every car that passed as I paused to observe the passengers.

It was methodical, as I made my way to "The Place", a nightclub. A joint about six blocks away, across the tracks. Skinny Kenny passed by and stopped. "Big Mike, Youngblood on the set", he said. I grabbed the door handle and slid into the Burgundy Riviera. "Don't say that name too loud man." I laughed as we drove off into the night. He was glad to see me. He supported the Black Panthers back in the day and we had put in some work together. He was loyal and could be trusted. A couple of years earlier we were busted together, and I rode the gun beef up in Victorville. It was me, Skinny Kenny and George Edward MacMahand that got popped.

As we pulled into the parking lot, he pulled out some reefer and I declined. I was already on full. Smoking reefer in public made me paranoid. I accepted a joint and put it up for later when I would be maxin and relaxing at the pad. People were pulling in already, but The Place never really started jumpin until about 1 a.m..

We sat in the car talking and going over old times. I asked him if he was packing and he said he had a 22 pistol. Not much, but it could keep the cheat off. I told him to watch my back, those lanes could show up at any time. They were no match for me head up, but I understood that over- confidence filled many coffins.

I saw Big Blue and I yelled, "Who's that "turnkey" on the stroll?" He had that million-dollar smile and got into the back seat. It was the first time that I saw him since I hit Broadway, but he was one of the crew along with my brother, Bad Habit Rabbit, that had put protection on the spot. He was a few years older than me and was fierce with his hands. He never lost a fight.

There was one thing for sure, it was this fact, I never wanted to get into a fight head up with Big Blue. I knew that I would come up short. "Young Mike he said, "You know I got your back. Them punk niggas better not try anything tonight." I asked him if he was packing, he laughed and said, "Oh man you know I'm still on parole. But I got these two pit bulls, one in my left hand and one in my right hand."

"Sure, you're right", I replied as we sat there quietly. Blue began to give me the lowdown. He said Big Hank had told everyone that he was neutral, because "Gangster Lane", was his father- in-law, whom he despised. And I was his young Homie and he would walk through hell with gasoline draws on for me. Yeah! He had always been my protector but his hands were tied on this one. We all understood and he had our utmost respect.

All of a sudden Anthony Lane appeared with his girl. He saw me at the same time I saw him. He raised his hands up to show he had no weapons and said, "Big Mike, I don't want any trouble. My dad said, 'squash it' and that's what I'm doing." He looked back once as he strolled into the club. Skinny Kenny said, "Now I don't trust that nigga." I said, "Let's get out of the car and go in." It was important to keep my eyes on him. I wanted to have a good time. Blue and skinny Kenny grabbed a table near the jukebox. I started to relax when I heard the "Temptation's" singing, "It was just my imagination running away with me."

Then I saw a vision of loveliness stroll past me and gave me the once over. She looked at the Fox next to her, they laughed and went towards the dining area and restroom. Wow! Who was that "high yellow Chiquita brand banana"? I cried. "I'll be back", I said as I removed myself from the table. I looked across the room at young Anthony Lane. His back was to me and he seemed to be minding his own business. I went to the door and peeked in to see if she was sitting at one of the tables. She was not seated and must be in the restroom. I posted up by the entrance into the lounge and waited for her to return.

Suddenly, I saw her come out of the restroom. I slowly stepped behind the entrance into the dim light of the club. She stepped through the door as I stepped to block the way and she bumped right into me. I grabbed her around her waist and she said, "Excuse me", as those panda bear eyes met mine. I replied, "God has sent an angel to mend my broken heart." She said, "Is your heart really broken?" As I pulled her closer, I said, "Baby girl, I'm laughing to keep from crying." She replied, "I can fix it." I swept her off her feet and pulled her around and kissed the sweetest lips I had ever tasted. It appears she melted into my soul as we made our way to the dance floor. The song "Stay in My Corner" was playing. It was the longest slow jam of all time.

We danced the night away and did not talk much. It was again joy and pain. You see joy had replaced the pain in an instant. It was about 4 a.m. when I told Skinny Kenny to drop us off at the "No Tell Motel Holiday Inn", well better known as the Big Six on University Avenue. We spent the next two days together. She had to be back at work on Monday morning at 5 a.m.. Now catch this, she was a guard at C.R.C. Prison (California Rehabilitation Center). We made love like Romeo and Juliet.

That morning as the sun was making it's ascension I looked at her and she started crying. I asked her what was the matter and she replied, "I thought this kind of lovemaking was only in books", as she smiled. "Baby girl you ain't seen nothing yet." I went to the restroom, cooked up some heroin and found a vein and went into euphoria. I came out and went back to work! She said five times, "Oh my God, Young Mike! I can't believe I love you, Michael Paul Sterling and I'm never going to let go." "Ditto", I replied as I gave her the once over again. Wondering if I was tripping or something like this was too good to be true. I called my cousin Leonard Norris. We drove out to Corona that morning and dropped her off at the prison.

She informed me she was supposed to get a car and would call me later. We drove away and Leonard said, "Who was that?", with a smile of admiration on his face. "That's my new squeeze Marcy Girl", I replied with the pride that one would feel as he captured a star from the very sky. I was feeling like a million bucks as I stepped out of the car at 2791 Ninth Street.

I entered the door and the kids were getting ready for school. I helped Leoshie with her Shirley Temple curls and gave Jakuma the once over. Rascheed tied up his shoes. Mama Bessie had given them an early breakfast. I took each one and hugged them with a father's love. These tender moments are the things that bring security to children. They scurried out the door as I walked to the sidewalk and watched them disappear into the next block. I went into my room, grabbed a bag of Heroin and went off into another dimension.

Yes, I was getting hooked on this stuff and I knew it. How could my life have spiraled into this. I said to myself as I shook my head and as I literally went out to lunch. What happens when the challenges of this world become daunting and unbearable to one's moral fiber it seems many of us look for ways of escape. I thought about the song, "I'm Doing Fine Up Here On Cloud Nine" as the cigarette I was smoking began to burn my hands causing me to instantly come back to reality.

Every morning I was high as a kite and doing about a quarter of powder for a wake-up. I contemplated, "How am I going to hide this from my new flame, Marcy Girl"? The phone rang and the clock was almost at 12 noon. I had nodded out for hours. As I arose, I heard Mama Bessie say, "Michael it's for you." "Hello", I replied. The voice on the other end said, in a soft sweet voice, "What's up Spicy Mike?" I laughed loudly, "Where did that come from?" She said, "You are full of spice and everything nice. Your sugar and cinnamon all rolled into one and I cannot wait to see you, my love. I just called to ask if you can take me to Vegas this weekend."

"They just approved my car loan and I'm going to pick it up after work. I took a little extra money out of the Credit Union and I'm taking Friday off. Baby, please take me to Las Vegas this week." I replied, "Just pick me up as soon as you get the car, I'll be ready." She said, "Gotta go love.", as she hung up the phone. I lit a cigarette and said to myself, "What a girl!"

I called Little Jesse and explained to him I was ready to go back to work. He asked what could I handle? I told him to send me three paquettes. I took a third out of every bag for my own personal use, and I still made about $500. I always made 10 extra bags which gave me a total of one hundred bags.

I walked down to Robert Earl and Lily May's house and dropped them off 30 bags. Then caught a ride to Papa Religh's house and left him with 30 bags. They would give me $200 and keep $100 and that left me with $400. I would do little or no work, giving Little Jesse his $500 and re-up.

We started off at 60/40 but over the years it turned out to a 50-50 split. Oh, and I had to put in a little work for him when some of his other people got out of line. It was a business relationship, but we became close, especially when some up and coming wannabes tried to take over. Those who know don't tell and those who tell don't know. We will tell that story at another time.

Marcy Girl arrived about 8:30 that evening. She gave me the keys and said, "Baby this car is yours." I played it off real cool and nonchalant. You know, like it was an ordinary occasion. Somebody had laced this filly up real tough. She knew how to treat a man, as we drove up University Avenue to the Motel.

My boy, steady Teddy, had gotten out. Him and that white girl, he liked, had posted up at the Ramada Inn. As we drove into the parking lot, Marcy Girl opened an envelope full of bills and said, "Daddy I got $1,200 here, can I have $600.", as she handed me an envelope. I parked and counted out $400. "I'm putting this up for emergencies." I gave her $400, pocketed $400, and hid $400 in the trunk.

Wow! this girl is a trip. I hoped she was not the feds on some undercover cop, as this is too good to be true. I looked at her again and said, "Get out of the car and come here." I held her in my arms and began to romance her by whispering sweet everythings in her ear. I ravished her with a poetic license.

"Let Me Pause For The Cause"

Sweet ebony pride in life of love...
I adore the very essence of your soul...
You mended my heart and melted the pain...
Captured my imagination when no one else came...
I was the hunter and you were the game...
But this love that I found can never be tamed...
Its a vision of life's ups and downs...
That have faded away the tears of a clown...
Into the sea of forgetfulness I gaze, I'm lost in your love...
and I'm found and amazed...
I promise to love until the ancient of days...
You're my Cleopatra, I'll love you always...
I feel I've been checkmated...
In the rhapsody of your love...

She cried as she placed her head on my shoulder, safe and secure. It seemed as if we were the only ones on the planet for life had faded away. While we were caught in a state of bliss, my heart skipped a beat. Our breathing became synchronized and the rhythm of our being became one.

Suddenly I heard a voice, "Big Mike Sterling." It was Steady Teddy, yelling as he came out of the Ramada Inn. "Who you got with you my man?" "Homie, this is my new squeeze 'Marcy Girl' and we're on our way to Vegas." "Let's go inside", he replied. "I got something for you". I said, "Is it snowing in the room?"

As we walked into his suite. Karen was in sexy lingerie making lines on a stained-glass mirror in her compact. It was Peruvian Flake, the best cocaine around. He was on his way to Montana and played a beautiful long-range con game that was about to pay off at $20,000. We left late that night and caravanned to Vegas.

Me and Marcy girl rode in her 1980 Malibu. Steady Teddy was sporting a Thunderbird. We got a room at the Flamingo and acted up. When you party, you party hearty and you party all night long. We broke Camp Monday morning about 1 a.m. and headed back to California.

He drove off and hit the road towards Montana. I saw him about a month later in a brand new 1981 Cadillac, with two white girls. He was rolling hard. But then I saw him again in the Spring and he looked like death on a stick. He was all alone, broke, and living in the drug house along with Kenny Appleton and Robert Mayo. All of them were real players back in the day-day.

I'm glad I retired from street life and whenever I did come into the neighborhood I would pass through one of the spots and offered to send a struggling O.G. to one of my training centers up in Northern California.

Most of them were stuck like Chuck, but I brought a few out that are doing well still today like Poppa Joe Talley, Pemo a.k.a. Benjamin Fludd, Michael McKnight, Lorenzo Allen a.k.a. Low Tracy, and David Reese just to name a few.

Steady Teddy is dead from overdosing. Michael died from gangrene. Robert and Geno Mayo both died in misery. Marcy girl had a stroke and died with her five children by her side. Margareet Ford was shot with a double barrel shotgun. Kathy Crawford was stabbed 36 times and thrown in a dumpster. El Dorado Butch and Olie J overdosed. Chocolate died in the hospital, but not before she came out of the life. She was born-again too and saved by the blood of Jesus.

Baby Seal had kidney failure and I saw him about 5 a.m. sitting on the corner down from the motel. He was the only one that was younger than me. I almost did not recognize him. He looked 70 years old. He had been on dialysis for about four years and got tired of going. It seemed he hadn't had a treatment in over a week and his skin was tough like an alligator. I u- turned my big Sedan Deville around and jumped out of the car. I picked him up, and took him to the community hospital. He just said he was tired and died two days later. Jesse James Jackson Junior died from cirrhosis of the liver. The list goes on and on.

There was a record that came out when we were all in the midstream and it was called, "Street Life." There was a line I always remembered. It was in street life that you better not get old. I thank God I retired from the life at 30 years old and believe me that was late. I started at 13, yes 13 and spent 17 years in street life. That was a lifetime ago.

As tears begin to fill my eyes even now. This book is very heartfelt and I did not realize it was going to be so emotional. If it had not been for Mama Bessie's prayers and the grace of God, which I did not deserve, I would be dead myself. You must understand, I was harder, rougher and did more wrong out there in the street life than most of them. But one thing I must say, is that I never was evil in my heart. Oh, believe me! Most of the people I encountered were evil. I always asked for forgiveness in my heart, but I also was stuck like chuck in street life and did what was necessary to survive.

"Pimpin Ain't Easy But Somebody's Got To Do It"

I hesitated about writing this chapter and I will try to be as polished as possible but it would not be authentic if I left this chapter out. The one thing that I regret the most out of all the things I did in the street life was "Pimpin."

I want to go on record by apologizing to my Black African Queens, those White girls, and all their children, mothers and relatives. It is not possible to undo the past, I am truly sorry. As Mother Shepard says so eloquently, "God's got me and I plead the blood."

My legacy now includes opening an 8 ½ -acre ranch for women with a swimming pool, horses, chickens and goats. My older sister, Bishop Claudia Marshall, ran the House of the Virtuous Women Ranch. I was the founder and visionary. The facility was dedicated to take women off the streets and help them realize the potential of becoming a Proverbs 31 woman. The house began in my home. Women slept on my couch, in my spare bedroom, and we put women wherever we could find space. How is that for a change in direction?

The men's center was a 30-bed facility called, "The House of Joseph." We had two other facilities as well. A transition home for women and children and an alumni house for those who graduated, but were not ready to re-enter society. My niece, Teresa Bush, ran the transition home and my ex-wife, Shawn Vaugh was an instructor for the whole project. We did this project for about 20 years in Maryvale, CA. I had graduated from Power of God Men's Home in Baldwin Park, California after sixteen months. I started my first men's home with Pastor Raul Genera in San Bernardino. I was on fire and determined to pull people out of the pit. From time-to-time I got a call from some girl's mother, whose daughter was trapped in one of those drug houses by a gang or a "want to be" pimp. I would go to the spot and literally put the girl over my shoulder and carry them out.

God had me and I did not have the spirit of fear, but of power, love and a sound mind. If anyone is reading this book who needs help, contact our ministry. Even though I am at retirement age, I'll still put in work and have trained up armorbearers, ministers and a five-fold ministry team to support me. I'm just paying some dues, not for glory nor for fame. I am Christ's slave and the rest of my life is dedicated to saving souls. It's payback time. This is from my heart because again, God's got me. I have no guilt. I'm covered in the blood and I understand its power. I'm still willing to give Satan a Black eye, as my Brother Jude said in the Bible, "And others saved with fear, pulling them out of the fire; hating even the garment spotted by the flesh."

I was a real O.G.. A Gangster in street life. I'm going to say it again. Not a gang banger, but a true O.G. Gangster who for the most part followed the O.G. Player's Rules. My Player Card was never suspended. I just retired from the game and went with Jesus Christ, my Lord and Savior. Do you hear me?

How it all started. It was 1974, about 40 years ago, I was in the prime of my life. I was driving a 1965 Riviera that had one owner with about 30,000 miles on it. It was clean. I was selling heroin and kicking back at Lincoln Park on the grass with big Hank and Count Drack. I was sipping on some white port wine with a lemon juice twist.

The day was fair, as autumn was turning into winter as seen on most of the trees. This cocoa brown Cadillac drove up, out jumped, sucker Victor Brew and when I say sucker I mean sucker. A wannabe for real. I had not seen him for some time, but he seemed to be sportin' real tough.

Victor never had the heart for the game. He was just faking the funk. Oh, by the way, I heard he got saved. A big thumbs up to my brother if this is true. He asked me, "was I holding" (still dealing drugs) and I said, "Yes man." He handed me a Benjamin and I told him he had to take me to the spot. I was just about to go and re-up. He hesitated and then said, "okay" as I walked towards his car. He went to the passenger side, opened the door and snapped his fingers, Pippen style, and out came two of the finest snow bunnies I had ever seen. They looked like they had jumped out of a Vogue magazine. These broads were classy with fur boots on up to their knees. One had on a micromini and the other had on a pair of Jordache Jeans, which were top-of-the-line back then. They both had on waistline fur jackets, as I smiled and said, "Pippen Victor", what's really going on?" He said, "Homie pimpin ain't easy, but somebody's gotta do it." Then he attempted to give me a high five. I gestured and pulled back my hand as he missed and left him hanging.

Those snow bunnies began to chuckle and he looked back at them with a frown, and they immediately stopped. I had him drive me up to Papa Religh's house - one of my dealers, but no one knew that he was dealing for me. I always cut and bagged my drugs up differently. It helped me to regulate traffic and at this time his drugs were the best on the east side.

I insisted that Victor get out of the car with me. I knocked on the door and saw Papa peek out the window. He immediately smiled and opened the door. I told Victor to have a seat on the couch while Papa and I proceeded to the back room. He shut the door and I said, "Papa how much cash do you got?" He said, "Man you just left here. I got about a C note you want it?" I said, "No take this $50 and go ask Victor for change. I want you to spy out his roll. I said to Papa, "He's got two snow bunnies in the car and I'm fixing to work him. I'm about to go into the pimpin business, this dope game is too tough. They done already run in on me twice and came up short. It's just a matter of time before I would have to pay the piper."

"I had been going good for about one year and a half. If I don't change up for a while it's just a matter of time before one of those suckers sets me up." Papa went out and got change from Victor. He came back and said, "His role had to be about $2,000 if not more. He must've went through about 15-100 bills before he got to a $50." I said, "Cool man, let me have half of your stash. I will be back in the morning and you can keep an extra

$50 on me," and he smiled. I walked briskly back out and said, "Let's go." Pimpin Victor smiled because he thought I was giving him his props in front of OG Papa Religh who had been in the life with Filmore Slim and the Ward Brothers up in the bay area. Jesse James Jackson Junior was one of my heroes who told me stories about Papa and how his name use to reign throughout Fresco and Oakland, California. Yes Jessie, B.N.A. JJJJ, had the biggest rep on the East side and was known as a six-time loser. He had been lacing me up and giving me the game over the last few years. Papa was now semi-retired.

Me and Victor got in the car and he drove me back to the park. I got out and he said, "Where is my stuff?" I said, "I got it, I'm going to follow you. I need to handle my business." He said, "Man I can't take no one to my spot." I said, "Listen Homie, I thought we were cool with both hands open wide, palms up and no smile on my face." He said, "We are." I said, "Let's go.", as I jumped into my river dog (Riviera) and we drove to the corner of Victoria and Denton. He lived right behind the golf course. It was a large home that belonged to his mother. There was a small Grandma house on the side that he occupied. It was right across the street from my big sister, Leona's house. I knew a few older women who were about my sister's age that dabbled in the life. They loved having me on their dance card as my reputation was fierce. We went into his pad and I retrieved a couple sets of brand-new works. I walked into the bathroom like I owned the joint. I said, "Blondie what's your name?" She said, "Giles", as she followed me in. I cooked up about a half a gram, threw in about a quarter of cocaine, drew up about 50cc's and blasted off into outer space. I gave Giles a syringe and told her 10 cc's only. She did as she was told and said, "Big daddy this is good." All of a sudden, Victor and Babs showed up at the door. Victor was demanding his stuff. I told the other chick to draw up 10 cc's and grab Victor by the collar and escort him out of the bathroom. I said, "Punk you know better than to push up on me like that." He started to talk some smack and I slapped him across the face while saying, "Nigga you better sit down before I raise up on you." He sat down and said, "Big Homie, why you do me like that?" Babs looked with concern and Giles pulled her back into the bathroom and shut the door.

I began to read him the riot act knowing they could hear me loud and clear. After about 20 minutes, I yelled, you hoe's about finished and they said yes and came out of the bathroom. I told them to sit on the couch and threw Victor two bags of heroin. He said, "Man, can I have some of that caine?" I said in a resounding voice, "Hell no man. This shit ain't free." He pulled out his wad and said, "Can I get a 50" and I said, "Yes and flipped him a 50 sack of cocaine. He went into the bathroom, and I said to the girls, "How much money you done gave this nigga today?" Giles said, "About

$2,000." I told Giles to tell that Nigga you need yo money back. He opened the door with a confused look on his face. He replied, "Are you fuckin' crazy?" I went to the door, grabbed him in the collar and said, "Giles take it out of his pocket" and he slapped her hand away. I hit him with a right cross and he went spiraling on the floor. "Sterling what's up?" "I said give her, her money" as blood began to flow from his mouth. He pulled the wad out of his pocket and said, "Man, I don't want any trouble." Giles grabbed the money and I said "here" as I tossed her the keys to my car. "Get your things both of you, you're going with me. Giles, you drive and whatever your name is you're riding shotgun. I'll be down in a minute. I reminded Victor of something he did several years ago, concerning me and his older sister. It was because of him that his mother came over to Leona's house and cussed me out and snatched up Stephanie. Oh, by the way, I was 15 and she was 17 but I always looked much older than I was. That punk had snitched on us when we went down into the basement and I never forgot it.

We drove off as I got into the back seat and said "they call me 'Young Mike' or better yet call me "M.P." I'm like the military police. Yes! I'm the regulator on the East side and you girls have nothing to worry about. If anybody gives you any trouble tell them you're rolling with Michael Sterling." For two years, we rolled and they never had any trouble in the street life. As a matter of fact, people did them favors to get in good with me. As we approached the Ramada Inn, I told Giles to go inside and get a double and she did as requested. I began to probe the other chick, who was really the finest. Seriously this chick looked like a fashion model. She was about 5'9", tall, sleek, with a body that would put Fleetwood to shame. I said, in my suave voice, "All right young lady tell me a little bit about yourself."

She began to tell me how she was raised in the Midwest and had come to Hollywood to be an actress but found herself "tossed up like a salad" by some fake directors. She said she had to run for her life. She had met Giles sitting on a bus stop on Sunset Boulevard. In L.A. Giles had taken her in about a year ago and she been on the track ever since. She explained that Giles had told her to go back home and offered to buy her a bus ticket. But she had refused for some personal reasons. So, Giles had taught her about street life and had laced her up and she still had a lot to learn.

She said, Victor was cool but she knew he was weak and was happy to be in my stable. She had some harassing experiences over the last year. As tears began to fill her eyes, a true rush of sentiment began to rise in my soul. I pushed it down so fast you would have thought the toilet had flushed. No time for that, I told myself, as my outward appearance projected a stony gaze.

Giles appeared and I told her to give me one of the keys and stay put. I would grab something from the restaurant and be back in a few hours. I posted up across the street and watched the door to the Ramada Inn lobby for a couple of hours. They stayed put. I then drove to Mama Bessie's house on the east side. Oh! By the way, I was married with two kids at that time to a square. Well, I mean to a very good girl. She was hip ghetto style but was not hard-core Street life. I wanted her to stay that way and she did for years. Barbara was truly my heart and our kids, Jakuma and Leoshie, were kept out of "the life." Barbara worked at Taro and in the early days she didn't have a clue as to my true lifestyle.

I soon found out that the dope game was different from the pimpin. I remember one time I had spanked this particular snow bunny real tough. It was not Giles or Babs, it was years later and I sent Brandy packin'. I drove my Cadillac to the house on Ninth Street. I had two spots at that time. There was a two bedroom flat in back of the Turners that I had rented out. **What happened was...**

I drove my Cadillac up to Mama Bessie's house and I parked the car and got out. I slowly walked into the house and to my surprise Brandy was sitting there and Barbara my wife was counseling her. I said to myself, "Ain't that a bitch." Barbara said, "Michael it's okay, I'm just talking to her." I was so stunned that I just said, "I'll be back." Believe me, I got ghost fast. You see nothing is surprising in street life.

Some of the things I've experienced, I'm re-living them now emotionally. As I sit here writing these memoirs of some things are causing me to be sad, others are embarrassing and most of them I can't believe myself. They are still unbelievable to me. I want you to know as I write this book, I am going to keep on thanking Jesus. You might as well get used to it. If it had not been for the Lord on my side, where would I be? As tears began to fill my eyes today, it's okay to cry - I'm free!

Let's continue with Giles and Babs. I left the Ramada Inn, drove to Mama Bessie's and went to the window sill to retrieve two paquettes

. I dropped off a grand and then drove to Papa Religh's house. I was in full effect and walked in grinnin' like a Cheshire cat. I was now in the pimpin' business. He smiled, I collected the cash and gave him a re-up. He said, "All right, 'Sporty Yorty'. How about a couple sacks of cane on the house since you're doing so well? I'm just a squirrel in your world trying to get a nut, an acorn or something." I smiled and flipped him a couple of sacks, through the screen door. I observed the terrain and slowly and majestically walked out of the house.

There was one thing about "Young Mike" no matter how high or how good God was, I was always in a surveillance mode. It saved me many times along with the spirit of discernment. I must remind you that the Bible says the gifts and calling of God are irrevocable. This means you can be a Cleo fortune teller on the dark side or you could use your gift for God. I'm so glad I made it out of the "rain"! Give God the glory. Let's get back to this autobiography.

I got into my river dog and proceeded back to the Ramada Inn. When I arrived, I looked at the room number on my key. I strolled through the lobby, pushed the elevator door button to the third floor and went to the room. They had actual keys back in the day-day. I opened the door and walked in and saw they had left a plate of food for me. It was steak and potatoes. As I grabbed two slices of bread, I made a steak sandwich and discarded the rest, while saying, "where is my money?" They looked at each other and placed about $1,000 on the night stand. I picked it up, looked at it and said, "break yourselves", as they looked at each other again. I said, in a very stern voice as I stood up, "Giles, you need to break yourself right now." Them broads began digging for gold like the 49ers. They had money stashed in places I had no idea. Them hoes must have had an additional $3,500 + $800 in travelers checks. I thought to myself "now this is the life." I must have been a fool to sell dope and commit robberies. I'm going to enjoy this.

Pimpin' ain't easy, but young Mike is doing it. I fixed up their evening shot and put two syringes on the counter with 10 cc's and told them to hit it. It was about 10 p.m. and the freaks come out at night. They complied, I rested as it had been a long day while my adrenaline was pumping. They came back about 3 a.m. with an additional $500 and said it was a slow night. I rose up early the next morning, showered, and told them to meet me at Denny's restaurant about a block and a half away. I never wanted people at the hotel to see us walking together because we did not need the heat. I gave Giles some money and told her to book the room for a week. We went shopping and I did not buy myself anything but spent about $800 on them, caught a matinee, and ate with them. It was a good day.

I realized that Giles was a gangster and a shot caller. Some would refer to her as a bottom woman. She had all the qualifications, far from being lame and tested me with style just to see how sharp I was and what she could get away with. I had read Iceberg Slim's autobiography and Trick Baby, but my real knowledge came when I was with OG Coco at his brother's house on many occasions. I would listen to EL-Von Carter, who had pimped hoes from San Francisco to Hawaii. He was a real international pimp. He did everything he could to lace his young brother, Coco, up with the pimpin game. Coco didn't have the heart but he was a M.A.C. for real. He could talk his way into anything but did not know when he had his mark sold. He would lose his mark as fast as he had caught it. Coco did not know when to shut up.

I remember walking into El-Von's pad and having to take my shoes off at the door for the first time in my life. His living room rug was snow white and about an inch high. His wife was fine and classy. She walked out of the house with a real sable fur coat on and jumped into a white El Dorado that year. I was applying some of the things I had heard and it was perfection. It became clear later on that I never was a real Pimp. I was what you call a Gangster. There is a distinct difference as I would come to find out years later from O.G Silk. Now, he was smooth as silk and took me under his wing. For about six months he let me be his sidekick. Now, that was a life- changing experience.

El-Von's bottom woman was a white girl with blond hair and fine as 100- year-old vintage wine. I was about 14 years old and Coco was 17. As I sat there with Coco I looked up and low and behold this fine Black ace of spades sista walked out with a miniskirt and still today as she bent over and kissed El Von, I could swear she didn't have on any panties. He had four broads, two white girls, this broad and an

Asian chick. El Von could also be seen because he was a headliner in the entertainment world. He would frequent the Top Hat, the Velvet Lounge and even the Place after hours as a favor to L.B..

This life seemed glorious, but the devil is a liar. Some 25 years later Coco had died. It was a stark revelation when I found out that no one came to claim his body. His mother was dead, his brother hated him over a property dispute and it appears he had forged his mother's will and he cheated them out of their portion. Listen! He died lonely and alone.

After establishing the men's home I picked Coco up and took him with me up North and put him in the House of Joseph Christian Men's Training Center. It was about 500 miles from Riverside, the city where I did most of my drama. He was near death at that time. He had kicked the heroin and stayed in our program about 90 days. Then he got a call that his mother was sick. I purchased him a bus ticket so he could get back to Riverside. We stayed in contact until his phone went dead.

By that time, Matthew 6:33 kept me occupied. After my second trip to Nigeria and about a year later I came to Riverside. Everything in the hood was gone. The gambling shack, the barbecue bar, was all torn down like it never existed. I checked on Coco who I had not seen for almost two years.

Every time I went to the east side I would visit him, Pee Wee and a few others. My mission was to pull anyone I could out of the muck and the mire.

As I was driving toward Coco's house and I saw this old man riding a bicycle and I stopped to ask him a question. He looked like a bum, but much to my surprise when he smiled it was pimpin, El Von. He was homeless. I shook my head as I pulled over and asked him where was Coco, his brother? He told me he had died and no one claimed the body. There was no funeral as he had burned every bridge. I replied, "El Von what happened." He said, "Man look at me, I couldn't do nothing. I gave El Von a few dollars, drove off and cried. I literally cried for two days thinking how cruel street life could be. Oh, by the way we buried El Von two years later. Shirley Butts, helped. He had moved out there with her in Perris, California. She had acquired the Marla Gibbs mansion. Do you remember Marla Gibbs, the maid on the TV show "The Jefferson's." Shirley would take in some of the OGs from time to time. It was her way of paying some dues. El Von died out there from a heart attack. He was still shooting up cocaine and had become lost and pitiful.

Back to Giles and Babs. I woke up early the next day and told the girls that I might be gone a couple of days and to stack my money on the nightstand in separate piles with Giles on right and Babs on the left. They were to hit the street at 6 o'clock every evening and come in by 8 o'clock and go back out about 10:30, at the latest 11, and not come back until they made those quotas. They did as I commanded and I went home for about 36 hours.

My supply needed to be replenished so I called Little Jesse, my connection. Money was coming in real fast. I could not really tell my wife everything. You see, my bank was getting bigger and my habit even bigger. I stayed sharp, but my life was out of control.

Oh, by the way, the two years plus I was with Giles and Babs I never had sex with Giles and had sex only once with Babs. I'll explain that later to those who do not understand the game, player style.

K.C. was my new girl. Things had been going good for a couple of years. It had its ups and downs but that was the life. One day Giles and Babs said they need to talk to me about something important. That evening after dinner, we were now posted at the Holiday Inn. Babs said that she wanted her walking papers. She had some personal business that she needed to take care of and if everything went right she would not be returning and she would give me $2,000 for her release. Giles would stay. Now I never read this one in Iceberg Slim's book or heard anyone speak on this scenario. If a broad wanted to leave, she just ran off. I was sitting there pondering the situation.

I remember saying this is going to leave the stable short and Giles replied, "We have a replacement, her name is K.C. "Do you remember," she said, "when I got busted and had to do 90 days for soliciting?" "Yeah," I said, as I lit up a smoke. She continued saying she had met this renegade chick named K.C and had told her about Michael Sterling. She said that she had heard about Michael Sterling and that he was a hard man. They had been communicating with her and had been to visit her a couple of times. She would be out next week and Babs really needed to go. Babs gave me $2,000 in fresh hundreds. I always wonder why those bills were mint fresh but sometimes it's best not to ask questions. Giles was informed that I would make my final decision upon meeting this K.C.

It was a beautiful summer day and we had moved to the Country Inn. It had a kitchen, lounge, living room, and two beds. It was so comfortable that I leased it for a month. I told the girls no business in front of the spot as all business must be done two blocks in all directions. All the time I had Giles and Babs I never laid a hand on them because they really liked the life. On that morning, I woke up and the girls were gone. It was somewhat unusual but I was not really concerned. We had a good understanding. At 11 a.m. the phone rang and it was Giles. It was a rule that nobody was allowed at the spot. She said, "Big daddy we got a surprise. K.C. is here. Can we bring her in?' I replied, "Yes, give me 10 minutes." I got myself together, did about a $20 speedball I had fixed up earlier. Lit a cigarette and took a pause for the cause. The door opened a few minutes later and they or should I say, "She walked into my life - K.C. Wow! What a knockout." I kept my composure but I could not help a slight smile as I was introduced to K.C. I said, "Come here young lady and let me look at you." I want you, the reader to understand something as far as being beautiful. Babs had her by a mile when it comes to looks. But this chick was amazing. She was short about 5'5" with natural flaming red hair and a few freckles on her face. She reminded me of Rebecca of Sunnybrook Farms. She was sporting 38 boobs, with a 24-inch waist, and an ass that would put a sister to shame. I said, "Turn around, young lady and let me see what ya workin with." Oh, she not only turned around but she modeled like she was on the runway or something. Her smile was glowing as if she was making a Colgate commercial.

Chapter Eight

Christmas

"Michael Sterling, I choose you", as she handed me a wad of bills. It was about $500 to be exact and I was shocked. I shook my head in approval as my "Johnson" began to rise. I cannot believe it, this chick, K.C., had quality and her sex appeal was captivating. She had caught me totally off guard. I reeled myself in and asked her how long has she been out? She said she had just got out that morning. I told Giles to hook her up with a speedball, only 5cc's fresh. We partied for two days and went to the lake with blankets, and picnic baskets, as I romanced this new Philly player style. I was true to the game and we took Babs to the airport. I did not see her again for about two years. K.C. and I became really close. Closer than me and Giles or Babs had ever been. Giles started to act up. She would come up short and disappear for long periods of time. I was not paying attention. Yes! I was slipping. After about six months Giles disappeared. I did not see her for about two years either.

Matter of fact, it was Christmas morning. KC was in jail doing a year. I was hustling hard, as I had inherited a bad sister. I really loved her. Her name was Margaret Ford, but that's a different story for a different time. Moving right along, my money was really short. I was chilly pimpin. Hustling was hard and my habit was out of control. As I sat at the table fixin to carve up the Christmas turkey at Mama Bessie's house. She was all smiles and everyone seemed to be in good spirits.

My wife Barbara Neil and my three kids sat there excited. Rascheed was born the year before. I had sliced a few pieces of turkey and suddenly I heard a horn blowing out in front of my house. I said to myself, now who in the hell would be blowing a horn in front of Mama Bessie's house. I thought they must be crazy and I left the table. I grabbed my Roscoe and went to the door.

As I looked out, much to my surprise there was a brand-new Black limousine parked in front of the house. I was cautious as I stepped out onto the porch. The back window rolled down and low and behold it was Giles and Babs. They looked just like they did the first time I laid eyes on them with their fur coats, fur boots, but a little more seasoned, if you know what I mean. They said, "Merry Christmas Big daddy and get in." I complied as Giles handed me a Christmas card with about $500 bills in it and Babs did the same. They said they had a suite at the Ramada Inn and we all laughed. I said, "I'll be right back." I went into the house to grab my leather jacket, gave Barbara $200 and said, "Merry Christmas." You must remember, I was down on my luck and Santa and his reindeer's had showed up. (I want you, the reader, to know this is real talk. I cannot make this stuff up.) This is exactly how this went down. It's called reaping and sowing. It applies whether you are good, bad or ugly.

The Bible reads: "It rains on the just and the unjust." It's the same principle. In the streets we say, "if you be good to the game it will be good to you", or "what goes around comes around". That is the short version. I asked "the girls" how long they were going to be in town? Giles said "Just two days. We got the limo for two days and here's our plane tickets to Seattle dated December 27. We just thought about you because you were the coolest. You never put your hands on us, and we knew we were safe while we were on your dance card. We both have gone through some tough times. I got a sugar daddy up in Seattle and he really takes care of me", replied Giles. And Babs said, "My old man is retired and we just wanted to come by and spend Christmas with you. If that's all right? I understand no strings attached."

I was really happy that they came by. "Let's pick up one of my home boys." We drove off to Count Drack's pad. He was located up on Pennsylvania Avenue. He stayed in what you call the "suburbs." I knocked on the door and found out he was just sitting down to Christmas dinner. I told him what was up and he also got ghost. We hated to leave our families, but as the Main Ingredients use to say, "we've got work to do," and real Christmas only comes once a year. If you know what I mean. Everyone knows that big daddy, Yours Truly and all the other brothers are the real Santa Clauses.

We drove off and made a stop at every dope house in route. We hit the LIQ, then went up to the No Tell Hotel Holiday Inn. We partied like it was 1999. Oh, by the way, that's when some fool predicted that the world was going to end. So, when you hear that saying, it means we partied like there was no tomorrow. Oh yeah! All you "want to be players", I did not spend a dime and told Giles to go in their stash and give me and my partner a couple of bills. She said, "No problem! Now that's the real game player style. Holla if you hear me! I knew KC would be out in a couple of months and I ran for her pretty good. Never visited but left money on her books and sent her a card every week, some magazines and a couple of photos. This gave her bragging rights and no one messed with my people. Well! **WHAT HAPPENED WAS…**

"Karen Tilly", a cold gangster dyke. The way this story was told to me, by Jesse James Jackson Junior an O.G. with a long rep. He said, "She was one of the coldest that I have ever known." She had become a notorious gangster with her own hoes. She was about 10 years older than me. Her mom and grandfather owned Tilly's Mortuary. One was in San Bernardino and one in Riverside. Now Karen was my homegirl and lived on the same block at the corner. It was 9th and Victoria. Their house was the nicest house on the block. The mortuary was around the corner on 10th St. Karen was off the hook crazy and had been to prison about six times. She was no joke and we were cool. She considered me as her young Homie and I had not seen her in several years. Jesse had told me when he and Karen were in high school something really bad happened to her. Karen was a Creole with beautiful long wavy hair, high yellow, sophisticated and spoiled. She wore brand-new clothes every day and she was fine.

Shirley Butts, my play sister, Jesse and Karen were all about the same age. Shirley Butts, would throw parties at her mom's house and this particular party would be the last. They had a nice house on 10th and Eucalyptus with a nice enclosed patio and a grandma house that was vacant in the back. At one of those parties, a jealous nappy head Black chick slipped her a double Mickey Finn, which is what we call a date rape drug back in those days.

Karen was a beautiful young virgin girl out at her first house party. She was drugged and taken to the back house and gang raped over and over again. They found her naked, and in a bloodied mess the next morning. The police were called. Karen was never the same. She cut off all her hair, took a razor to her face and disfigured herself for life. She wore baggy pants, and she'd put tape around her breast to keep them from showing. Nobody was ever convicted of the crime, but I hope they paid for it. Sometimes we wonder why things like this happen. I'm convinced of what the Bible says, "The sins of the Father are visited unto the children unto the second and third generations." Incest is like this. When innocent children are raped by their grandfathers or what happened to Karen can be a viable explanation to these types of events. **Moving right along …**

Karen had come down from the Pen after doing another couple of years. She was released but still had a misdemeanor case in Riverside and was sent to the County Jail and had to go to court before she could be released. When she got to the County Jail, she was put in a cell with this white girl who had my pictures posted up on the wall by her bunk. Karen noticed that it was me and said to K.C., "What the hell are you doing with my Home Boy, Michael Sterling's picture on this wall. Take them down that's Barbara's old man. Take it down." As K.C. rose up to defend herself she never knew what hit her as Karen spanked her ass. K.C. had a Black eye and a broken leg. Three weeks before her release and I was hot. I mean smoking when I heard the news. I could not believe it. All I heard was that some Black broad had beat her down. I had great anticipation and all kinds of plans for K.C. I couldn't wait for her to hit Broadway.

You must remember, I was hustling hard and had obtained the sack once again. Most of the Christmas money I used to pay Little

Jesse half of what was owed and we started over with the rest. I had messed up bad with Little Jesse. It would take thirty miligrams a day of methadone to keep the edge off of a $500 a day habit.

Casey got out a few weeks later, after her encounter with Karen. I had to take care of her for about six more weeks before she could go back to work. Karen got out and I wanted to jack her up. She had posted up on Park Avenue, and was handling her business. As soon as I saw her, I made my move. But Karen had been in the game a long time and saw me coming. As soon as I stepped up to her and started talking smack, her stud brought Cynthia, who stepped out with a sawed-off shotgun and drew down on me. They had me cold and said, "Homeboy, I know you're mad, but I just couldn't stand by while that white girl was sitting up there flossin with your picture on the wall. Before I knew it, I had tore her a new ass hole". She said here's a little something on the strength Cynthia handed me a five-O and $50. It wasn't much, but it was respect. I walked away and she said, "Are we cool?" I replied, "Yeah we're cool." She knew I meant it. My word was bond.

Throughout the life if you were really an O.G., number one you never had to prove anything to anybody. A real O.G. would give passes every once in a while. You had to be careful. The up-and-coming player, gangsters and hustlers were always looking for a weakness in your game. So, in the life, I've given passes and I've received some passes, and that's part of the real O.G. code. A dying art. Not that I'm glorifying that lifestyle, it's just the way it was in street life. Things began to change rapidly as a new era was unfolding. You see in this new era of street life where our young men are bound by gangs and separated by colors. Some red and some blue. Where fratricide seems to be the order of the day. We never participated in the gang culture that still exists. When I began to challenge the gang culture and the destruction that was caused by Black-on-Black crime I almost lost my life. I then realized that I had become a dinosaur. The O.G. code that I grew up in had begun to fade away.

This new gang mentality had no ethics and was morally depleted. We've come from a dynasty of Kings and now have been demoralized. As I went into the prison system I found our men brutally sodomizing each other. There was no way I could be in an environment where this existed. No real O.G. was going to stand-by and watch as younger weaker brothers were being de-masculized, not on my watch. **Moving right along...**

I remember one incident, where K.C. and I were posted up at one of the less affluent hotels on University Avenue. We had been there for a couple of months. I was laying low and knew the police had a warrant out for my arrest, for one thing or another. Things had gotten pretty slim again. K.C. seemed to be on her last leg, so I was playing it close to the vest. I had a red Firebird at that time, but it was in the shop. All of a sudden, the alarm went off in the motel. K.C. yelled as she looked out the window, "The Motel's on fire!" "Oh shit!" I replied. Knowing the police would be on their way if they were not already out in front already. We grabbed what we could and made our way through the parking lot. Bobby Bonds Park was across the street and I decided to make our way over there, as the cops were already at the office and a huge fire truck blocked most of the driveway. Police were everywhere.

As we got to the curb, attempting to cross the street, I looked up to see my real mother, Gloria Hilton, in her white station wagon. She smiled and yelled, "Michael Paul, get in this car, boy." I told K.C. to get in the back and I got into the front. My mother acted like it was no big thing and was genuinely glad to see me. I know we must have looked a mess with me and my Jerry curl. We were a sight to behold. I found out several years later, at the Thanksgiving dinner, when my mom told that story of me and this crazy looking white girl coming out of the burning Motel. All the family laughed for days. She dropped us off at the Thunderbird Motel down the street. I sent K.C. to get a room and Mama and I talked for a while. She said "I'm praying for you" and kissed me as I got out of the car. I was feeling a little low and ashamed. I hadn't seen her for a couple of years as she staying in Pomona, at the time, some 40 miles away... "you figure that out." I've been telling you all through the story about Mama Bessie's prayers and how they never stopped working. The question remains. How was my mother, that I had not seen in years, was right there when I was about to cross the street. Police everywhere and I was a wanted man. Even in my mess, I had to give God the glory. I knew right then I was going to fight my way out of this mess one day. There was a calling on my life and I knew it. Eventually I would reach for the prize of the high calling in Christ Jesus. A few months later I looked up and K.C. had disappeared. I never saw her again. I hope she got saved.

The Mexican Mafia
Little Georgie Lopez

Earlier in the book I described how Floyd and I took off Tom Tom, a Mexican Dope Dealer. I must have been seventeen or eighteen at the time. Well let me tell you one thing, they never stopped coming after me. You must understand, that they don't forget, but am I worried? No.

For there is another code and it is the highest code in the world, which is God's code. Even in street life most O.G.'s, Veteranoes and even the Aryan Brotherhood follow it. If you have a come to Jesus moment. I mean a real genuine come to Jesus moment. There exist in the ranks of these organizations the code, blood in, blood out. This means that when you come into these organizations you may get a beat down, or you have to shoot someone as part of your initiation. Blood must be shed. It's the same thing when you try to leave. You either get beat down, shot or stabbed for trying to leave. But as I stated earlier if you have a real come to Jesus moment and you're not faking the funk, most of these organizations will let you go. You ask me why? First, most of the people that are in these organizations, the shot callers, have mothers, fathers, sisters, brothers, aunts, and other family members that are Christians. So, when I retired from the Street Life, I said blood was shed for me to come in and Jesus blood was shed for me to get out. The blood of Jesus has already made the way. You better not be playing a game, because it would be a harsher punishment if they thought you were faking.

Well anyway, it was a warm summer night and the moon had filled itself full of glory once again. They say this affects the very sea, its movement and its calibration. They also say that the very nature of man is affected by the fullness of the moon. With all that being said; one of my home girls and I were standing in front of the apartment next to Tilly's Mortuary. Chocolate and her old man, Lonzo, had a spot there that I frequently used from time to time. Now Chocolate had been on "the track" for a very long time and was a veteran of the game. She did more robberies and con games then she flat backed. She was a part of the Love Clan so she was considered one of my sisters and I looked out for her and she looked out for me. We were down by law. I was feeling pretty good. I had not blasted off in a while and but decided to come in for a Belushi or some call it a one-on-one.

As I was saying, Chocolate and I were standing on the sidewalk when Lonzo called her. She said, "Just a minute." He said, "Hurry come now." I continued to stand there lighting a Camel cigarette when all of the sudden I saw them. When that Chevy hit the corner I knew something was wrong. It was like everything happened in slow motion. They were coming. This was it, and I knew it. Ask me how I knew? It was that alarm clock, that would go off, in the back of my neck and begin to surge throughout my body.

I thought, here we go again as the shotgun was lifted out of the car. The pellets showered over my head. They shot again as I hit the asphalt and felt something hit my arms inside from the second shot. I was not packing at the time. I jumped up and ran to the apartment as Chocolate and Lonzo opened the door saying, "I think they got me." Low and behold, the second shot must have hit the asphalt and some of the particles had splattered up and hit me. "They missed again!" Lonzo replied, "You're the luckiest man in the world." I thought to myself, "Luck had nothing to do with it." They called me lucky so much I had to change the acronym to "L.U.C.K." Living Under Christ's Kindness. I ran to my car and drove off.

I lived out on North Main in a brand-new condo. I was not getting high every day and I was involved in a lot of more sophisticated long and short range cons. I loved it, because you could shut it down at any time. We had put together a small syndicate and we were getting paid from a lot of different revenue streams. It was me, my brother "Bad Habit Rabbit", JJ Stewart and Bruce Love. We were the core with a few soldiers at our disposal. We would meet at the Roundtable once a week and divvy up all the proceeds from the different operations we were involved in. When I got back to the spot, I told them what had happened. I had identified one of the shooters as Georgie Boy Lopez, an up and coming Lieutenant in the Mexican Mafia. He had gotten involved with Danny's son and supposedly they had taken off the police armory in San Bernardino. Now Georgie Boy was in that car and got paid for that hit. They really thought they had gotten me. Later that night some work was put in on the East Side. Least I say anymore, Omar handled that one. I caught up with Georgie Boy Lopez about six months later delivering a paquette to Lonzo.

I was posted on the Avenue and no one knew I was there. I was on the roof of the gambling shack. I saw him get out of the car as I shimmied down the back wall between the buildings and came out on the 11th Street side. He had walked around the corner and he and Lonzo were talking. I approached with a 38 revolver in my hand. Lonzo saw me first, saying, "Oh, Mike don't shoot him" as I was about to pull the trigger. "Lonzo, what the hell are you doing?" I yelled. Georgie Boy looked at me and said, "Sterling let's talk." I said, "Lonzo get out of the way man." He refused as he pleaded for Georgie Boy's life. You know I never thought about it. It never even crossed my mind. But as I sit here writing my memories, I just figured out that nine times out of 10 Lonzo set me up. It is now December 2014 and this happened back in 1980 some 35 years ago, and I just now figured it out!

People always said to me, you're more loyal to people who are not that loyal to you. It's okay, I still got to be me. It's the O.G. code and I'm a dinosaur fading into the night. It all makes sense. I had just come over for a visit to get high. It had been awhile. I had just walked outside with Chocolate and we had been talking about 20 minutes. How did they know I was even there? I had only been there about 30 minutes and I remember it like it was yesterday. Lonzo came to the door and called Betty. In less than five minutes later, they were coming around the corner shooting. And now he was pleading for this punk's life, who had tried to kill me six months prior. Well! It all makes sense, wow it is what it is. The Angels and the Spirit of Discernment saved me yet again. I'll give God the glory and move on. I am glad I did not realize what he did. Even back then when I would see him in church, he'd look at me and put his head down.

They tried again when I got busted and went to jail. I was taken to the Back End. It's called High Power in the Riverside County jail where there are six eight-man cells on each side. They were all in the

Day room when I arrived. It was mostly Hispanic. I was so messed up about being busted and was exhausted as I sat down at the table in the day room. On the way, I saw an inmate who reminded me of someone who was being escorted to high power on the other side.

This was the unit that had a one-man cell with a security walkway, called the Cat walk. I was placed there twice in my life. As I was sitting contemplating my next move, I was hit from behind with a bunch of punches. It dazed me as I finally got my legs from under the table. My back hit the dorm wall with a thud. Unable to see my target, but I felt a connection, I started just throwing my hands. I was hitting flesh. My arms began to extend and I made a step forward still punching in the midst of my dilemma. One step, two steps. These punks were retreating. My eyes began to clear as I threw punch after punch. Then I threw a powerful left hook as my assailant hit the ground. I was victorious once again. Before I could celebrate, I heard a voice from the corner yell out, "The Mexican can't lose" as five of them stood at attention. One of them headed towards me. It was Boxing Joe, he was a veteran and shot caller. I looked over towards the few Blacks that were there for help. They turned their heads in the opposite direction to signal they were not in it. I knew I was in trouble, real bad trouble. I stood up like a soldier at the Alamo, outmanned and outgunned, but I was going down like a real "O.G." **AND, WHAT HAPPENEDWAS…**

All of a sudden the gate cracked and everyone paused. The police were escorting some more prisoners in. I could have yelled to them for help, but this would have been a P.C. move, but I was no snitch and would never wear the green jumpsuit.

Five people came in from the morning court line, two Black and three white boys. I didn't recognize any of them, as I secured a place on the wall and waited for the drama to ensue. They began to approach. One of the new arrivals yelled, "What's going on?" Boxing Joe replied, "It's none of your business man." This little short brother stepped in front of me and said, "Wait a minute! Youngblood what's up?" I replied, "They jumped me as I was sitting at the table. I whipped the first one and now I was about to get down with the whole bunch. I had a beef with them on the street. I did not know who this man was but evidently they did. He looked towards the same Black brothers that had turned their heads 15 minutes ago and said, "You better lineup." They came to attention and surrounded me as he said "Ain't nothing goin' down like that." In a high voice, he said "My name is Edward G. Bailey O.G. Shot Caller, B.G.F. (Black Gorilla Family) from the cradle to the grave. Yeah, from the Gladiator School, T.I. my juice card reaches from San Quentin to Soledad. You better be careful what you do here today. You may win this battle but you will not win the war." Then he looked at boxing Joe and said, "It's your call. Put up or shut up." They backed down and he looked at the Brothers and said, "You punks sit down. Let me talk to this young warrior." It is amazing how I look back over my life and I think things over. I can truly say, God has been good to me. If this were ever turned into a movie that song will play because I was ready to die. But my Father in Heaven looked into eternity and saw He had a plan for my life and protected me in my mess. To God be the glory!

I received my inheritance early and sold my first house at age 24. It went for $45,000 back in those days but today would sell for $100,000-$200,000. I split the money with Mama Bessie and went and bought a 69 Riviera, Coco Brown. I then purchased a couple of ounces from Pimpin, Robert Bratton. He's out of the life and has one of the baddest soul food restaurants in Riverside, right behind the Mission Inn. It's called, "Graham's Place." He is also saved and off the street. He is my big Homie, I give a big thumbs up to Robert Bratton.

1975 New Orleans

It was 1975 the year of no jive. We had mounted up in the city of Rialto about 50 miles south of Los Angeles. We had moved into a track of brand- new townhouses. Jimmy Zan had the first house off Willow. My house was about a block and a half away. We could see each other's front doors. The way everything was situated, "Bumpen Bill", who was from Denver, Colorado was across the street from me and Leonard Coleman was down the street in the back house. We were protected on all sides. We had formed a Black Power Syndicate, which we kept under the radar. We were all about the "Benjamins". Most of us had legitimate jobs as fronts. We began to enjoy life without a care in the world. We were disenchanted with the movement. The struggle and the so-called revolution and its leadership. Things had gotten so bad that H. Rap Brown, a general in the movement was supposed to be underground awaiting the revolution. He had become so desperate that he pulled a small-time robbery just to survive. We the people were supposed to be taking care of him.

(The Revolution) The movement had fallen apart because of all the infighting. The different organizations who all thought they had the only solution to the great African American struggle in the confines of America. We had great ideologists, visionaries, statesmen and orators alike, who had led great organizations, but refused to come together in brotherhood. This led to the systematic destruction of the Black Panther Party for self-defense, Core, the B.L.A, the Nation of Islam, the NAACP, US organization, Urban League and the list goes on and on. The B.G.F. (Black Guerrilla Family Prison Gang), the Southern Leadership Christian Conference and many, many, other organizations who attempt to fight the beast, 666, the devil and its cohorts. Which has many faces but few disguises.

I became so disenchanted I decided to party like it was 1999. We would listen to Gil Scott, "Winter In America" and reminisce about the good old days. I was driving a brand-new Firebird. It was a 1974 which I bought off the showroom floor. The year prior I had beaten the Coors Beer Corporation robbery in the city of Riverside. This all had happened before I hooked back up with Jimmy Zan. There was a whole lot of events during that time. I do not think it would be wise to discuss, but I will say we were making money hand over fist. We were living large with cherry trees right in the front yard. This was one of the most unbelievable sites I had ever seen in my young mind, being born in East LA, Leso Village. Having lived in Compton and Watts, I was then raised up in Riverside, a block from the tracks in a one bathroom two-bedroom house. I thought the three-bedroom townhouse with a 2 ½ baths was heaven. I did not want to leave. There were no helicopters flying overhead and you barely heard the sirens or gun fire. We would throw a party on Friday night that would last for three days. On Sunday morning, the girls would cook a meal fit for a king. Nobody, I mean nobody, wanted to miss the big Sunday morning breakfast. After the breakfast, we would either go horseback riding, or to a baseball game and a picnic. Yeah! We were gangsters not gang bangers living the life.

I can remember one night when we partied so hard we ended up in New Orleans, Louisiana without clothes. It was all on a dare, involving me, my older brother, Leonard Sterling, "Bumpin' Bill, Jimmy Zan, who worked for Santa Fe Railroad and Leonard Coleman who was the parts manager at Toyota. When I sobered up, we were in El Paso, Texas with snow on the ground. We all shook our heads in disbelief - Texas and snow! We then took a vote and voted to either turn back or continue. That night we later arrived in New Orleans. Oh, by the way, we rode through the middle of Texas with 2 pounds of marijuana and two pistols! This was surely not our intent. I forgot these items were in the van. It was rumored that if you got caught with one joint of marijuana in Texas you could spend 99 years in prison.

As we arrived in New Orleans, we went straight to the Ninth Ward, a place called the Desire Projects. I had heard a lot about the place and remembered that Jimmy Zan and his cadre had a Black Panther headquarters right in the middle of the Desire Projects. One day the National Guard even brought an army tank along with 250 police officers who initiated an unsuccessful raid on the Black Panther's headquarters. The citizens that lived in the projects surrounded the B.P.P. headquarters. Over 400 people who supported the Black Panther Party had a lengthy standoff with the police who ultimately withdrew. They came back a few weeks later in disguises. Some came as priests and others as Post Office workers. During the under-cover raid, sister Betty Powell was shot and six of the Black Panthers were arrested. They were acquitted and all the charges were eventually dropped. This occurred in 1970.

The Desire Projects consisted of 262 two-story all brick buildings. They looked identically alike and was composed of 1,860 units that were on 98.5 acres of land. For the life of me, the conditions of these projects were deplorable! I could never understand why they were called the Desire Projects. I thought the Nickson's in Los Angeles were bad, but by comparison they were worse than the "Imperial courts"! I wonder how anyone could even find their way to their own house, There must've been about 5,000 people trapped in these units! America, give me a break "your slip is showing"!

When we arrived, we were told to be on our "P's and Q's" because it was well-known that some of the people that went into the Desire Project were never heard from again. We were told that a few nurses that went in to see about the elderly, were never heard from again. Well, I myself, Michael Paul Sterling, better known as "Youngblood", just laughed and said, "man if you shoot me to the moon, I'll be selling moon pies in a week." This is just another part of "Hell in America. Baby, only the strong survive and nobody better step up to me. It will be rock-a-bye baby". "Just be cool Youngblood", Zan said, "This is my turf. I've been gone a few years. Just let me get my bearings." By the time we found his dad in one of those speakeasies, I was toasted. We had been drinking White Lighting, like it was going out of style. As we got to his dad's house, I showered and put on one of his dad's suits. It was a bit big, but seemed like a grunge look. We continued to party like it was the end of the world. Yeah we were doing a dance called the LA Bump. But believe me, the New Orleans girls had something to bump with. We partied from the projects to the French Quarter for the Mardi Gras Fat Tuesday.

Believe it or not we ran into Cinque and Patty Hearst along with another white boy. Now! Cinque is long dead and Patty Hearst cannot be affected. It was a good time. We had shrimp and crawdad coming out of our ears and everyone knows that there is no Gumbo like Louisiana Gumbo. Please do not get me started on the Shrimp Creole! We were partying and having a good time while things back in California had gotten out of hand.

Back to Ground Zero – L.A.

WELL, WHAT HAPPENED WAS... I'd gotten a call from the set and it was told to me that Bumpen Bill's, main squeeze, Melody, who stays across the street from my spot had been set up by Bumpen Bill's side chick. She was a real chicken head. Now understand this is not a term I would use lightly, but they tricked Melody, who was high yellow, and I mean triple fine with long Black hair running down her back. This tender Roni was the choice of the boys. A number 10. At the same time, my wife, Ms. B, flipped out, and was taken to the hospital to be treated and admitted. It was hospital policy for people to stay for three days, but she refused and walked out of that hospital, got into the car and went to work the next day. The truth was I never was interested in Doll Baby. 'Barbara' was the love of my life, but tricks are for kids and I did not play games. Save all that drama for your mama. Because I was born at night, but not last night. We went home and life went on.

The years seem to fly by so fast when you're high everyday all day in the subculture of life. You the reader must understand that we had our own systematic government. There were rules and regulations that have been handed down from the University of the Street. It was called the Code. This code was in full effect when I was coming up through the ranks. Our people had been degraded to exist as chattel. During the time of slavery and most of those physical chains have become mental. Even our family values had been morally corrupted through things like the " Willie Lynch" method of control. Which caused a divisionary system of checks and balances that manipulated and controlled our people.

Our ancestors had been taken from a great civilization, where they ruled as King's all throughout Africa. They often built great dynasties, which included the great pyramids of northern Africa, that they labeled as Egypt. A lie that they had perpetrated through Alexander, "the not so great", who had Conquered Egypt. After his death, there arose Cleopatra, who was a member of the Ptolemaic Dynasty. She ruled Egypt and was born in 69 BC in Alexandria. She was of African descent. Cleopatra had become a Pharaoh in her own right. She thus consummated a liaison with Julius Caesar. After Caesar's assassination, she aligned herself with Mark Anthony. This bad sister ruled and reigned in Egypt/Africa for 20 years.

We, as a people, must begin to understand the lies, hypocrisy and fiction of America's hypnotic influence on a Black culture where Elizabeth Taylor played Cleopatra in the movie. This further perpetuated white supremacy. Where in reality, Cleopatra, reigned during the occupation of Egypt by Caesar and Mark Anthony of Rome. Cleopatra the VIIth was a beautiful African Queen whose seduction of Julius Caesar led to his downfall, because he was mesmerized by her beauty and could not leave her side. Even his general, Mark Anthony, also lost all credibility and killed himself. In Cleopatra's distress over his death, she committed suicide at age 39.

Our people have been subjugated to historical lies from generation to generation. These lies which caused a dissimulation and suppression of a once proud race. When you enslave a nation of people while taking away their identity, culture, heritage and language, their ultimate destruction seems inevitable.

But as Maya Angelo wrote, "Still I Rise" like a blade of grass that shoots up through a concrete jungle that seed will push through the very cement that covers it and tries to hamper its growth and development. We, as a people, must forever reach for the sun. We started to develop a subculture for our very survival. In a society where the Willie Lynch plan is in full effect, along with the modern three strikes law, Planned Parenthood, covert-mafia and FBI drug infusion programs, along with the modern-day slavery called the prison system, a once proud people are destined for failure and destruction. The penal system even has the audacity to offer stocks and bonds in its development and construction.

We ultimately had to invent a subculture, with our own code of ethics, where we were able to rule and reign as kings. I do not want to justify this behavior, however, this is why pimps became pimps and hustlers became hustlers, shot callers, gang leaders, and mini-mafias that would control neighborhoods, territories, city blocks, the projects and the street corners, where cash money would flow. It was our system of checks and balances, our Modus Operandi. It is how we were forced to live in a society, where the rights to life, liberty and the pursuit of happiness, had been denied a once proud people. We thus created a lifestyle, whereas when something went down on the streets we controlled it from an aspirin to an assassination. "The Code" was that no one would talk or cooperate with invading troops, the "po po", the man, the pigs, the cops, the one time, the fuzz, and the police. There were repercussions and consequences for the snitches and the finks. I'm not justifying the behavior nor do I condone it. I'm, just giving the facts of street life so that you, the reader, can have a better grasp on the reality.

We must say it again, to fully understand that when you take men and women, who were descendants of kings, that ruled great empires and civilizations and now subjugate them to chattel slavery where the very documents that you hold so sacred, now become an indictment against the order in which it was established. To wit; the Declaration of Independence, and The Emancipation Proclamation. The Civil Rights Acts of 1964, The Brown versus The Board of Education. This nation's idealistic thoughts, while written on paper seemed to be mere rhetoric which ruled the day. The Laws which were passed seemed to be symbolism of a society that is yet to live out the true meaning of its creed. Thus, many blood driven warriors rose up and said no; and began to go out to lunch on your social construct and refused to abide by your laws, your government or your established order. For the true meaning of the word justice, is best described as, "Just us." The concept which had fallen in the streets.

There seems to be no justice for us in a system where our young men, for survival sake, seemed to have little or no choice but to create and maintain an underground society. Even though we were infamous in scope and broke every law of moral and civic mandate we were in charge and produced warriors, shot callers and for lack of better terms, pimps and hustlers like Bumpie Johnson, the Ward brothers, Iceberg Slim, Tootie Reese, Doc Holliday, Ray Ray, Stanley P. Williams, Raymond Washington, Jack Daniels, Nicky Barnes, El Dorado Butch, Frank Lucas, Alprentice Bunchy Carter, Jesse James Jackson Junior, George Jackson, Pee Wee Reese, Big Chuck, I.E. Mob, Eddie & Pee Wee Fitzgerald, Hugo Yogi Pennell, Flores Forbes Romeo, the Gangster Disciples, the Black Mafia Family, the Black Gorilla Family, the Blackstone Ranges, the Crips, the Blood's, just to name a few. We did not just wake up and choose to be criminals. Life in the ghetto molded our character, and we became notorious as the blood of kings rose up in our veins. We refuse to be denied life, liberty and pursuit of happiness. The first African slaves came to this land in 1619 – 400 years, and still seeking the same rights and acceptance guaranteed by the Constitution.

No matter how we had to get it, for a few minutes in the sun is better than no sun at all. Although short-lived, they were free and lived as a king. It is sad as I look back at the stark reality of life in America. **"The man-child inthe not so promised land"**. Let me pause for a moment and give you a personal look into my psyche. I became homeless once in my life for about four months. I refused to sleep in a cardboard box, or sleep on a park bench, or under a bridge. I was in

America. The greatest country on the planet earth ''. Oh, by the way, who has my 40 acres and my mule? I want it with interest. Moving right along. So, I became homeless and I would get dropped off close to the new developments. I would walk in and find a place with electricity and break in the back door and fix it so it looked untampered with. I would set up shop in one of those houses and just live. I had said to myself if I ever got caught, I would say that my ancestors built this country and until I got my 40 acres and my mule, with interest, I refuse to sleep in the streets. I do not know how you feel, but that's exactly how I feel.

"Still I Rise" by May Angelo

You may write me down in history
With your bitter, twisted lies,
You may tread me in the very dirt
But still, like dust, I'll rise.

Does my sassiness upset you?
Why are you beset with gloom?
'Cause I walk like I've got oil wells
Pumping in my living room.

Just like moons and like suns,
With the certainty of tides,
Just like hopes springing high,
Still I'll rise.

Did you want to see me broken?
Bowed head and lowered eyes?
Shoulders falling down like teardrops.
Weakened by my soulful cries.

Does my haughtiness offend you?
Don't you take it awful hard
'Cause I laugh like I've got gold mines
Diggin' in my own back yard.

You may shoot me with your words,
You may cut me with your eyes,
You may kill me with your hatefulness,
But still, like air, I'll rise.

Does my sexiness upset you?
Does it come as a surprise
That I dance like I've got diamonds
At the meeting of my thighs?

Out of the huts of history's shame
I rise
Up from a past that's rooted in pain
I rise
I'm a Black ocean, leaping and wide,
Welling and swelling I bear in the tide.
Leaving behind nights of terror and fear
I rise
Into a daybreak that's wondrously clear
I rise
Bringing the gifts that my ancestors gave,
I am the dream and the hope of the slave.
I rise I rise I rise.

Maya Angelou

I wonder if Abraham Lincoln's assassination was attributed partly because of Special Field Order Number 15; which was issued by General Sherman and was supposed to be enacted by General Oliver Otis Howard, of Howard University, but was derailed by the President assassination.

As we began to look at a system of injustice where new laws and the legislations were being enforced every day to stifle the growth and development of a group of people. These laws, such as: Three Strikes legislation, the Big Bitch (habitual offender) or the Little Bitch which were the enhancement laws, running wild. Where many of our young men after incarceration felt, they were better off dead, than to live a castrated life in America. The book of Revelation in the King James version of the Bible tells us, in Revelation 12:17, *"And the dragon was wroth with the woman, and went to make war with the remnant of her seed, which keep the commandments of God, and have the testimony of Jesus Christ."* Satan's war was and is against those who have placed their faith in our Savior.

Yes! War has been made, by Satan, against the Black male seed in particular and the male seed in general. The Bible says in Hosea 4:6 "My people are destroyed for a lack of knowledge; because thou has rejected knowledge. I would also reject thee, that thou shalt be no priest to me. Seeing thou has forgotten the law of God. I will also forget thy children." I am so happy I had a praying mama. Yes, Mama Bessie MacDowell or should I say, Bessie Parthenia McDowell. She adopted this man-child and became my chief intercessor and stood in the gap until this man-child could wake up in the very subculture that was geared to ultimately destroy him. This destruction of the male seed, was a systematic plan that would ultimately erode the family unit. First, starting with the man and then the woman and ultimately a whole nation of Kings. This was Satan's plan Perpetrated in America by White Supremists and their cohorts.

"Now listen" and remember that I'm not condoning any of the previous statements. I'm just giving you, the reader, a review of what has happened. White supremacy and racism has caused a division in the human race. Their main goal has been to ultimately destroy the man-child, the male seed, through division. We as a people, must develop a righteous system. We can live and grow as kings and priests, while establishing a Commonwealth, with a legitimate infrastructure. Whereas we can begin to re-educate our people through self-worth and the value of human life. We can become builders and not the destroyers of our own neighborhoods, cities, states, and nations. We must cultivate and thus motivate the next-generation of kings. We refuse to be denied, yet not compromise our moral and social values. Our scale model is to be structured after a ''Black Wall Street'' pattern.

As we look at that great community in Tulsa, Oklahoma, we need to realize, that it was bombed June 1, 1921, by racist bigots because of hatred and jealousy. Black Wall Street was one of the most affluent all-Black communities in America. It was bombed from the air and burned to the ground by a mob of envious whites. In a period of 12 hours 3,000 African- Americans were killed, 6,000 successful Black businesses were burned to the ground. 21 churches, 21 restaurants, 30 grocery stores, 2 movie theaters, a hospital, a Black-owned bank, a post office, many libraries, schools, law offices, half a dozen airplanes, and even the bus system were all destroyed. Right there in Tulsa, Oklahoma. Yes, this was America, this is your legacy America, this is your heritage America, but God, Jehovah has the final say. The Last shall be first and the first shall be last. Justice shall prevail in righteousness. This was less than 100 years ago. America "your slip is showing." This event was led by the Ku Klux Klan with support of local government officials. They destroyed a mini Black Beverly Hills. It was the golden door of a Black infrastructure that proved that Black people could be successful and not adhere to the fratricide that plagues our inner cities today.

We must begin to mobilize. "FOR US BY US"'. We must begin importing and exporting goods and services to and from Africa, our Mother land. We must educate and train diamond cutters, goldsmiths, engineers, scientists, ambassadors, statesmen, farmers, lawyers, bankers, investors, surveyors, architects, builders, doctors, and the list goes on, while refusing to let another Black business die. We must adhere and develop the spirit of excellence on all levels of life. We must be at the table doing business and engineering our own future. Which is what is necessary for us to be about our Father's business. We must seize the time and enact dominion and power in a lawful manner, whereas we can come to the table of brotherhood and do business, from a place of power. Yes, capital financial power. We must do business on a corporate level with the Jews, the Italians, the Arabs, the Greeks, the Spanish, the Japanese, the Chinese, the European, the Russians, the people of India and all the nations of the world, who make up the world's markets. "We can do it! United We Stand Divided We Fall."

CHAPTER NINE

Prison My Salvation The Born Again Experience

My road to recovery was long and arduous. One day my baby mama, yes, my ex Barbara drove up in a money green Thunderbird. It was sharp. She said, "Michael, the guy who owns this car just went to jail and told me to keep his car until he gets out. I don't want nothing to do with it." She threw me the keys and walked away. I had hit rock bottom and the police had chased me the day before. I was on foot and ran about 15 blocks and barely got away. I ran through backyards, jumped fences and faced down a Rottweiler, a German Shepherd and knocked out a baby Pit Bull! And panicked as I tripped and fell into one yard. He leaped at me and my right cross caught him on his chin and to my surprise, he was out like a light. I finally made my way to Papa Riley's house and layed low until midnight. I knew they were going to catch up with me sooner rather than later. I took the keys to that Thunderbird and drove over to the next county, San Bernardino. For the next eight months, I drove that car like it was my own. When I got to San Bernardino I must of had a half of a paquette of heroin and about $100 to my name. I did not stop for clothes or anything and did not go back to Riverside for about five years.

I shook the spot; the air felt good as I jumped on the 215 freeway and headed for San Bernardino. I knew quite a few hustlers in this area and a few notorious con-men, short changers and a cold creep thief whose name was JT. Now JT was from the East Coast and we were tight. He ran a squad of hustlers called the A-team. This was back in the day-day before they had all these cameras everywhere. It's really something how society changes over a period of time. During that time the flim-flam was so cold these teams were netting 20 to $50,000 without the use of a gun. Even a good till tapping team could net large amounts of money by hitting six to seven spots in one day.

The first till tapper would be called the "Grifter"; the second would be the "Blocker" and the third would be the "Hitter" who would lay in the back until the cash register was left open by the Pullman. Anyone else near the register was distracted by various methods. The hitter would come up to the cash register and pull the money out of the till taking tens and 20's if he was good. He would place the money between the newspaper he had under his arm and walk out the door while no one was the wiser. I could hit three trays at a time fives, tens and $20's. This was unheard of. I had trained myself when I went to school at OIC, a training program that was developed by the late Rev. Leon Sullivan of Philadelphia. I studied solar conversion and air-conditioning while attending the school. They had a program downstairs for cashiers. So, at lunch time I would go down and practice on the register. I even got so good that I placed a little bell on the lever and could pull the money out without the bell ringing. I practiced for six months and there was a lot of hustlers I knew that were not that good.

When I arrived in San Bernardino, I went straight to the Elks Club on Mount Vernon Boulevard. The place was thick with hookers who lined up from the Velvet Lounge to Baseline Avenue putting in their work. I had to be very careful how I approached the set, because there had always been a feud between San Bernardino and Riverside County. The O.G.'s knew who I was and I had a little juice because several years earlier, I had been the protégé of a famous pimp named Daddy Glenn. His name rang from San Francisco to San Diego. From the inland Empire to the Empire State Building. He had gotten old but still had juice and style. I was his son. He had gotten killed a few years earlier by one of those young wannabe Crips. Old School Daddy had gotten into a debate with this young fool and daddy verbally clowned him and this youngster drew out his gun and shot the old man, who was about 79 years old. He was 150 pounds and this wannabe Crips was about 22 years old, 250 pounds and could have slapped daddy Glenn down.

The times were changing and the code was eroding right before our eyes. I looked for that youngster along with several of the real OG's. I'm glad I never found him, in Jesus name. I did not want to end up like King David with too much blood on my hands. I was still looking for information on two other boys that had killed two of my Comrads. They were off-base and they both were in violation, as far as the movement was concerned. But at last! A lot of us were messed up and disenchanted. **Moving right along…**

My two Comrads that were poisoned were Alfred Hassan a Muslim minister, who was a standup brother and Iman in San Quentin prison. Chino was hooked up with the BGF, (Black Guerrilla Family). Prior to this, Chino had been waiting on a lawsuit for about three years. It finally came in at about $10 grand. That was big money back then; it would equal to $30,000 today. He decided to go back to San Bernardino and get a quantity of heroin. And get back in business real fast. When he and Alfred Hassan went to San Bernardino, you should have seen them when they left the Eastside. They came down to the avenues sporting brand-new leather jackets along with those Stacy Adams. They wore the Old Man Comforts and were sharp as a tack. Hassan had come by my spot, but I was in Los Angeles. They went to the Bucket of Blood and bought drinks for the house. They paid all their debt and spent big money. Several hours later they were found in a vacant house buck naked, having OD'd on some bad dope. They had been robbed and left for dead. One thing about street life, you better not get old! To this day we do not really know who, how, when or where this set up really went down. We have some ideas but most of it was speculation.

As I was saying prior, when I arrived at the Elks lounge on Mount Vernon Avenue the night was still and I could sense the nostalgic moment of time slipping into darkness as the undercurrent was calling me deeper and deeper into the asphalt jungle of despair. As I pulled into the parking lot, all my training began to captivate my soul as I found a spot where I could check out the landscape. As I slowly stepped out of that "money green" Thunderbird, I lit up a Camel cigarette and gave the parking lot a once over. When I arrived at the entrance to the club I took a pause for the cause, hoping to see a friendly face or two.

I slowly entered the club, and sat at the bar and ordered a Long Island Iced Tea. My money was short and there was no turning back after sipping on that iced tea until the ice melted. I was not about to spend any more money than necessary. I needed to get my bearings. Finally, the night was fading to day and I had gotten the location of Littles Scotties, who had a spot off of G St. He was in the back. I headed over there and when I arrived it was about 4 a.m.. I located the back house and laid low in the car across the street and began to check out the traffic. Suddenly I saw Bubba and JT arrive on the scene. They were moving fast. I jumped out the car and yelled, "A-Team on the block" and the response was, "Hey man don't say that name too loud. As I approached, I heard JT yell, "Oh my God, it's spicy Mike! Say my man, Harry's up. Let's get off the street it's hot out here." I gave Bubba the salute and we strolled into the back where little Scotty lived. He was there with that white girl and had set up shop. As JT gave the one, two knock at the door, it opened and we were let in.

JT had just made a big score earlier that day and was there for a re-up. He asked, "Spicy what are you doing in this neck of the woods?" as he gave me the once over and said "Hmm" under his breath. I guess I was a sight. I had not slept in two days. I replied to him, "I'm just a squirrel in your world trying to get a nut. I slipped him, bubba and little Scotty a few bags of H, it was the best around. I knew I was short but this was a good investment. I crashed at little Scotty's spot and laid low there for about a month. I made an additional $150 off the H before the night fell into day. My bankroll was almost $300 now and on the next day I spent about $150 on toiletries and clothes. I went to the ragman and he gave me a double up with a promise to pay.

I cleaned up and rested for a couple of days. I was down to my last $50 and knew I had to make a move sooner or later and low and behold! Late one night about 11:30 p.m. in walked this chick talking loud, and strutting her stuff. I could hear her from the back room saying, "This is "Little Bit" back on the Boulevard and you better tell those fake crack hoes to vacate the spot because a real bitch is back in town!" She said, "I'm taking names and calling shots. My real man is in prison and there's no pimp, player, hustler or gangster that can control or attain this bitch. I'm a renegade to my heart step up to the plate Little Bit is back in town now it's on me. Who needs a shot, a snort or a drink, it's all on me, I'm paying the tab. I've been down in that hell-hole, the penitentiary for the last two years but I'm back on Broadway now."

I was in the back room rolling. This little "Filly" spit game and it tickled me until I laughed out loud. I had to get out there and see who this was. You see back in the day-day every real top notch hustler, player or pimp, had a mack. There were also a few top-notch hoes that could spit game, too. I fixed myself up real fast and strolled into the front where the drama was unfolding. I began to spit game as I entered, and this is what I said. "This is Spiceman, O.G. the original gangster, the macaroni, yeah. I'm the pimp player and the hustler all rolled into one. I'm that mean mother son of a gun. I'm colder than iceberg and smoother than silk. I'm a regulator shot caller and big Baller. I'm the one your mother warned you about. I'm soft as doctor's cotton and sweet as apple pie. I'm that bad mother that made Dolomite cry. I ran the Klu Klux Klan from the federal building. I knocked my first police out at age 17. I'm a pimp's nightmare and a gang bangers threat. I'm a dinosaur stalking, whose come back to the set. I'm howling and growling from deep within, you better get on my side or be gone with the wind. There's no dollars moving, nor drugs being sold, there's no flat backing, unless I say so. The Spice man is here now, run and tell that."

As I finished my repor, the crowd went wild whistling and high-fiving. The houseman, little Scotty, replied, "This is the spice man I know and everything he said is colder than that. When "little bit", Dawn Branch, spun around and said, "So you're the notorious spice man." I replied, "Just keep looking into my eyes, baby doll, and you will see my soul." As she gazed long and deep, she became mesmerized by what she saw. She quickly pulled out a roll of bills and placed it in my hand and said, "Daddy can we shake this spot?" I replied, "Sit on daddy's lap and let me take a breath. After a deep pause for the cause, I strolled out into the coolness of a new day.

The roosters had not yet crowed as the moon smiled its pleasure and slipped into the darkened sky. I knew we had a few hours before dawn. I gently opened the car door of that "money green" Thunderbird that had been lace with a gold package. Little Bit, my new girl stepped in and purred like a cat. As I pulled the car out of the driveway, I headed for Mount Vernon Blvd. a well-known stroll in the inland empire. While heading down Mount Vernon Boulevard, I spotted the Bank of America, made a left on 18th St. and pulled over about a half block from the stroll. I bet Little Bit thought we were headed towards some hotel or Holiday Inn. But I slowly let my seat all the way back, so anyone passing could not see if anyone was in the car. I lit a Camel cigarette and said, "All right girl, get my money hooker." While simultaneously popping the unlock button on the bird. Little Bit looked at me, shook her head and got out.

She knew the ropes, was back in about 90 minutes and knocked on my window. I cracked the window about 6 inches and she dropped the money in and walked away shaking her head. I counted the money she had given me at the spot, which was about $200. That's gate money, I assumed. In California when you are let out of prison they are mandated to give you $200, plus any money you had acquired while in custody. Now along with what she had dropped in the window, my bankroll was now up to $500.

I had fallen asleep and heard a knock on the passenger's window. It was Little Bit. Her wig was crooked, her makeup had faded and I saw she was not the best-looking girl in the world, but she had a body made by Cadillac- The Fleetwood brand. She handed me an additional $250 and we sped off to the No-Tell Motel Holiday Inn. I checked in and went in immediately. I took a shower and she did the same.

She mentioned, "Daddy, I don't have any clothes. I just got home. I lost everything during this last bid." I replied, "Get dressed, let's go." As we stepped out of the hotel we stopped and got a couple of egg McMuffin's and some coffee and headed towards the Mall. When we got to the Sears entrance, I handed her $200 and said, "Handle your business and be quick." As we arrived back at the hotel I let her off, told her to get some rest and said, "Baby if I'm not back be on the track by 10 p.m.. I laced her up with the do's and don'ts, the signals that we use for occupy, vacant or danger - a piece of paper in the side of the window meant "shake this spot."

I went looking for Felipe Rey, a Mexican Mafia drug dealer, who is now deceased. I had gotten hooked up with him through Daddy Glenn, also deceased. Street life can be cruel. They both died a very violent death. Oh, by the way, Little Bit a.k.a. Dawn Branch now runs a drug rehab center. She's saved, sanctified and filled with the Holy Ghost, too. Helping other girls that are trapped in Satan's grip and doing it clean and sober is a miracle. Some of us did make it out, but sad to say most died in the grips of street life. I was able to find Felipe's younger brother. Let's call him, Danny Boy. I'm not sure if he is still alive or not, but, he and his old lady were stand up people back in the day-day and I do not want to front him off.

Danny Boy made a few calls and introduced me to Black Tar (top Mexican heroin). He got me a good deal, made the connection, and the rest is history. I headed back to the hotel. It was about 2 a.m. that morning. The all clear sign was up and I walked in. I immediately blasted off with a "Baluchi." It was about 10 a.m. when Little Bit walked in. She had breakfast in her hand and handed me $400. I told her to keep $200 and get some more clothes and she blasted off with a Baluchi. We just chilled that evening and early the next morning she left. I paid the rent for a week and told her to put my money in a certain spot and I would be back when I get back. I left her a little to get high on and was gone for a couple of days.

One of my old friends, Melvin Murphy, had a spot on 16th St. It was a small duplex with a lot of traffic. I quickly made a deal with him and set up shop. I turned over the packages that I had and my bankroll was now up to $1,500. On my way to re-up I ran across Denise Williams. She and her sister were two gangster girls. They did a little bit of everything. Denise joined my family and her mother and I became cool. We partied that night and I dropped Melvin off a paquette and went to check my two-day trap. When I arrived at the hotel it was about 3 a.m. and the all clear sign was up. I walked in and Little Bit said, "Daddy where have you been? I was worried." I replied, "I was at where I was at." I looked over to see if my "paper" was where it was supposed to be and I told Little Bit to go count my money. She said, "It's about 300." I replied "Girl you're a little bit short, you better stop playing games." She pulled a roll out from her bra and said, "Daddy I didn't know where you were at." She purred and handed me an additional $400. I shook my head, took $500 and left her $200. I said, "In the morning I want you to get me an eight ball of Coke and keep the rest." Later that night we went out to the steakhouse, caught a movie and chilled. As we got back to the hotel, I told her she can take the night off. She cleaned up and tried to make a move on big daddy with a red silk negligée. I was not having it and never had sex with her. She was with me about six months and got busted in Pomona.

By that time, my stable was strong. I had acquired a young "Cripette" out of Grape Street. Her name was Re-Re and she was a piece of work. I then purchased an El Dorado and a little Pinto station wagon. I had abandoned the "money green" Thunderbird which was parked at a spot in Pomona. Unfortunately, there was a raid going on and I barely got to walk away. Something told me to get out of the Thunderbird and walk down the street. When I was about a block away I saw the Police cars rushing to the spot. I never looked back.

A cousin of mine who lived in Sin town gave me a ride and we headed back to San Bernardino. The Bible says that the gifts and callings of God are irrevocable. That word gift translated into the Greek is charisma which means spiritual endowment. Michael Jackson had it, but did not use it for God. Elvis Presley had it but did not use it for God. And, Cleo the television fortuneteller had it but did not use it for God. Most of the fortune tellers, psychics, clairvoyance have it but choose to use it for the Dark side. Romans 11:29 in the word of God says, "For the gifts and callings of God are without repentance and are irrevocable." Certain people are given the gift of charisma and no one or anything can disallow the gift. They have the gift until the day they die. To use it for God or the Dark side.

One of the gifts I was given from birth was the gift of discernment. I knew when danger was imminent. In the early years, I always knew when something bad was going to happen. But, when I had foresight, I did not pay attention and found myself saying to myself, "If I had just followed my first mind, I would not be in this cell or this predicament."

Moving right along. I do not in any way shape or form begin to glorify street life. It is a cold bitter hell, designed to destroy all its inhabitants. I just want to keep this book authentic. I realize that I barely escaped. There are just a few more episodes I would like to explain before I get to the good part: Being Born again!

I had gotten established on the Dark side and now realized I was going deeper and deeper into the pit of despair. The Devil should've killed me when he had the chance. I was so caught up in street life or should I say street death, I knew if I was killed during that time I would have busted hell wide open. I had acquired three spots from which I operated and I was making money hand over fist. One of my spots was on the border line of a turf war. This gang war was claiming many young lives. I was a young Player, Gangster, Pimp and was trying to stay out of the gang banging Crip/Blood, i.e. mob conflict. The territories were sized up like this; The i.e. mob claimed the territory on the other side of G Street going west. The Los Angeles Main Street Crips, Hoover and Grape Street, claimed everything east of G St. One of my main spots was, believe it or not, right on G St. I was in the middle of this turf war. They tried to move in on me several times but I had an O.G. crew that was fierce. Now from time to time they would try to recruit me. I had to make them understand, I may be caught up on the Dark side but there were certain things I would not be a part of. Number one, no fratricide on mine. There was enough genocide going on without my participating in Black on Black crime. I was messed up but not that messed up especially behind the color of a rag....

Poem

Color Of A Rag

How can I be happy... When everyone seems sad... How can I have Joy, when the whole world is going mad... My brothers are flying colors... Some red rags and some fly blue... They're shooting each other down and they're killing babies too... It's an accident they cry...I did not see that baby girl... I was trying to kill that blood who crossed into our world. You midget minded nigga, the whole world is at your feet... And you're killing up our warriors... For a corner, a set, or a street... O'cuz you say, it's not my fault... They started all this mess... They killed low down and baby doll, that summer at Watts fest... So, we're going to run down slobs and kill all bloods, until we revenge our set... Boom!... Hey man what happened here... Why did you kill that man... Oh he just a cuz from crippled street... Getting what he deserved... And we're not going to stop the guns from popping, until the blue rag is to the curb... Say Grand Wizard of the Klu Klux Klan all is going well my friend, tell the Knights of the Klan, the Nazi party, and the Aryan Brotherhood if we wait a little longer... We could grow a little stronger and they will kill each other off for good.

By Michael P Sterling a.k.a. Spicy Mike better known as Mao Mujedi, written while in Chino Prison.

It was an ominous night and the summer was blistering. We were all at the spot where "Pimpin Scottie Glenn" and the white girl lived. He had recruited her on the East Coast. She was a real looker and really wanted to be a Black sister. She had that high-class look and made good money. She just didn't know the game and did more flat backing than was necessary. I knew she was not going to last long at that rate. Jules, who was retired, was house mama and my play sister. I always made sure she was taken care of.

This particular evening Scottie and the white girl were in the kitchen. Jules, ReRe and I were in the front room. ReRe was passing around the pipe while I was sitting at the table with my briefcase open. It contained a sawed-off shotgun, a 9 mm, and a 380 automatic which was on my waist most of the time. All of a sudden, I felt that strange feeling creeping up the back of my neck. I slowly got up from the table and looked out the corner of the window. Low and behold they were just getting out of the car. It was the Main Street Crips.

I could see the shotgun under the coat as three men arm to the teeth started up the driveway. I grabbed the 9 mm and shoved the briefcase under the couch, this is it! "Come on let's go", I commanded. The girls had already been drilled and headed towards the bathroom as we passed through the kitchen. I yelled, "Scottie they're here!" They also headed towards the bathroom. By the time the knock came to the door all three girls were laying in the back and Scottie was on the floor with a 38 revolver. I immediately jumped out of the window and duck walked up to the porch. As soon as I got there, C-dog got in the door. I guess they were tired of knocking with no response. Boom! I fired and C-dog went down as he kicked the door in. I fired two more shots in the air and shouted drop it. They dropped the shotgun and 22 pistol. I shouted get that fool up and get the hell out of here. This is O.G. Spice Man and the next time there is going to be a body count. They grabbed C-dog and ran to the car, he had a leg wound. I knew if they were smart they would take him to a hospital in the next county. I never heard any more about it.

The only thing I knew was I had to lay real low. They outnumbered us 10 to 1 and at any time Spicy Mike could come up real short. That's real talk. My Pinto station wagon was parked out front and my El Dorado was in a garage parked across town. I had not driven it in several months. I was trying to maintain a low profile and keep the cheat off. I took ReRe and we moved over to Peggy and brother's spot. They had a house in the back, across the bridge down from the old Kato's liquor store. We rested there and got high and chilled for about a week. I knew ReRe really liked this and this young tender Roni could have me at will. One night ReRe informed me that she had a regular trick that was a high roller. She was laying, to take him off. I replied when she said that, "It's no time like the present."

So about 11 the next evening I drove her over to Tropicana Street. She told me to park down the way. I parked, she got out and I let my seat down. I knew I was probably in for a long wait. This was not my first rodeo. As I lit up a Camel cigarette, I adjusted my mirrors so I could see the perimeters and it looked like no one was in the car. Then about 3 1/2 hours later I heard a knock on the window as I had fallen asleep. It was ReRe. I opened the door and she jumped in, butt ass naked. She had a small bag in her hand and shouted, "Let's go!" I started up the car and sped off into the night. She seemed to be in a panic as she said ,"Let's get out of here." I replied, (Okay baby girl, take it easy." She said, "No we got to get out of here. Look…", she said, as she opened the second bag and began to pull out rolls of bills with papers on it and small writing. I shook my head and pulled into the nearest gas station. I looked into the bag, took off my shirt and gave it to ReRe. I said, "Baby girl you're right. We got to get out of here, you hit the mother lode!" I sped to the freeway and cut across the county line and pulled into the parking lot of the No-Tell Motel Holiday Inn. I rented a room and we went in. I told Re-Re to jump into the shower as I poured the contents of the bag on the bed. She had hit it big. It must have been over $20 grand + 2 ounces of weed and an ounce and a half of powdered cocaine.

I came to realize later that she had robbed Old Man Jimmy, one of the last numbers runners of his time. There were no lotteries back in the day- day. The numbers racket was still in effect. The next morning, I went to pick up a couple of paquettes and an eight ball of rock cocaine. I then made a run to the L IQ we kicked it for several days I bought her a few outfits and stashed a couple of G's and paquettes in my El Dorado. As I opened the garage, it was dusty with spider webs. I stashed the money and the drugs in the El Dorado, for hard times. I had not opened the garage in over four months and that's another story.

As night turned into day, the days turned into weeks, and the weeks turned into months, the slogan I remember was "Chicken today and feathers tomorrow." One night in the middle of summer I was on full with a 30 balloon paquettes and a pocket full of money. I strolled out into the back at one of the spots and decided to chill. It was Scottie Glenn's spot and there was an old chair set in the cut. I pulled to the back in this dark spot and set down and fired up a primo. I was tired of this life as I looked into the sky. I said," Lord forgive me of my sins. I plead the blood," as tears began to run down my cheeks. I began to think about my children, Mama Bessie and all those lives that died in the street life. As this gangster mask began to fade, I realized I was stuck like Chuck. I asked God, "If you cannot get me out of this madness, please take me home." I sat there for about an hour, in a deep emotional query.

Then suddenly I heard someone call, "Spicy Mike, there's some business out here, you better come and get this money." I laced myself up, put on my gangster swag and went back to work. Two days later I was at the spot-on G St. and the place was raided. I was charged for possession of sales of Heroin, possession of a sawed-off shot gun, possession of a loaded firearm, to wit a 380 automatic. Well, all I can say is you better be careful what you pray for. Your request may not come like you want it and may take a minute for you to understand. But it is all Kum-ba-ya, baby. I found out later that the Bible says in Proverbs 18:21 that death and life are in the power of the tongue.

San Bernardino County Jail

The Hon. Judge Kennedy

It took me several weeks to shake the effects of drugs and the street life. I knew I was in serious trouble. I had about a five-year run as I sat there in the preliminary hearing. Some Public Defender came with an offer of 10 years. He said I could probably get 17 to 25 years if I fought the case. He led me to understand I could get five years for the sawed-off shotgun. Five additional years for the loaded 380. Three, five, or seven for the possession of sales, and 5 to 10 years on the enhancements. Wow! I was dizzy to say the least. This was way over my head. My oldest son would be 30 years old by the time I was released. "Tell him no deal", I said. "I'm putting 12 in the box." Six months later I was in pretrial. I started off with a Public Defender and I was now going Pro Per, which means I was my own attorney.

I now had access to the law library and was given a private investigator. They also gave me a stipend I could use for trial clothes or material. Over the course of the next six months, I had been in several fights and one riot. The first fight, I was still weak coming off all those drugs, when a young Crip about 6'4" and 275 pounds ran into my cell while I was laying on the bunk. He said, "Nigga this is it!" I jumped up and got the first two punches in. I busted his lip and then ran out of gas, still weak. He got me in a headlock and before he could go to work, the deputies ran in. He was slow but strong and I knew I was in trouble. I was offset and didn't know anyone on this block. I asked the deputy for a mop bucket and a mop, so I could clean the cell. As soon as it arrived I turned on the shower and broke the mop making me a Shaka Zulu spear. I had made up my mind when the gate racked for chow, I was going to get a 187 for real, come what may. One way or another I was not coming up short even if it meant sticking my homemade spear in his gut, his eye or his ass.

The next thing I knew, some crazy deputy came yelling my name, saying he was tired of me making trouble on his row. He demanded me to come out of the cell and come up to the front. I was totally confused, yelling and talking head. I said, "Man you got me mixed up with someone else, I just got here." He snatched my 185-pound ass up and threw me against the wall and gestured to me to be quiet as he let go. He continued to rant and rave and put on a show. He quietly said, "Go back and get your stuff man, your cousin and some friends are next door in the next cellblock H South. They told me you were offset and if anything happened to you they were going to set it off."

I shook my head and cautiously complied. As I was escorted down the tier, I heard a familiar voice say, "Hey Big Homie, it's me Willie Boy from Paris." I was all smiles as I stepped into the cellblock number two. I had heard that Willie Boy had got a double murder charge almost 2 years ago. He was still here fighting the death penalty 18 months later. He introduced me to Romeo, a shot caller for the newly formed inland Empire Mob. It was comprised of two counties, San Bernardino County and Riverside County, the second and third largest counties in the United States. It was formed because the Los Angeles Crips started migrating out of Los Angeles into those counties. They laid seize to those counties taking over drug territories, murdering, robbing and literally running amuck. Now, do not get it twisted, some of the notorious gangsters had come out of those areas. They just were not organized, Big Chuck, the Wizard, Romeo, Big Bob, O.G. Frank Houston and several others had put a protection racket together to fight off the Los Angeles Crip rampage. The Black Guerrilla Family was already in existence, but was primarily a prison gang. Highly publicized by Doc Holliday and Ray Ray two O.G.'s from Pasadena. So now H South Block was controlled by the I.E. mob (Inland Empire) and H North was controlled by the Los Angeles Crips.

I now saw my mistake. I was born in Los Angeles at the General Hospital and we stayed in the Leso Village East Los Angeles. I had spent a lot of time in Compton and Watts, but I grew up in Riverside. On the jail application when the question popped up, "Where are you from?", my crazy ass put down Los Angeles. Now I never was formally inducted to the I.E. mob but on occasion I put in work and took quite a few contracts for Big C. He was a general and a real Gangster Double

O.G. who had juice all the way up the ladder. His brother had been hooked-up with Doc Holiday, Ray Ray and one of his nephew's played for the Green Bay Packers, that Woodson boy. As a matter of fact, the first time I saw a cold million-dollar cash was several years later. I was in the Valley and had gotten out of prison and ran into big C. He had taken a liking to me and invited me to one of his spots and low and behold, on the kitchen table set a cool million dollars cash.

He just let it sit there as a showpiece for all the "would be want to be's." For several months, he controlled the I.E. mob with an iron fist. Big C was a cold piece of work and a very dangerous man. One of my Ace-Boom- Coom Homie's, was big Frank Houston, now deceased. Frank and me, dated two sisters that lived in the projects in those days. I would come to the spot and no one could spend any money. I was hitting the Tri-County tough and this was one of my hide away spots. I could relax and take a breath because I knew Big Frank had my back. No one knew my real name or where I was from. I was known by my friends as the "Spice Man O.G.." Everyone else called me Spicy Mike. I would be gone for several weeks checking my traps and supplying the houses, but when I showed up it was party time. You see in the life I lived, I never relaxed. Not at the G St. spot with Scotty Glenn, nor N. 16th St. spot with Melvin Murphy. I wore the mask and lived the tough gangster life.

Several years later after I got out of prison, I found Melvin Murphy homeless, at Sacombe Lake during one of my Jesus Street Rallies. I snatched him up and put him in one of those vans. He arrived eight hours later in Marysville, California, which was about 40 minutes away from Sacramento. I had founded a 30-bed facility which was called "The House of Joseph", a Christian recovery home for men. Melvin Murphy had become a great asset to the ministry. After a year and a half, he became assistant director and married my secretary. He also became a deacon in the church two years later. God blessed him with a baby boy, Ananias. I was with him later when he took his last breath. His wife, my daughter in the Lord, Colette Murphy, at that time walked out of the hospital. It was during a sweet and gentle rain that he went home to be with the Lord. He had about five good Jesus years after being born again. Me and his wife walked down the streets of San

Francisco weeping and laughing at the same time. It was joy and pain, sunshine and rain. Let's just take a minute and give God the glory for Deacon Melvin Murphy, Junior.

As I finish this chapter of **"The Man Child In The Not So Promised Land"**, let me pause for the cause and drop a tear for Big Frank Houston also, who loved Jesus too, in his own way. He came to the program up north and stayed about eight months. One day he disappeared and left on my door a beautiful gold silk suit which looked like it was tailor-made for me. Several months later I found out he had been beaten to death and found in an abandoned house in the City of Fallen Angels, Los Angeles California. I cried for about a week in my alone time. I really loved crazy Frank, he was my brother in street life and in the Lord. Let's turn it back a page or two!

Now, as I think back to the San Bernardino County jail and piece the events together, I remember that when I arrived, I began to eat everything and exercise regularly. After several months, I could do about 500 push- ups. Brother Romeo and I had gotten real tight and we competed to see who can do the most push-ups. He always won with a smile. If I did 1,000 push- ups he would do 1,050 push-ups. I got up to 1,200 push-ups and he did 1,300. I was through! He would always beat me. Oh, by the way, not all at one time. But sets of 50 back-to-back.

I started to do push-ups with someone on my back. Then in the dormitories we would lift the bunkbeds with someone on them. Sometimes it would be two people on them. We would prop the legs up with books then get up under and push it up. We were doing back arms off the side of the bed and curling plastic buckets full of water. We made our own gym. Then with a towel we could do isometrics. These 19 inch arms turned into motor 21's on the hang.

One day as I was coming from the jailhouse library there was a big commotion in the hallway. "Big C" had arrived from Folsom Prison. As I was going down the hallway to my cell, I found out that my cousin Willie Boy was sentenced to life without the possibility of parole. He cried in my arms that day as his sentence came. No one saw this but me and I have not seen him since. Anyway, as I was passing cell Number One, I saw "Big C" out the corner of my eye. He yelled, "Oh! you're the "Spice man" that I've been hearing about. Young man we've got to talk." He looked like a huge short guerrilla about 5'7" with a massive chest. So big you could set a cup of water on it as he stood upright and it would not fall. I.E. Mob in full effect.

Two days later, he put everyone out of his cell except Wizard and Brother Hurricane, let's not get mixed up with "Hurricane Carter." For 2 weeks, Romeo and I were holding down Cell 4. I saw Big Chuck knock 4 men out cold and one defecated, and the other peed on himself. Big Chuck Woodson was nobody to fool with. He loved talking to me and was fascinated by some of the exploits of the Black Panther party. I knew the 10-point platform and program by heart and could quote sections of "The People's War", by Mao Tse Tung. Better known as The Red book. Big C blew me away one day when he showed me paperwork on how he had been ordained as a minister. But I never saw any of that at work in his life.

I was there in the county jail for about 18 months. One day Romeo and I were sent on a mission. I found myself with Romeo in the "hole", Solitary Confinement, for 60 days. I was now called the "Slasher." Some fool that had been snitching was stabbed and cut 47 times. He said that two Ninjas attacked him and he did not identify them because they were masked. You see Big C had put together a crew called the Ninjas, who would wear masks and "put in work." All through the County Jail this Folsom influence was having the full effect and taking no prisoners.

On the way to court people were stabbed and beat down by contract. In the hospital chow line, snitches and b***h's were taken care of. Those L.A. Crips had bowed down under Big C's rule. After getting out of the hole and barely escaping a hot 187 attempt, I was shipped to a dormitory called, Jay Tank or should I say jumping J.. Romeo and I had been split up and Big C was back in prison. I continue to exercise and as I came into Jay Tank, I located my bunk and could hear cries that could upset your ego if you are not careful. "Spicy Mike, that's Spicy Mike - hey what's up big Homie?"

I heard these cries as I was settling down into this new atmosphere. All of a sudden, men began to dump bags of commissary food all over my bunk. My reputation was now off the Richter Scale. I was now

6'3 and 265 pounds, all muscle with a Ho Chi Minh beard that ran 2 inches below my chin. I was bald headed with a 6-inch braid in the back of my head. I must have been a sight. One day on my way up the ladder, I found those white boys who had beaten a brother half to death. In those days the jail had been segregated. You see every once in a while those racist deputies would throw a Black brother, into an all white cell, at about 2 a.m. in the morning, just for laughs.

So, for payback one day I slipped out of the chow line into one of those cells filled with white boys and I knocked two of them out. It happened so fast and no one was the wiser, except the men on the row. They were laughing and shaking their heads, saying that "Spicy Mike" is a real fool. My Reputation kept growing. Meanwhile... The D.A. had offered me a seven-year deal plea bargain and said if I went to trial he would make sure I got 27 years. Let me take a brief moment to explain my case: the raid on G St.

It was a warm summer night around 11:30 p.m., almost midnight. I was walking in from the kitchen when the police kicked the door down with a no knock warrant. My briefcase was on the dining room table with a shotgun and a 9 mm inside, an ounce of rock cocaine and two 8 balls. I had left it on the table and little C, ReRe's brother, was in a chair about 6 feet away. He was strapped with a 9 mm and had pleaded out to 16 months.

There was also two hookers sitting on the couch about 9 feet away from the briefcase. There was this crackhead, Larry, that used to be a Gopher for Kibble and Bits. Altogether there were four people in the proximity of that briefcase. My name was not on the briefcase or in it as I recall when the police came to the door. All three doors were kicked in simultaneously. I was coming from the kitchen, at least 8 feet away from the briefcase. It could have been anybody's briefcase legally and that was my defense 18 months later on the way to jury trial.

An Epiphany

I started praying again on a regular basis right there in J tank. I would wait until late at night between 12 and 1a.m. in the morning. Not because I was ashamed, but because it was usually quiet. I would start off with "Jesus, I plead the blood, please forgive me of my sins."

127

One particular night I was on my knees praying with my eyes wide open and an OG named Louis, came over to me and knelt down beside me. He said, "Spicy I've been watching you pray for the last couple of weeks, do you mind if I join you? The word of God says, "One will put 1,000 to flight and two 10,000" and that began our prayer routine and the midnight watch. Soon we were joined by several more, who asked about a Bible study during the early evening hours. The dorm had about 50 bunks which legally housed about 100 souls and most of the time we exceeded that number with at least 25 to 50 men on the floor. The tension was high. Louis began to teach the Bible study and I would lead the midnight prayer circle. After about a month the prayer circle had gotten up to about 70 men. It was awesome. I had cut a hole out of the middle of a sheet and made a belt out of toilet paper. I was truly born again. I was not perfect, but born again. I told everybody I was retiring from the life of crime, gangsterism, and pimpology. The time had come for me to write my farewell toast to "the game."

Fair Well Toast To The Street Life

As I think about the moon, the stars and sun... I think about the crazy things I have done... I've lived a carefree life with a debonair bliss... I've had a Burger King attitude that could not miss...I was gifted and talented beyond compare...I was a honeycomb Mack with charisma and flair... You know I strutted like a rooster without a care... You know pimping came easy there were hens everywhere...I was nigga rich maybe two times or three...I rode a Palomino horse down on Rosarito Beach...I was at the Mardi Gras in 1975... I've seen a Super Bowl game on the East Coast live...I've flown in the best airlines in the world, always first class just kickin the breeze... Champagne flights with caviar dreams... I've lost it all and gained it all back... I was a continental joker... a silver tongue Mack... there's only one thing that I regret to say...I haven't seen Marcy Girl 10 years to the day... if I die before I decay... Tell Marcy girl there was something else to say! I've lived a life that was sweet and mean...But Marcy Girl you were my queen.

Moving right along. One thing about being born again, while spiritually you do receive a new lease on life, one thing's for sure; you still have to reap what you have sown. The word of God says: "God cannot be mocked." Now in some cases mercy and grace can show up. If divine favor shows up, you might even be eligible for a miracle. But for the most part the precept is found in Galatians, chapter 6 verse seven: "Be not deceived, God is not mocked; for whatsoever a man sows that shall he also reap." There have been many convicts, inmates, and detainees that have received a jailhouse religion. Let me explain this. Jailhouse or prison life can be real rough on an individual. These people live under such harsh circumstances with unimaginable stress and death threats; such as bleed on my knife or s**t on my d**k. So, a lot of individuals choose not to bleed.

I remember one time, I was in Riverside County jail and a young white boy was thrown in by his father to teach his 18-year-old son a lesson. I guess the father's plan was to scare him straight. I will not go into detail, but it was a horrible night for that young man. He was soomized and raped by at least 18 individuals. It was a white on white crime. Yes! The jails and prisons can be a cold, heartless environment.

Now because lockup can be so tough, a lot wanna B's play like they found Jesus under some bunk or at some chow hall meeting. You know back in the day-day when an inmate truly turned Christian or Muslim, for the most part all hands were off that inmate. This was a part of the O.G. code. Now if someone got caught playing the God card and doing things that were not in the book... Oh, his A** was out! He received the worst beat down, even disfigurement or being sodomized. One thing you do not do, is play with God in prison. This is a no-no. This conduct means you better act like the Pope, as you walk the yard. There's no gambling, no getting high, no drinking "Pruno", nor sexing of any type, no jacking and no playing games. You better be churching 24/7. On the yard carrying your Bible and not mixed up in any altercation. There was only one exception: if a race riot broke out all hands on deck. That's the code!

I remember when I arrived at Chino Men's Prison, my butterflies were trying to change to fear. Yes, I was scared but I was not afraid. Like a boxer, you can be a little scared of the unknown, but you're still moving ahead forward with no retreat and no surrender. Everyone had been strip-searched in classification and given the necessary clothes. To my surprise, everyone that I drove up with was sent to the gym. But my paperwork read: Sycamore a.k.a. Stick-a-more. It was highly unusual for a first-time offender to be sent to a high-powered section, especially one who had never been in the system before. But my dance card read "Black Panther Party affiliation, high security risk." Yes, the Black Panther Party; they had made me and now it begins.

As I sit here today, December 3, 2015, reflecting on the past, I'm in Paris, France with pen in hand. Nostalgically looking at a time gone by. Prison life is far behind me. I am amazed and in wonderment as I am allowed the grace this liberty and freedom has bought me. Indeed, God has been good to me. The world is in turmoil, Paris has been under attack. The terrorists called, Isis, have hit six major targets with guns and bombs. Many lives have been lost and I have been sent by God to declare and decree over the territorial evil in this region. We must understand that there are true principalities and powers controlled by the rulers of darkness. We do not wrestle against flesh and blood, but against wickedness in high places, which have captivated some of Abraham's illegitimate children, which claim to be descendants of Ishmael. He was the firstborn of Abraham who is the father of many nations. His mother was Hagar, the bond woman.

The Bible declares that as a man sows, so shall he reap. Our father, Abraham, like so many of us did not wait on the promise of God. Abraham tried to manipulate the hand of the Almighty. His two sons, Ishmael and Isaac, thousands of years later, their descendants are still fighting over the heritage and the legacy of father Abraham. You see Abraham and mother Sarah tried to speed up the process. Often we hear the voice of God clearly, but find ourselves in the same place without the patience or discipline to endure the process.

Example and point. David was anointed to be king by the great prophet Samuel, but he had to endure the trials of process. Like a fine wine or good cheese that must be aged to perfection, it is a process. It's all part of the plan. We find in today's society that many people are given prophecy and leave ministries prematurely. They go out and print up business cards when they are years from that prophecy being fulfilled. It all started with father Abraham. It would seem by now, that we should have read his account and learned from Abraham and Sarah's mistake. We have enough Ishmael's running around, having been created by our own lust.

It has been a wonderful day here in Paris. I have been to the Eiffel Tower and there I began to blow the Shofar under its space, scattering principalities and powers. I rode on the subway and train praying over and under this great city. It seems to me that we're going to be pushed into destiny. The enemy is coming in and so like a flood, God will raise the standard. In the Book of Jeremiah 51:27 it reads "Set ye up a standard in the land, blow the trumpet among the nations. Prepare the nations against her. Call together against her: the kingdoms of Ararat, Minni and Ashchenaz, appoint a captain against her; cause the horses to come up like the rough catepillars. Refer to verse 29 for further insight. Just a moment. Let me not get too far ahead of myself! Back to prison life.

"Sycamore", the cellblock. It looked like I was being escorted into Dracula's Castle. This dark place, would give anyone the creeps. The walls are burned, because of prior riots and abuse. The stench of death is everywhere. As I walked along this great hall, I was consumed by its terror and could barely hear the Deputy's voice as he spoke those forbidden words. "Step inside." I could feel the eyes that peered at me as I walked down the row. They seemed to be sizing me up, to see if I was a warrior or prey. As I stepped in, the sound of the gates closing seemed to seal my fate. I'd been placed in a two-man cell, alone on a row of about 50 inmates. I adjusted myself and fixed my gaze, as the floodgates of hate began to rise up like a volcano ready to erupt at any moment. I refused to be a prey. I would die first, before I became a victim to a savage end.

Now the warrior "Mao Mujedi" rose up! I could now once again hear the words of Elaine Brown's album, "Seize the Time", (Black Panther Party Anthem). The words began to resound in my soul. I quoted "Seize The Time." *Have you ever stood in the darkness of night screaming silently, your man? Have you ever thought the day would come that you must stand up in the noon day sun. Well believe it my friend that the silence must end. We just got to get guns and be men."*

131

I yelled at the top of my voice "Mao Mujedi", on deck; Field Marshall Southern California Black Panther Party." The reply came back in a sharp steady voice, "Be still 'young blood'. B.G.F. on deck." "Now, sing that song would you please, young warrior." I replied.

"Three the Hard Way"

By Mao Mujedi ... Better known As, Michael P Sterling

"The gorilla stopped the panther... the other day... He said what's happening man you've been away ... I've been laying low and being real cool .... But things have gotten crazy ... I've been hearing about you ... Now I don't like the things that ... I've been told ... How so many of my people, Have been dying from this snow ... How little Black babies, Are laying in there cribs ... With no diapers on their asses ... And you can see their every rib ... How little sister, Tizzie, is turning kibble tricks ... Just to get her daddy a snort, a bump, or a fix ... I heard you had a meeting in one of those troops up north ... and you justified this shit ... For revolutionary art ... Not by any means necessary ... Does not mean by decay ... You have set our people back ... 50 years this way ... And what about the dead ... Who died for dope are vain?... Now wait a minute panther ... You cannot talk to me this way .... Ain't nobody seeing you ... We thought you ran away ... and What about your boy ... Was shot out ... to the max ... he was seen riding a bicycle in Oakland ... Begging for kibbles and cracks ... He was supposed to be your number one man ... Now tell me Mr. Panther ... Was that part of the plan ... And what about that author ... The one who talk so hip ... He ran away to Algeria's and then came back, with a line of undies ... You know that G string shit... .... Ya! The one who wrote Sucker On Ice ... Hold on Mr. gorilla ... There's some things you got to know .... How that brother up in Oakland ... Was never really let go ... Now mission impossible ... was the order of the day ... They fooled a lot of people ... But Huey P Newton died in the state ... Just like, Brother George ... never made it home ... Different plan, same old trick ... To stop the warrior song ... Aw! Man ... I didn't know ... Never really thought about it .... Like that before ... I guess that penthouse lie ...Was a joke on me ... I guess I was blind ... And did not really see ... Now it ain't no thing, my brother .... We want to leave this allbehind ... Is time to get busy

*brother ... let's seize the time ... Now youknow the Praying Mantus
... The one who faces East ... Call him on the phone ... He really hates
this beast ... Not the one who embraced the flag ... We're talking
about the O.G. who stayed with the program ... Of the others old
man, you see ... Solidarity is the orderof the day ... They're not going
to take us out .. That divide and conquer way ... Over time ... The
gorilla, the panther, and the Praying Mantus ... Solidarity three the
hard way."*

After the dialogue the block started to take on a life of its own
and settled back into its normality. The first tests were over and I was
accepted into this dark society. I slowly positioned myself on the top
bunk. I was glad that I was by myself for the first night. It was a chilling
experience. I dozed off to sleep, not heavy, but a light reflective sleep
almost nostalgic. All of a sudden, I was awakened by a loud scream,
as the prison guards and hospital staff came rushing in. They stopped
at the cell next door. "What's going on now?", I said. As a gurney was
pushed along the walk, they went back and forth for several hours. I
heard one deputy say, "Well he's free." Now what the hell is he talking
about as a body was placed on a gurney along the catwalk. I saw as a
sheet was placed over some white inmate. They left him lying there
for hours. As this dead man was laying in front of my cell, I thought,
"Now this is unbelievable. I just got here. Now, what the hell is this.
I've been on this row one day and there's already a dead man in front
of my cell. What part of the game is this?" I thought to myself. "Why
don't you roll him down the ramp." Why does he have to be dead in
front of my cell?" I shook myself in disbelief, only to find out that he
had committed suicide.

The next bit of information really unnerved me. I came to find
out this fool only had 18 months and cut his wrists. I said to myself,
"I'll be damn. This nut only had 18 months." I had been sentenced to
seven years. I thought that I was prepared in my mind for somebody to
get stabbed or even thrown off the top tier. But this fool had gone and
cut his wrists right next door. This was a little much. I rolled over and
softly cried myself to sleep. I woke up several hours later and saw the
body was still in front of my cell. As the next guard passed, I shouted,
"Man, why don't you push this fool's body down the ramp. Why did
you leave him here?", I yelled.

133

What's your name he inquired, I replied Michael Paul Sterling. He laughed almost mocking. "You just drove up. Welcome to Sycamore, you might as well get used to this. You're going to be here a long time. If you're not next?" "The devil is a liar," I replied and began to do some push-ups. I didn't stop until I'd done about 1,000 to be exact. I paced back and forth and took my mind off everything outside my cell. "This is my environment", I said to myself. I don't know when they removed the body. I just settled into prison life.

A brother named "Easy", approached me on the way to chow. He said, "O.G., we got you. I'm family, but there's some trouble. A kite has come down from one of those Crip Sets, with your name on it. "Main Street?", I replied; "Yes, Main St.", he said. "Crips, that young crazy crew." Everything was fine until one day I had to step out into the yard. Now understand this, just to keep it real and to let you into my psyche. Up close and personal, I was no punk. My persona was like Humphrey Bogart. I stepped out into the yard. I looked into the sun, and began to take inventory, as a small crew of brothers walked over and said to me, "Walk with us."

Brother Easy was among the crew as a low-ranking soldier. The tension was high as I heard one of the gang bangers say, "That's the nigga from the I.E." Even though I was not from the I.E. Mob. I had some close affiliations with the "shot callers" and would always help a real Black man in trouble no matter where he was from. Number one, I was not into fratricide. As I masked myself and strutted along the yard taking giant steps, I began the panther walk, left leg forward, then I would drag the right. Young blood walking, "gangsta stalking." I pounded the ground and paused briefly, as I checked out the terrain.

This could be a set up. But I was ready, and I would go down fighting like the lion I was. I was led to the "500 club weight pile bench." In those days the yard was full of Olympic weights. Much to my surprise, there sat Baby Ray Townsend, a cold killer, who I had favor with on my juice card. One day when he came and hit our set, he had some trouble with the homies and I helped him out of a jam. We had become very tight over the years. If you remember earlier in the book, he and my Indian brother, "Ron Dear", had helped me out back in the County Road camp, when that buster killer tried to make a move on me. I even stopped him and his crew from running in on Big Judy, a big-time drug dealer. **AND WHAT HAPPENED WAS...**

Reflections: I had been up all night smoking cocaine and had gotten the jitters. Little Danny, my connection, had brought me a high grade of powder cocaine and I was making money again hand over fist. The day was breaking and I knew I had to come down. I decided to go over to Judy's and get some H. I knew that would bring me down off this "go fast." I liked getting high, it kept me out of life's reality. Anyway, I could not wait till the sun came up. Most of the dope houses shut down late and would open up about 7 a.m.. It was about 6 a.m. when I arrived over there off of Linden. It was me and Shelby and it was still dark. I had Shelby park down the street and began to creep up to the spot. As I was moving along, I saw that a car had pulled up and stopped. It was a bad 63 Chevy, a low rider. It seemed a little out of place. I was attracted by a lit cigarette, as I cautiously approached the vehicle. I looked and baby Ray Townsend stepped out of the car with another brother. I noticed immediately he had a pistol with a raw potato on its barrel. "Hold it baby Ray", I said. He looked back startled, "Oh my God, Michael Sterling what are you doing here? Man, I almost shot you!" We all got back into the car. I laughed and said, "Not today Homie." He smiled that big O gangster smile that was deadly. I knew he could shoot me at any moment and continued on about his business. It's called respect and I had earned it with him.

When he had first came to Riverside a few years before, he had been running from some drama out of Los Angeles. Big Blue and some of the homies had him "hemed up" on the Avenue one day. I approached, took one look at Baby Ray and knew he was a soldier. I lied and said, he was my cousin from Los Angeles Big Blue and his crew gave him back his merchandise and me and Baby Ray were cool from then on. We rode together for several weeks getting paid. He was a cold robber, killer for real. I stopped him from pulling the trigger several times during a caper. My slogan was; this is a robbery, do not make it a murder. I was young and angry and getting paid. But I still, even then, placed human life over dollar bills. I wish some of my ancestor's slave traders felt the same way. Yes, I'm talking about, your grandfathers, your great-grandfathers, their grandfathers, uncles, cousins and brothers that killed, maimed and castrated my people. Yes, I needed to get high, so I would not go off on your asses. You know you are wrong, so be glad I found Jesus. Yes, Jesus, who set the slave and the slave masters free. Moving right along…

"Now Big Homie, what are you up to?" I asked Baby Ray, as I gave the driver the once over to make sure he was not calling the shots. When I looked at him, he looked down, so I kept my attention on Baby Ray. I was not healed at that time, but my reputation preceded me. I was known to always be packing. Baby Ray replied, "Young Homie, you need to split. We did not drive all the way from Los Angeles to go back empty." "Wait a minute Ray", I said, "These are my people, this is one of my undercover spots, let me do this. I will lace you up with a few Benjamin's and get you at least 15 bags of H. Here take these three bills, I will be right back."

Yes, I lied again as I ran to the door and knocked loudly. Judy opened up. I cried, "This is Michael Sterling. What are you doing here so early? Just open up the door I demanded." She replied, "What's wrong", as she opened the door. "Give me a quarter, I have the jitters." I was shaking because of the cocaine I blasted off and settled down. I steadied myself and explained the situation. She got a broom and walked outside and played like she was sweeping and waved. I demanded a couple of hundred dollars and 15 bags of H for "Baby Ray", who would leave with almost $400. She never knew who he was and complied without hesitation. She peered out the window as we drove off. Judy moved in a week and got out of the drug business. As me and Baby Ray drove off, he said, "Young Homie I was prepared to lullaby all them folks in that house," as he laughed to himself. Judy put me on her dance card for the rest of her life. She and Baby Ray are both dead now. Baby Ray was found shot five times and left for dead in his car after a botched robbery two years after he got out of the pen. Judy OD'd and was pronounced dead on arrival about five years later.

Now, here he was on this bench. He smiled, "Young Michael Sterling, now what are we going to do with you?" As he hoisted up 500 pounds. He did about three reps, then landed it on his chest and took a breath. He did two more reps and put it up. He jumped up and gave me a hug. He whispered in my ear, "Do you feel this shank? I'm supposed to be putting in work on you. As he let me go, he looked over to one of his lieutenants and said, "Tell them fools, this is my people, Michael Sterling and nothing better happen to him on this yard."

The next thing I knew gangster Marv approached from the PO (Pamona, California), Tray 5 7 Crip Set. "What's up big Homie?", he replied to me. He then told baby Ray, "This is the big Homie that saved me when I was in the I.E. and some fools try to bum rush me. Your right Marv, you're going to have to stand up with me. They want him bad and we're not having it." The next thing I knew, here comes Big Vic out of Texas with that gold tooth smile. You cannot make this stuff up. They came one after another, people that I have helped during street life, only God could orchestrate something like this. Like Humphrey Bogart said to Lauren Becall, "out of all the gin joints in the world!" The situation was soon diffused and I was protected.

I was soon shipped to Donavon Correctional Facility in Southern California, near San Diego. I did my time fairly easily and another "shot caller" out of Oakland, California told me to just be cool, do my short time and go home. He was a lifer, a B.G.F. Lieutenant that controlled the whole yard. He said if he needed me he would call. He knew I was hooked up but, doing the Jesus Program. I turned my head quickly and said, "What did you say?" He smiled and gave no reply. Now how did he know who I was? I thought about that for a long time. Only the OG Black Panthers knew I was Mao Youngblood back in the day-day.

The funny thing is, I remember years ago, it was in the late 70's, the FBI would come by my Mama's house on ninth Street where I lived. They came off and on. I remember the first time they showed up. It was about 8:30 one morning. I was already awake and heard that familiar Gestapo knock. As I looked out the window, there was one white man standing in the middle of the walkway and another standing on the street opposite the car. There were three altogether. As I reminisce, they looked like extras from "Men in Black". "Open up", I heard the one at the door announce. "This is the FBI." This would occur once a year for the next few years and then they went Undercover.

When Mama Bessie and I reached the door, I immediately stepped outside as Mama Bessie replied, "Can I help you?" The man answered,

"I need to talk to Michael Sterling." "That's me." I said quickly, "What do you want?" "Michael Paul Sterling? Is that your true and correct name?" I said, "Yes." The other man in Black approached. "We just want to ask you a few questions."

As I reflect vaguely, on how this interaction went. "Are you now or ever have been a member of the Black Panther party or the national committee to combat fascism?" I really did not know how or if I should answer that question. So, I stalled and said, "Mama what are they talking about?" in an adolescent, dumb voice. The agent replied gruffly. "You know exactly what I'm talking about!" Before I could say another word, Mama Bessie spoke up and rolled out of her chair. "Now wait a minute, you have no reason to talk to Michael that way. You know I work for Judge Rex Escondido downtown. Are you placing him under arrest?"

The agent eased his tone and skipped to the next question. "Do you have any information about the whereabouts of Jimmy Zan, Tok Abara, Mao, George Edward MacMahan, or Kibo?" I replied almost laughing inside, "No!" Just as I thought. These fools are asking me about me and I'm standing right in front of them. Mao young blood in full effect! I finally said, "You mean the free breakfast program on Dwight street? Yeah, I used to go up there and help feed the children. If that's what you mean."

After about an hour of an evasive dialogue. You the reader must remember this; the slogan remains "those who tell don't know and those who know don't tell!" Moving right along… I just heard the news a few months ago, as I was ministering at one of the churches in Northern California, that Yogi, better known as Hugo Pinell of the San Quentin Six, was assassinated on the yard at Folsom Prison. A big ups for you Yogi Hugo Pinell. May you rest in peace. Dare to struggle, Dare to win.

As I continued on in prison life, seconds turned into minutes, minutes turned to hours, hours turned to days, days turned to weeks, and weeks to months. It seemed as if time was flying by. As I did my time and time did not do me. I would study long into the night and the day would sneak up on me like some unwanted stranger. There seemed not to be enough hours in the day, as my poetic license took full effect. Even then preparing this long overdue book, *Man Child In The Not*

So Promised Land, some of those long overdue thoughts could now appear in the essence of this true life account of times long past. When I reflect, and bring back to memory the tragedies of a struggle to be free, my heart often aches as I realize I'd become a dinosaur trapped in a time warp or even a changing environment. As I sit here at my desk, in Phoenix, Arizona, having left Paris, France traveling through Brussels, Belgium and the Netherlands with Everlasting Salvation Ministries; I thank God for the great Apostle Evelyn Kuwoe, my host and daughter in the Lord. I'm happy and sad at the same time. It's hard, as I often reflect on my mortality.

How am I still alive? Almost all my friends, Conrad and Homie's are gone. It's lonely out here while I have these thoughts, memories, and accounts of life's trials and tribulations. Things have gotten crazy in the world. They're even cutting people's heads off, execution style, right here in America! Oklahoma for an example. While I have evolved far above some of the ideology, I once professed, you must understand that I understand and have identified the true enemy. Satan, the devil and his principalities and powers. The rulers of darkness in high places that have the whole world hoodwinked. Listen my brothers and sisters whether you be Black, white, Hispanic or another we are all a part of the human race and it's time for us to stand up in brotherhood and put Satan under our feet. My life has changed and the Bible says, "With all thy getting, get understanding." "I'm writing this auto-biography to give you, the reader, a chance at life and life more abundantly. You may not have the grace that God gave me to rise from darkness and despair and be a voice crying in the wilderness.

Now, let's 'pause for the cause' and go back. There's a few more things that I need to say concerning these harrowing experiences. One day as I sat in the prison yard, at the time I had been bench-pressing about 400 pounds. I had just pushed one, two, three reps. I got up from the bench, as one of the runners from the "500 Club", came over with a kite, saying, "Look out there's some youngsters on the yard coming at you. As I surveyed the terrain, I spotted "Mad" from San Bernardino County Jail. He was the one who I had the fight with a few years earlier. "Well I guess it's reckoning time", I thought to myself. They were traveling fast coming across the yard straight at me. I played like I did not see them knowing the whistle would blow ending night yard.

As I headed for my cellblock, in these newly designed pods, which were somewhat round or oval in shape, a door would open and you would find yourself in a long hallway which was about 25 to 35 feet long with a door at the end. It would be shut. Once the hallway was full of inmates. The front door would shut and the pod would open. The gun tower appeared above while all the cells lined up in top to bottom in a circular pattern. This would eliminate the blind spots from the old Folsom and San Quentin prison designs.

As I was getting closer to the door, they were catching up to me. My timing had to be perfect. I could not allow myself to get trapped in the hallway with them. As I paced myself, I watched as the group ahead of me entered the hallway and the door shut. They had almost caught up with me. I could turn around and go for what I know or slip into the hallway at the last second and be the last man standing. I turned slightly to see them. There were three men behind me as the door opened again. The hallway began to fill fast. I had slowed up to keep from being trapped inside with them, if I enter too fast they could rush inside with me. All of a sudden, the door began to shut and I made my move and barely made it in as my arm almost got caught in the door. I slipped in sideways. As I peered out the little glass window, Mad's face appeared. I smiled and said, "I'll see you tomorrow." He was furious.

I slowly looked around and saw "shot caller", Ray from Oakland, California sitting at one of the tables. As I slowly approached, I placed myself in his view. He summoned me over. I said, "Look man, I need a shank. I must put some work in on the yard tomorrow. They just made a move at me. I have no choice, I must take it to them at the first opportunity." "Slow down, Youngblood", he replied, "We've got you." After your work detail, I'll have someone waiting on you, he'll have the white handkerchief hanging from his right back pocket. Now, understand the rules; if you lose it, or fake with it, you're in trouble. Do you understand this, this is part of our arsenal, shot caller Ray said, "At the end of the day, it must come back bloody or someone must fall on the yard. We're giving you one shot, one day. Don't blow it. We like you. Are you sure this is how you want to play it?" he said. "I have no choice if they jacked me up, then one of my stores belongs to you. Put the other one up for me. He nodded in agreement. I made my way to my cell. I pushed the button, the door opened and I walked in. I sat down on my bunk and sighed, "My God." I said to myself, "now ain't this a b***ch."

I sat there motionless for the next couple hours contemplating this new development. I thought about my children and never seeing them again, "My Jesus", I cried, I never figured out how to turn the other cheek let alone, just let someone stab me and die. As a warrior, I must be the aggressor, I refuse to play cat and mouse with this fool all night long!" I cried unto the Lord. I rolled over on my bunk and fell asleep. It was about 4:00 AM when I woke and began preparing myself to go to work. I was part of the AM kitchen crew. They would unlock my door from the tower about 5:15 AM. I sat there ready as I began to realize my cell door did not open on time. It must be about 5:30 AM. I looked out the cell door window and saw the rest of the kitchen crew assembling. I pushed my intercom button with no response and sat there wondering, did someone snitch about the incident.

What's going on? I said to myself then suddenly I heard these words "Michael Paul Sterling roll it up for release", I said to myself, "What the hell is this." My door opened and a deputy was standing there. He handed me an envelope and said, "You got 10 minutes to gather all your belongings." As I began to read it, it was from the third District Court of Appeals. The words were in bold letters: "**CEASE AND DESIST RELEASE IMMEDIATELY.**" I could not believe my eyes, as the tears began to run down my face. I began to gather my things running from cell to cell. I left my TV and most of my goods with the family. My legal folder, which obtained most of my writs, writing, and poetry, I placed under my arms as I said my farewells. In the processing, I would be sent back to San Bernardino County Jail and released from there. I did not realize there would be a catch 22 awaiting me.

I sat there in the transportation area with my hands and legs chained once again, while my soul and my spirit danced among the clouds. I began to sing softly to myself these words: "God has smiled on me, he has set me free. God has smiled on me, he's been good to me. Amazing Grace how sweet the sound that saved a wretch like me. I once was lost but now I'm found. I was blind but now I see. God has smiled on me he's been good to me..." If you are reading this book, this is indeed a miracle. Let's reflect on the fact that a few hours ago, I was about to commit a murder on the yard before many witnesses. If I was not careful, or be killed myself and die on the prison yard, I would have become a statistic, then placed in a wooden box and buried in the Potters Field. Never to be seen again. Only God could orchestrate this miracle. Once again, I must reiterate Mama Bessie's prayers were invincible. There is no power in Satan's kingdom that can defeat, stop, or hamper the prayers from a mother, grandmother or anyone that has a connection with the Kingdom of Heaven. The only thing that can hinder it is unbelief, a lack of faith. So keep praying for your children, your grandchildren, and all of your loved ones because God is listening.

I arrived back at San Bernardino County jail and I was booked in and sent back to H North. Now 3 1/2 years have passed and as I told you before, I still had my massive 6'3", 280 pounds, all muscle frame. My biceps were 21 inches with a chest that look like a gorilla's. I was still sporting that Ho Chi Minh beard, 2 inches long and the seven-inch braid on the back of my bald head! I probably looked like a movie extra or the new barbarian with Arnold Schwarzenegger. It was about one in the morning when the gate opened. I trembled as I was placed back in H North. I was curious as the deputy opened Cell 3, knowing that as the saying goes, "there's not a horse that cannot be rode and there's not a man that cannot be thrown." The tank was still segregated. I slid in as quietly and as humanly possible. I found one loan top bunk and placed myself there. Everyone seemed to be fast asleep, but I can feel those eyes piercing at me from the blankets below.

I sat on the top the bunk for most of the night. I knew better than to fall asleep in this new unknown environment. The lights came on about 5 AM. I watched several men relieve themselves; each looking up and quickly turning away. I had tied the top of my jumpsuit around my waist using the arms as my waist tie, purposely revealing my massive frame. Yeah! Hollywood in full effect. A picture is still worth 1,000 words. No one spoke as the hour passed by. It was about 6 AM when all the cell doors banged open. Like thunder, they announced chow in 30 minutes. It happened so fast that two men ran into the cell and grabbed a man off the bottom bunk and said either you give me those shoes or get a beat down. He was sporting some brand-new Jordan's.

They didn't see me being so confident in their endeavor. I swung from my position and yelled, "Who the hell do you think you are running up in my cell. This is O.G. Spice Man and this is my house." I grabbed the one closest to me with one hand and effortlessly threw him out of the cell. He hit the wall and fell to the floor. I swung and faced the leader who is now trembling and said, "Big Homie I did not know you were in here."

He's just a wannabe buster from IE, "Get out and next time get permission before you enter a man's house." As he hurried away, I stepped out onto the tier and yelled thunderously, "Spice Man O.G. on deck, this is my house. Where is the shot caller on this row?" Silence filled the air and there was no response for several minutes. I looked back into the cell at the young man who had been accosted. He was putting on one of his shoes. I said, "Were you going to give them your shoes without a fight?" "It's too many of them", he replied. I answered back, "If I get you a head up, one on one fight, will you defend yourself?" "Man, I don't want no trouble" he said. I immediately slapped him across his face. "If you're not going to fight for your own self-respect, you cannot stay in this cell." Another man spoke up, "Big Homie, they started off by taking people's stuff and then sodomizing them at night totally dehumanizing the brothers." "Not on my watch", I replied.

Oh, believe me I had acted on instinct but I meant every word. If you're not willing to fight for your stuff roll it up and get out of the cell. The next thing I knew bags of commissary stuff was being dumped on my bed once again. One bag said, "Hurricane" i.e. Mob, the word began to flow throughout the system, from tank to tank. "Spice Man, O.G. is on deck." My reputation seemed to be stronger than ever as the chow line began to assemble. I told my rag tag crew to assemble at the front of the line, as I looked down the row and took a survey. I could not see any real O.G. Hogs on the row. There were a few real big youngsters that looked stone faced, as they examined me closely. As we walked to chow and one of the deputy's said, "So you're back." I ignored him and walked on. I saw a couple of O.G.'s in the cafeteria. We acknowledged each other with sign language as we played out the drama.

As we entered back into our cellblock, I stood in the doorway and examined each man as they passed by me. After several minutes about five L.A. Crips approached and said, "Big Homie this is not your problem, but this punk must give up those shoes." I said, "I do not think so, let one of your shot caller gangsters come and take them from him by himself." "Man, this ain't your business", they said. "I'm making it my business as two of the other young men in my cell stood up beside me. One said, I'm with you, Spicy," as a crowd began to gather. Several of the other man on the row began to say, "Hey spice man do you remember me? I was with you last year in F tank, we are all from the I.E. they yelled, "Go get your champion and he cannot weigh over 20 more pounds than the little man." "Little man, by the way, what is your name?" "Eric", he replied. "Are you ready?" He said nervously, "I will fight 1:1." "That's what I'm talking about," I said. They walked away and one replied, "We'll be back."

As they left a young man approached me and handed me a bag full of zoo zoo's and wham wham's. He said, "You know the Joneses? I said, "Big Jonesie? He said, "I'm his nephew." I smiled and could see the resemblance of the family and gave him a high five. I called the young man, James Jamison, who would later be known as JJ and said, "Are you ready?" He replied, "Yes!" I said, "Put your hands up", as he did I hit him with a 1, 2 in the chest. He fell against the wall and I laughed, "Did that hurt?" He said, "Yes!" As he slowly got up from the floor. I said, "It was just pain; are you dead?" He said, "No", as he slowly came up from the ground. "Now when this young Crip walks into the cell to challenge you, you better hit him first without saying a word and just keep hitting him non-stop!" "Do you hear me?" He shook his head. I grabbed him and repeated: "Do you understand what I'm saying to you? Once again when we find out who you are going to fight, as soon as he walks up to you, you start swinging. If you do not do as I tell you, I'm going to whip your ass myself and afterwards, pass you around like a B***H" He replied, "Okay, I understand!" I said, "Then handle your business like a man. Win, lose or draw. It doesn't matter. Be a man. I had them do a few push-ups and told, Lucky to do some sparring with him. Later, that day, they came with their champion. Now it was the whole crew, about 25 of them. I told them, "This is a one on one fight. And no one better interfere."

He outweighed my boy, J.J. by about 25 pounds. He was also a little taller. He walked up to JJ and said, "Nigga, are you going to give me those shoes?" And before he could finish talking, JJ went to work. I mean JJ fought like a champion, but Crip Rider was a young seasoned veteran and could take a punch. JJ lost the fight. But Crip Rider gave him his respect and walked out of the cell and said, "Man keep your shoes. I see you are nobody's punk." It was a good lesson for everyone on the row.

It took almost a week before I went to court. When I got there. Judge Kennedy was already on the bench. When they called my case. He said, "Mr. Sterling, you made it back." Then he smiled like a Cheshire cat. And put my case on the end of the calendar. I sat there puzzled as to what was going on.

I was approached by a Public Defender. He said that he was assigned to my case. He explained to me that the District Attorney had two choices. It was all up to me. Number one, because of the decision handed down from the Third District Court of Appeals, he had to drop the case. But the catch 22 was that he was going to refile and by refiling we would start the proceedings all over again. I said, "What the hell, are you talking about?" He went on to inform me, that if I did not take the new deal. He was going to guarantee that I got no less than 17 years. I almost went berserk. As the bailiff approached and told me to quiet down. I said, "What new deal?" He said that I could finish out my original sentence. Which left me about 14 more months. I had already served about 3 1/2 years on a seven-year bid. I was eligible for one third, good credit. Because of the gun allegation I said, "Ain't this a bitch", and sat back in my chair. I was fuming. Judge Kennedy looked over his glasses and smiled and went on with his next case.

At the end of the day, I asked for a two-week continuance. It was granted. The DA then snickered and said, "This deal is only on the table for two weeks." They had me in a pickle. I felt like a cat caught between second and third base. They had the ball and was throwing it back and forth. They were closing in. When I got back to my cell dismayed, I knew I had to go to sleep. I was in deep despair. I was hoping to wake up and shake myself, and come out of this nightmare.

I did not go to chow and was awakened about 3 a.m. I came out of a cold sleep. It seemed I had an epiphany. As I began to go through my legal documents, I found it, "The Marsden Motion".

While I was in prison, studying in the law library, an old veteran named Joe, handed me some documents and said this might come in handy one day. I looked over it briefly and filed it away and never saw Joe again. As I began reading over it. It was a motion that was to stop all proceedings and render them moot. Time would literally stop concerning my case. Then my case would go straight back to the Appellate Court. I believe, they would have to render a decision in 90 days. When I got back to court I had it ready in triplicate and filed it immediately with the clerk. I sent them the transcripts from the entire case, along with the Third District Court of Appeals Cease and Desist Decision. Judge Kennedy was hot and the DA said to me, "Now you're going to get 17 years. We're going to make sure you do every day."

I began to sing praises unto God for the word of God says, "When the enemy comes in like a flood. The Lord God will raise up a standard." 65 days later, I heard these resounding words that would, in this chapter of my life, and forever would be a testimony to the glory of God. "Michael Paul Sterling, roll it up for release." Hallelujah, hallelujah. As the gate opened, I began gathering my belongings. I was escorted to the Booking Desk and then released. I wasn't given any gate money because I was not considered a number. I was not on parole and I'd been completely exonerated from the system. I hit Broadway a free man. Almost four years of my life had been taken, but free at last, free at last, thank God Almighty I was free at last!

CHAPTER TEN

BACK ON BROADWAY

The term Broadway has been constantly used as, I'm back on the stage of life; where everyone plays a part. Life's drama is real and like an actor on the stage, most people wear a mask that hides the true nature of their character. Like a mayor, a judge or a sheriff, that sit in the halls of justice, by day as jurisprudence, then like an actor on a stage during the night they terrorize like the Klu Klux Klan.

They have a blatant disregard for Black Americans, who are citizens of the United States. Kidnapping, burning out neighborhoods, lynching, shooting, castrating, raping and murdering because of white privilege. These are some of the people who smiled in the day, while promoting genocide under the cloak of darkness. I often wonder, not really, why they do not want to have the conversation about the genocide right here in America. The Jewish Holocaust is widely known and often spoken about. But, the holocaust happening here in our country, where unknown numbers of Blacks were and are being slaughtered is being swept under the rug. They do not want to talk about these atrocities that have taken on a new method of operation, even today. This is no longer hidden under a mask, but people wear badges and commit genocide under the cloak of law and their order of white supremacy.

As I collected my property and walked out of the County Jail, in the City of San Bernardino, California. I had about $350 cash to my name. There was also a phone number to the Inland Empire (I.E.) Mob. It was a notorious Black crime organization, where Willie B. was in charge because Big Chuck was down. I dared not use that number. I thought, "No, for me it's Jesus all the way". I strolled down the street, and the air was crisp and clean and I could hear the birds chirping in the trees. As I walked, I stooped to feel the grass. You must understand some of the simplest things in life are taken for granted. Having been in the concrete jungle of prison confinement the mere touch of God's green earth was awe inspiring. My first stop was to eat some greasy fried chicken, with jalapeno peppers and fries. I smiled as I saw all the pretty girls. Some with baby strollers and others with paper bags going about their merry way. The city seemed somewhat different.

I purchased an all-day pass and jumped on the bus headed toward the nearest "No Tell Motel" Holiday Inn. As I checked in and opened the door, I was contemplating my next move. After paying for five days, I walked to the swap meet across the street to buy underwear, Jeans, and a couple of shirts. This was all I could afford for now.

I began to think about my family and my children, but decided not see them until I could be Daddy all the way. This would be a journey which would take about 18 months. Yes, it was 18 months on Broadway, before I went to see my children. Yes, I badly wanted to see them. But I refused to go over to big Mama's house, "hummin' and bummin', torn up from the floor up". When the time would come that I could walk back into their lives, I was going to let them know that Daddy's home. It happened about 18 months later, a few days before Christmas. I drove up in a fully loaded, 1966 Chevy Impala Super Sport and the car was loaded with bicycles, clothes and presents galore. And, my pockets had the mumps. I was sharp as a tack and had received my Chaplain certification. I was operating a Christian men's facility in the City of San Bernardino. Yes, that's how I walked back into my family's life. I took Jakuma, my oldest son, to live with me first and enrolled him in San Bernardino High School and Rascheed followed later.

But before that happened I had to make a lot of changes. What did I have to do? I had been out of the pen five days and I could not afford another day at the Motel. It was about 5 p.m. and it seemed I was going to have to call the number I dreaded, but I had no other choice. I slowly dialed the number to the Inland Empire Mob, Mr. Willie B. As the phone rang, my imagination ran wild. Then suddenly, I was reeled in by a voice. "Hello this is Willie B." "What's happening man?" I replied, "This is Spiceman O.G., I just got out a few days ago. Big Chuck told me to give you a call." He replied, "Where the hell are you man, we've been waiting on you." "I'm on Mount Vernon Ave. at the No Tell Hotel Holiday Inn." "I'll be there in about 20 minutes," he said. "Just hold on."

By the excitement in his voice, I knew he had been given my credentials by the higher-ups in this gangster society. I was a valued commodity and my reputation was off the Richter scale. I dropped the phone and lit up a Camel cigarette. I had not smoked a cigarette in a while, but I knew the environment I was stepping into was extremely real. I was going to have to "mask up" and be real tough. I sat on the bed contemplating my life and saw that big Lincoln Town car drive up. I walked out, as this short brother jumped out of the car and ran up to me. "Spice Man O.G., I've heard a lot about you man what are you doing? Get your things and let's go." I retrieved my few belongings and got into the car. He handed me a roll of bills, "This is for you", he said. It was about $500. I played it cool and lit a cigarette as we rode down Mount Vernon Blvd. He made a right turn on Baseline and soon we pulled into the shopping center. The sign read, "Ragman Clothing." I smiled and retorted, "I know this is not Bob that used to sell clothes out the back of his van." "He's family.", as we exited the car. I walked in as Bob yelled out, "I know this is not the notorious Spice Man that I've been hearing about." "Willie B this my homeboy, Michael Paul Sterling."

"Bob", I replied, "Do not say that name too loud, Ragman, nobody knows it. Just call me 'Spice Man" or 'Spicy Mike'." "Homeboy stop being so serious", he said. "And come in. Willie B, you said to give him $500 credit on the I.E. Mob, I'm going to double it. This is my young Homie and he is no fool. I remember when he knocked that policeman out, right next to the pool hall. He was just a baby boy then. "Okay", he replied, "Pick out what you need, it's on us. I've not seen you in years, young Homie", "They finally caught up with yo' bad ass. He laughed and smiled and was delighted to see me. I guess I was a big shot in reputation and it had grown.

All of a sudden I heard a cry from the front door, "Spicy Mike baby, what's up Big Homie." It was Bogart. One of my pupils, while he was in the Big House. He was no longer the short snotty nosed kid I remembered. To my surprise, he picked me up and laughed, "Big Homie, how long have you been out? He retorted, "My Appeal finally came through from the Third District Court of Appeals. It said, "Cease and Desists, Release Immediately. I remember you stated writing that in the Law Library, when we were down." I thought to myself, the devil really knows how to reel you in. It's called life in the fast Lane. No holds barred. We made a quick stop at the liquor store. I purchased a bottle of Remy Martin, some cigarettes, a beer and some chips. And we sped off into the night. When we got to the Spot, there were two workers there. One male and one female. Willie B. had laced me up. I watched as he rode off into the night. He had dropped off the night packages to the runners. It included an ounce of rock and several eight balls for the street workers. It would net about 4-5 grand. This was now to be my spot. It was a back house right behind the Meadowbrook Projects, which looked like New Jack City.

A big war had been waged there between the I.E. Mob and the Los Angeles Crips, to wit, Main Street and several other notorious Crips sets. At this time the I.E. mob had gotten strong and was in full control. Back in the day-day they sent me there to hold down the territory. Yes, I was protection. It would've been an easy task, but now my heart was not in it. I was stuck, like Chuck. This would prove to be a tough assignment. I was given a choice between a 9 mm and a 45 revolver. I chose the nine, it was a Beretta. I lit a camel cigarette, and took a couple of shots of Remy Martin. I popped the can of beer and went to work. Willie B. had said he would be back in a couple of days.

I sat down with the crew and read them the riot act. The crew consisted of "Double Fresh" and Tina. They both were crackheads. I opened the O.Z. and started to package the rocks. Ten dollar packages, some twenty, some five-O's and a few more eight-balls. I gave them the crumbs, which consisted of about a good hundred-dollar sack. After about a month, I had so much money, I became paranoid. One thing for sure if the police raided the spot, even though I was not doing any hand to hand sales, I knew with over 5 grand in my pocket, I would be deemed the connection. I dug a hole in the backyard and buried about five grand. One night some wannabe buster came in and tried to take over. I was told he had come twice before to rob the spot. When he came I could see he was a rider and there was going to be trouble. Willie B. had laid in wait for him twice before, but he never came. Now here he was, on my watch. **AND WHAT HAPPENED WAS…**It was 2 o'clock in the morning and I had been posted up about a month and a half. I was in the back-room chilling and heard somebody say, "break yourself." I jumped out the back window and ran to the front door and busted in. "Drop it', I said, as I fired a shot into the floor. Blue boy was startled and dropped his 22 pistol on the floor. I slapped his homeboy in the head with the 9 mm and watched him fall bleeding profusely. "What the hell do you think you're doing, this is the I.E. mob territory", I cried out and said, "I'm Spice Man O.G. in full effect! I got a shovel and I'm ready to dig some holes. The Cajone Pass, is full of you Wanna B tough guys. So, you break yourself. You're leaving here butt-naked."

They complied with a lot of kicking and screaming. But they both left there, butt naked. I was breathing hard and my adrenalin was pumping. I almost killed those fools. That was the day I packed up quietly and said I'm out of the game. I no longer had the heart for Street life and what goes with it. The next day I left the spot and got a room on Mount Vernon Ave. I called Willie B., who is now deceased, and said, "This is the Spice Man

O.G. and I'm out. I'm retired. This is it. You tell Big C. and them, I'm gone." He said, "You cannot do this, at this time Homie. It doesn't work like this man. I like you, but don't get caught in my crosshairs", he said. I replied, "Listen and listen well son, I'm out for good. Call big C. and tell him to chalk it up to the game. I'm retiring and I'm going back to Jesus. I'm not going to kill some young Black fool, behind some drugs or drug money. I just don't have the heart anymore." About a year later Willie B. was found shot in the head, floating in the canal. Street life, I thought you knew; now you do. It's cold out there!

I posted up on Mount Vernon Boulevard in one of the flea bag hotels. I think it was "The Oasis", now a vacant lot. This once thriving hotel is gone; lost in the destruction of the street life. This was the way of life where there were pretty girls with pretty smiles, all turned out with their charisma and style, taken from crayons to perfume. The lust and the glow is like a spider's web, colorful and enticing, that would ensnare our sweet innocent children. You know the Hollywood Swingers on Sunset & Vine, Mount Vernon & Baseline, University & Park, Hope Boulevard & Town Avenue are just a few places where the glow of street life and its web of deception helped to topple a Bloodline of Kings and even a Prince or two. Where notorious mack men, players, gangsters and pimps sell their spiritual endowment, "charisma", to be used for the dark side. To the Hip-Hop generation, gang bangers, Rap artist and all that seek the limelight. All that glitters is not gold. You know Humpty Dumpty set on the wall. Humpty Dumpty had a great fall. What more do I need to say except, don't fall on the dark side. Mr. Satan, you should have killed me while you had the chance.

Back In Africa

Reflections: Let's take a pause. While here in Sierra Leone, West Africa writing my memoirs I am watching the house being "spiritually set on fire" by one of my spiritual daughters, Prophetess, Jane Brown. This love I have for the continent of Africa overwhelms me. It is my first trip to Sierra Leone where we are being hosted by Apostle O. who has been very gracious. I realize that this will be a Covenant relationship. It is my turn to speak.

They have been waiting for me for several days. Even though I'm late getting here, "fresh off the boat." There was a three-day delay. Satan thought he stopped us. I arose from my seat and began to pray in my spiritual language as the Holy Spirit took over. The people were on their feet. I grabbed a young boy in the fifth row, hoisted him in the air, and then put him on my shoulders and ran around the church. The crowd went wild, and everyone knew, except me, that he was a child of a visiting pastor. They all knew that he was destined for greatness. The Holy Ghost had identified him when I first walked into the church, and my spiritual antennas went up. I had never done this before, but I was prompted by the Holy Spirit. The Word of God says, in Romans

8:14, "He that is led by the Spirit, they are the sons of God." Oh, by the way, his name means "wisdom." I began to impart to him the virtues of a young Solomon and said, "He would not make the mistakes of David's, son, King Solomon, in his old age."

Now back to the story. As I stepped out of the motel, my caution light was on. I had about $2,500 cash, a pistol and an 8 ball of rock cocaine. There was an ounce of powder left and I really did not know what my next step was. I gazed across the street, because there was someone yelling. There was a young Hispanic preacher shouting Jesus this and Jesus that. One thing for sure he had passion. I smiled and yelled, I know Jesus. Stop talking about Jesus and show me some Jesus. He acted as if he didn't understand what I said so I crossed the street. I said to myself, my God what have I started now. He introduced himself as Brother Joe, a member of Joy Harvester Church. Little did I know this would be the crossroads of my life. It was what I had been looking for since leaving the Penitentiary.

The Bible says, "... with the temptation also make a way to escape…" As Brother Joe continued to minister to me. I heard the voice of the Lord speak through him. Finally, after about an hour of this soul saving dialogue, he prayed for me and we walked toward the church. I was going to meet his Pastor, Raul Genera. Ultimately, he would become my mentor and friend. As I informed Brother Joe again, I did not need to hear about Jesus, I needed to see some Jesus. There are a lot of Bible thumpers who stand on corners, quoting the Bible. But there is a lot of talking, with little or no action or any remedy. Listen closely. The Word of God says: "For I was an hungered, and ye gave me no meat: I was thirsty, and ye gave me no drink. I was a stranger, and ye took me not in: naked, and ye clothed me not: sick, and in prison, and ye visited me not." (Matthew 25:42-43)

The Word of God that they preach has little or no substance. In reality, God's Word is so powerful and one day there will be a reckoning and awakening. Jesus said these words to the religious zealots of the land who had passed by the wounded soldier of the Lord. Those who have been church hurt, or have made bad decisions, that caused them to fall into the pit of despair. The fivefold ministry is supposed to use the pulpit, to pull people out of the pit of desperation. Those who have fallen and love Jesus and just need someone to care like me, an O.G. Gangster for real. The 9 mm in my waist and a half ounce of rock cocaine in my pocket.

We must begin to understand that the harvest is ripe but the laborers are few. But alas God has heard my cry. I know that Brother Joe had been divinely sent here before the beginning of time, just for me. I was at the crossroads of life and I needed Jesus desperately. My heart was ready - my situation was bleak. If God's man did not show up that day, then my survival skills would have begun to take over again. And that would have been another story, never to have been written. I refused years ago and vowed that I would never push a basket down the street with all my belongings in it. Or never would I sleep under the bridge. Surely, I would never hold a sign or stand on the freeway saying, will work for food. Not in America, the land of the free and the home of the brave, Dodger's baseball and mom's apple pie. My ancestors built this country and I'm still wondering about those 40 acres and that mule. *This passage was "Written in Liberia"... MAY 11, 2016*

"PASTOR RAUL GENERA"

As I crossed the street with Brother Joe, I felt that his Pastor would be another religious zealot and when he first saw me, I would be stereotyped and rejected. I could tell Brother Joe had been in street life to some degree. Now do not get it twisted, I was a sight to behold. I was still sporting a bald head with an 8-inch braid running down the back. With the Ho Chi Min mustache, and a heavy goatee. As I told you before, I weighed about 285 pounds and I'm 6 feet 3 inches tall with 20 inch biceps and a massive chest. The fire in my eyes could probably pierce steel. As we strode into the church, Brother Joe told me to have a seat. He walked to the Pastor's office and came back quickly and I was escorted in. As I inventoried the room, Pastor Raul rose from his seat and quickly scurried around the desk. He extended his hand and said welcome to Joy Harvester Church. I am pastor Raul Genera.

He grabbed my hand and I detected a powerful hand shake. I'd come to learn later he was an former Marine, who stood about five feet 8 inches, 210 pounds. His smile seemed genuine and infectious.

"How can I help you?" he said. "Tell me now, what is your name." "My name is Michael Paul Sterling. I just got out of prison. I heard this young man from across the street shouting "Jesus this and Jesus that", and I shouted back to him, "Stop talking about Jesus and show me some Jesus. I needed to see some real Jesus", I said. As I sat down, he said "Brother Mike, I am a part of "The Power of God Ministries". I'm under Pastor Eddie Macias and we have a men's home in Baldwin Park, California. Would you like to go there? We have an 11 month - "A live-in program?" I replied, "When can I start?" He smiled and said, "Let me make a call."

As his fingers dialed the numbers, my mind drifted off as I began to paint a picture of what my future could hold while I was writing the script to a movie in my head. I heard him say, "Pastor Eddie, I've a young man here that I need to send to the program. He has just been released from prison after doing 3 ½ years. Can you help him?" "Is he on parole and where is he paroled to?" Pastor Raul asked me this very important question. They were both startled by my answer. "No, I'm not on parole." I already knew what the next question would be. "How long have you been out?" I replied, "Almost two months." Now they were really in a query because no one coming out of prison could be off parole that fast. After some debate, Pastor Raul hung up the phone and said, "Brother Mike, we're wondering how did you get off parole so fast. It seems impossible." I took a copy of the letter out of my wallet and handed to him. It read "Third District Court of Appeals, in the case of Michael Paul Sterling, prison number E77897. Cease and Desist. Period. Release immediately no parole. Because of an irreversible error to wit; A Writ of Mandate has been issued and the jurisdiction of the Court rules that all findings be dismissed and erased." It was signed, dated and sealed." Pastor Raul smiled and shook his head. "You must've had some kind of lawyer" he replied. "I was in the law library, I wrote the writ myself. Most of those lawyers are dump trucks. They do not care about inmates who are truly innocent. There are those that have been railroaded just to clear some cases. The California Penal System is a joke.

The three strikes law is really double jeopardy." I replied. "But the way it has been written. It is almost impossible to reverse."

We sat there talking for a brief time. He finally said, "Are you ready to go to the home today." I said "Yes!", knowing this is my way of escape out of every temptation. "They have a bed waiting for you, but I cannot take you until tomorrow evening. I want you to go get your belongings then we'll have dinner. You can spend the night in the church and I'll take you tomorrow. I'll have to lock you in. I will be here early in the morning. Is that okay with you, brother Mike? I want you off Broadway and locked in a church, because I do not want anything to take you off course. I believe we have destiny to fulfill." I replied, "Are you absolutely sure this is going to work?." He said, yes in a very reassuring way. I removed my gun from my waist and sat it on the desk. "Well, I guess I won't be needing this." He did not blink, I then handed him the bag of rock cocaine, street value $5,000 and we flushed it down the toilet, period! Tears began to fill my eyes.

It was a new beginning, as I arrived in Baldwin Park. The number eight had popped up and destiny and purpose had collided. As we drove up, there was a little short Hispanic brother watering the grass. I would find out later, his name was Kenny and he owned the property. He had collaborated, with Pastor Eddie and together they started the men's training center several years before. Kenny was a very down-to-earth brother, and very mature. I liked him right off. Brother Kenny, who was the director, interviewed and checked me in. Then, he escorted me to a room, where there were two bunk beds. I was given a bottom bunk; the top bunk was empty.

There were about 20 men in the facility, dormitory style. This was a spacious six-bedroom house, right in the middle of Baldwin Park. There was only one other Black man in the program and he was the assistant director. His name was Vince. There was also Big Saul, he was an old Veterano, and a Northanio. We started working out together. I began the program and study the fundamentals of the program. Time went by quickly and one day I was baptized in the Holy Spirit with evidence of speaking in tongues. It was strange to me at first, being brought up in the traditional Baptist Church. I later embraced a Pentecostal environment. It seemed to be on fire. The church was electrifying. Everyone was dancing and worshiping the Lord. The nine gifts of the spirit were in full effect.

After about six months, I read Dr. Kenneth Hagan's book. "The Intercessor." After reading this small pamphlet several times and taking notes and comparing it with my King James Bible I began to understand something that I missed. You see I had already read the Bible from cover to cover several times, while in prison. But this new revelation that I received, enlightened me to the Rhema Word of God. When the Apostle Paul stated in Ephesians 1:17-18, "That the God of our Lord Jesus Christ, the Father of glory, may give unto you the spirit of wisdom and revelation in the knowledge of Him. That the eyes of your understanding being enlightened that you may know what is the hope of His calling and what are the riches of the glory of His inheritance in the saints." Period! When our Lord Jesus Christ ascended on high, He gave gifts unto men. These gifts are commonly known as the Five-Fold Ministry. The apostle, prophet, evangelist, pastor, and teacher, which are in full operation today. He also gave nine gifts of the spirit, which include prophecy, healing, miracles, tongues, interpretation of tongues, a word of wisdom, word of knowledge, discerning of spirits and faith. There is also the fruit of the spirit found in Galatians 5:22-23. The closer we stay to Jesus the more these right principles develop in our lives. I wish more people had the fruit of the Spirit rather than the gifts of the spirit. You see the gifts of the Spirit are given. The fruit of the spirit must be developed as we grow in our life as a Christian. **Moving right along...**

One night, about 14 months into the program, I went into the backyard of the facility. It was around 3 a.m. and the night was dark and ominous. I had been awakened with a prayer burden. As I looked into the night sky, I felt this burden begin to intensify. I started to make intercession and pray with increased fervency. I was lost in the total concept of time. All of a sudden I saw an open vision and I could see a man trying to rape a little girl. The city seemed to be somewhere in Chicago. As my intersession increased, the man stopped and ran down the stairs because someone was knocking at the door. The man answered but it was the wrong address. He began to pace around the living room for some time. As I stopped my prayer of intersession I had an epiphany. Unbeknownst to me I was in prayer for about 90 minutes.

As I started toward the back door, the burden returned. I stopped in my tracks and began to pray earnestly again. The open vision happened again and I saw the man at the girl's bed. It seems he was a relative. As he began to mess with her undergarments, my prayer intensified to an unfamiliar level. The phone rang in the girl's house and he stopped in his tracks. I sensed that he was being distracted. I knew it was just a matter of time until he would complete his mission and the girl would be left scarred for life. I then went into a warfare prayer like never before. The tongue seemed to be a native language or an Apache dialect. I believe the girl peed on herself and he stepped away from her in disgust. Then I heard someone cry, "Uncle Bob we're back". "I think she just peed on herself", he replied. And I awoke. My face was full of tears and my shirt was wet as if I had been crying for some time.

Relief came over me and I understood that something had been broken in the spirit realm. I questioned, "Was this prayer a mere coincidence? Then the phone was ringing, the girl peeing on herself - prayer or coincidence, no! These are all elements that came because of intercessory prayer. It stopped the assault. This is one of the most outstanding revelations of the Kingdom of God. Our Heavenly Father told His sons and daughters, "I give you power over serpents and scorpions and all the works of the Devil." As this realization came over me about true and real intercession, I looked into the sky and I shouted these words, quoting Isaiah 6 and 8: "Here I am Lord, send me. The Bible declares also: "I heard the voice of the Lord saying whom shall I send and who will go for us." You see, our God in Heaven is always looking for someone to go, on His behalf. But the problem is, who will answer the call? When you have been called, you should always say, "Here I am Lord, send me." You may never have an open vision, but the essence is, you must pray until there is a breakthrough. The code is P.U.S.H., pray until something happens period.

A few months later, I graduated from the program and left Power of God Men's Training Center in Baldwin Park and returned to Joy Harvester Church in the Inland Empire, San Bernardino. I knocked on the church door. Pastor Raul Genera answered and gave me a big bear hug. He seemed to be excited at my return. I stayed in the church for several weeks and then moved in with Lenny and Pat, two deacons at the church. I became an usher and enjoyed greeting people at the door. It was an exciting time. Pastor Raul was "some kind of great preacher" and his wife Fabie, was a real jewel. She made sure that I had the best of everything. I'd been at the church about six months, when we finally found a place for the Men's Training Center.

This was a two-bedroom facility and I quickly took the back room, which had a side door that led to the driveway. It was used as an office and living quarters. I turned the living room into a dormitory, with three bunk beds. In the other room, I installed a single bunk bed. The house was full instantly. There was Richard, one of the mother's son from the church. He was a character. Soon my oldest son, Jakuma, arrived. I enrolled him at San Bernardino High and told them not to mention any gangs. He was stubborn and began to uphold his set, PJ Watts Crips, (PJWC) right there in the newly formed I.E. Mob territory. The gang epidemic began to get out of control, throughout Southern California.

One day I decided to look up Chaplain Gregory Payson, who is now deceased. He was the head Chaplain and the one that would visit me in jail and help to convert me back to Christianity. It was a time when I thought there was no way home, there was too much water under the bridge. It seemed impossible to make a turnaround in life. He would come by my cell several times a week, during my two-year stay in the San Bernardino County jail. While I was awaiting trial, one day he asked me if I ever went out of my way to harm and kill Christians. I had been involved in many things, that I have mentioned in this book. If I decided to record it all, I might be on my way back to prison for good. But as I pondered over his inquiry, I replied, "No, no way." He smiled and then told me the story of Saul of Tarsus and how he was involved in the death of Stephan (Acts 7:58), who was one of the first deacons of the Jerusalem church. Saul obtained warrants so he could pursue, capture and execute any of the Christians he could find. In Acts Chapter 9, it tells how this man was knocked down off his horse and the Lord spoke to him, then he confessed Jesus Christ as Lord. Read about it in Acts chapter 9. Chaplain Payson went on to make me understand how this man Saul's name was changed and how he became the Apostle Paul. That was the day that I turned my life back over to Christ. I was not perfect, but I was called by God and chosen.

As I entered the old San Bernadino County Hospital, I went directly to the Chaplains office. Lo and behold there he was Chaplain Gregory Payson. One hundred and 80 pounds soaking wet. His wiry frame and smile that would melt the coldness of men. "Chaplain Payson", I cried. He turned and looked around, grabbed my hand and jokingly said, "Sterling, I see you have on a different uniform!" Chaplin Payson knew I had a life sentence or something, "I thought that I would not see you this soon, if ever!" he retorted. "Tell me how have you been and what brings you here today." He motioned for me to sit down and I quickly updated him on my life. After about 30 minutes of dialogue, I informed him of my desire to become a Chaplain. He smiled and said, "When can you start?" I replied, "Right now!" He got up briskly from his seat, grabbed a handful of Bible tracks and said, "I'm fixing to make my rounds come along with me." My heart began to pump faster, as we walked down the hospital hallway. He began to explain to me the do's and the don'ts of a hospital Chaplain. I began to come down twice a week. The training was intense and it was more than on-the-job training. He explained the functions of the different wards and once a week we went across the street to the dialysis unit. After about four months he gave me a Chaplain's badge and assigned me to the H. Ward. It was for patients who had been in the hospital 30 days or more. It was there I met George, an old dope fiend. He was lying in bed. Our relationship would take on a new meaning. I'll come back to George in the next chapter about our encounter.

I began my first day on the job, as an official Chaplain. It was an experience of a lifetime. **AND WHAT HAPPENED WAS…**

It was a beautiful Tuesday morning, as I got off the bus in front of the hospital. It was my first official duty as a Chaplain. I was on my own. I was indeed excited as I strolled across the street. I entered the hospital and began greeting everyone that I encountered. I took the elevator up to the second floor, and my mind was flooded with thoughts. The butterflies began to dance around in my soul in anticipation, but after I'd been there awhile, I settled down. As I got off the elevator I passed the nurses station, giving them a hearty greeting.

As I entered the first room, there were two women there and I asked them, did they need prayer today. After introducing myself I proceeded to pray. Then continued down the unit examining each room with caution. When someone was sleep, I kept on moving. When someone was awake, I stopped at the door and asked, "Would you like prayer?" I walked from room to room praying and discerning and leaving tracts. I finally came to the last room on the unit and walked in on a young man doing something unusual. He straightened up when he saw me. I saw that his arm was in a sling and his leg was in traction. He was a new patient. I said, "Hello young man, I am Chaplain Mike." It felt so good to hear myself announce my new born again position. "And what is your name?" He replied, "James; James Armstrong." "Well, Mr. James Armstrong what happened to you?" He began to cry, as his soul erupted! The details of his life began to well up out of his mouth, as tears ran down his face. He replied, "This is not fair, I was supposed to die." He rocked back-and-forth violently. "James, God sent me here to help you. He heard your cry." "God is not real!", he retorted. "He is indeed real and I'm his servant." "I just wanted to die," he said. As I began to pray a song came to my heart, an old familiar gospel tune that I learned as a boy, while in the Baptist Church. Now, understand this, I cannot for the life of me, hold a note! But every once in a while, the anointing would hit and the Holy Spirit would take over and minister to whosoever was in attendance. I sang, "He Lives, He lives, Christ Jesus lives today, He walks with me and talks with me, along life's narrow way. He lives! He lives! Salvation to impart! You ask me how I know He lives? He lives within my heart."

As the chorus filled the air the Holy Spirit ministered to James through my mouth. James told me the story and how he had been fired from his job and went home early and found his best friend in bed with his wife. They had a big fight. He lost the fight and they put him out of the house. Yes, his wife and his best friend put him out of his own house. The next day he said, they repossessed his car. He decided he had nothing to live for and stepped in front of a truck. He was angry that he did not die and was still alive. I talked to James for over an hour. Finally, he repented and gave his life to Christ Jesus. After giving him information about the House of Judah on E. Street, which we started through Joy Harvester Church, I assured him there was a bed with his name on it. "James", I said, "I will be that friend that will stick closer to you than a brother."

I gave him one last prayer and walked out of the room. He stopped me and said, "Chaplain Mike, take this, I don't need it now."

He reached into the hem of the pull curtain that separated his bed from the next. He then handed me a scalpel. He repeated, "I don't need this." As I walked out of the room I fell against the wall. As tears of joy filled my eyes. The experience caused me to be in a state of bliss, that was intoxicating. Never before had I reached, nor felt this feeling of self-gratification, that can only come from helping another person in their time of greatest need. As I sowed the word of God into James, ministering life's compassion and care, my life had a new purpose and meaning. This was the drug that I was seeking, and the high that satisfied the soul! I believe God used me to save James' life. I understand this. I indeed became the beneficiary of giving. The Scripture comes to mind that says, "Love thy neighbor as thyself." These Scriptures had taken on a new meaning to me that day. Also "As a man sow, so shall he reap."

The House of Judah Christian Men's Training Center developed quickly. Soon we opened the house of Ruth, for women on the adjacent property. It was a high time. There was Richard, my son Jakuma and brother, George, the Veterano. The church was friendly and everyone worked together. There was a Deacon there named Louis Garcia and he became my best friend. It was amazing. One day he invited me over to his house and gave me the keys to a '69 Chevy Impala low rider. It was sharp, it's called a glass house. I sported that ride for over a year. Louis never questioned or asked anything about it. I was working hard for the ministry and I needed transportation. I guess God was "supplying all my needs according to his riches in glory by Christ Jesus", as I was literally touching the hearts of men that would listen to the spirit. The key is this: the Bible says in Romans chapter 8 verse 14. "For as many as are led by the Spirit of God, are the sons of God." If more people move in the Spirit, the true church, the Body of Christ would develop more quickly, as one entity.

There was another Deacon in the church, named, brother Saul. He had a wife named Becky and some wonderful children. Brother Saul became a good friend and a year later he gave me a Buick 225 Electra. The ministry was about 90% Hispanic, but from the top to the bottom I felt at home. I also continued working at the hospital, along with the men's and women's home.

There was a fine white woman, named Sheila, in the church. She had been the church secretary for several years. Then she began to take over some duties at the Women's Home. She was streetwise and no nonsense. She also became a good friend. For the next two years, I diligently served the church. I painted the church, different brothers and sister's homes, did landscaping and hauling, too. Wherever I was needed there at the church you would find me. I worked like a "government mule." Not forcibly, but willingly. It seemed I was trying to pay back some dues from the past. I was looking for nothing and was gaining everything.

Life seemed to be so simple, I rose up as pastor Raul's Armor Bearer. I remember, taking the men from the home to Mexico on a missionary journey. We were invited down to kilometer 15, to a mission, where we stayed for a week. We served, cooked, prayed and ministered. Brother George came with us and it was a good lesson for the men in the program. When we came back to the church, they were grateful for what they had. Having seen the poverty and alkali poisoning that flowed into Mexico from the Colorado River disaster, when sludge from an old closed mine contaminated the river water until it was finally cleaned up by the EPA.

After about two years of diligent service. The church pastor and elders decided I was due a vacation. I did not get paid for my work and I was not looking for pay, because all my needs were met. So, one bright Sunday morning I was asked to stand up in front of the church and they took up a collection for me. Wow, it came to about $900! I called my Mama Gloria and we decided to drive 500 miles to Northern California, where my eldest sister, Claudia Marshall lived. She is now the Bishop over the Northern Region of our ministry! It was a beautiful trip. I never had a chance to live with my real mother, so the drive was truly a blessing. It was indeed God, restoring the years that the canker worm had eaten. (Joel 2:25).

I was grateful and felt free for the first time in my adult life. It's something special when you can take the time just to hear the birds singing in the trees. I would wake up in the morning and could smell the dew upon the roses. Life's subtle pleasantries were always there, but sometimes we just need to stop and "smell the roses." When you're living in the fast lane of life, one must be on his P's and Q's!

The death rate is high and there are many casualties. You need insurance when living in the fast lane. Not the kind you can buy with money. This insurance comes from praying mothers and grandmothers, that know how to get on their knees and touch Heaven on your behalf.

It's called intercession. Maybe you, the reader, need to make a covenant with our Lord and Savior, Jesus Christ, and begin to stand in the gap on behalf of your family. It works!

We arrived safely. The town of Marysville consisted of Sutter Buttes on the one side and Beale Air Force Base on the other. The Twin Cities had Sutter County and Yuba County. It was a quiet place and there were no bars on the windows and most of the residents did not lock their front doors. It reminded me of Mayberry R.F.D.. I expected to see Opie, come walking down the street at any moment.

There were no helicopters flying overhead, as in the asphalt jungles of America. Everyone knew who you were and they also knew if you are a stranger. Their greetings were warm and friendly. For me, this was indeed a strange, but friendly, welcoming environment. I liked it. I took a breath of fresh air. Yes; I would never have realized that across America, nestled in these unique places there exists tranquility and peace.

One day when I was sitting on the couch, "maxin and relaxin", in walked Miss Shawn Vaughan, my future wife. As soon as our eyes met the chemistry took over. I was smitten and so was she. We laughed, we blushed and we cried. She was a looker and she was smart. You know, "fine as wine – just my kind"! We talked for hours. One year later we were married at the church in San Bernardino. The church and her family went all out. There were trumpets blowing as we entered, and dancers dancing. It was a Cinderella fairytale wedding. The reception was held at Auntie DD's house in Ontario, California. There were gardenias in the swimming pool and you know they even roasted a Pig. That was Bobby Hilton's idea. He was a professional chef and worked at Caesars restaurant in Hawaii and Las Vegas. He was my brother, Robert Hilton's, dad. There were also two beautiful ice sculptures. The theme was, "It's a Luau, Hawaiian style". Everyone was happy for us and everything was going well.

We moved into a beautiful apartment townhouse with a swimming pool and Jacuzzi. There was also a sauna and a small gym. Life was good. I soon realized that taking on this ready-made family was not going to be an easy chore. There was her sister's son, Lavell, a very troubled teenager, who was eventually killed by the police. I wish I could have done more in his life. But we were divorced by then and my focus was elsewhere.

Then there was Krystal, who will always be my beloved daughter. She came to live with me in Arizona several years later and completed a pharmaceutical technician program. She now has her own business and is doing well in Sacramento. Last but not least, there was Jonathan. He was a handful but has turned into quite a young man, with the emphasis on man. I may not agree with everything that he is doing, but he is definitely handling his business and helping out family members as the need arises. I'm really proud that he is a man. Protector and provider. A big thumbs up. Life has a way of getting you to your destiny.

I guess I had revealed a little too much to my new wife, about the ministry. Now understand, there are no perfect churches nor perfect people and love covers a multitude of sins. Needless to say, our family soon left Pastor Raul's church. We landed in Montclair, California and one beautiful morning, I found myself, preaching at Claremont Theological Seminary with Pastor Charles Harrell. I began to make several alliances. There was Pastor Ricky Porter in the City of Pomona, also the Mann's. Sister Mann was a School Teacher and her husband owned a tile business on Gary Blvd. They were great supporters. Check this out. I remember one night at one of our meetings a young man came in talking about Artesian Wells and bottled water was going to be a million-dollar business in the future. He had great investment opportunities and we could get in on the ground floor. Yeah!

And is the Brooklyn Bridge still for sale. The song writer said, "If, I could hold back the hands of time", or maybe I could get a do-over. Smile...

I was soon introduced to Apostle F.L. Person of the Greater Upper Room Apostolic Church, located on Hoover Blvd. He became a great instructor. After several months, he ordained me as an International Evangelist. Apostle Person was some kind of preacher! Talk about fire, brimstone, and holiness. He would preach himself soaking wet. Then change clothes and start all over again. The Holy Convocation there at Greater Upper Room was inspiring. I learned a lot about the Apostolic faith. As my wife, Shawn and I settled into married life, things seemed to be going well.

One day after the service at Pastor Charles Harrell's church, I was in the hallway and this Native American Indian woman came up to me. She gave me an envelope with $500 cash inside. She said, "This is for you, not for the church. God told me to give it to you every month." You must realize this is the very first time I ever saw this woman in my life. And, for the next two years like clockwork, she would give me an envelope with $500 inside. Then she just disappeared and I never heard from her again. The bible says in Hebrews 13:2, "Be not forgetful to entertain strangers: for thereby some have entertained angels unawares." Her name was Myra.

Myra soon moved in with our family. She had a few problems, but that's life in Christendom. The Word tells us to take care of the widows, the orphans, and those that are in need. One morning while Shawn was at work, Jonathan knocked on the door. I realized he had a startled look on his face and said, "My room is on fire." I rose quickly and ran to the bedroom only to find it engulfed in flames. We only had seconds to get out of the house. Lavell and Krystal were at school. I quickly grabbed Jonathan and Myra and ran outside. I could hear the fire trucks coming down the street. I guess someone else had called. After all was said and done, we had lost everything. To my surprise the community came all out to help us. The fire department gave us a food voucher for $200 plus a clothes voucher for $500. Krystal's school gave her a clothing voucher for $200. Between the church, family and friends we had a new start. Where I came from you did not see this kind of support, especially in the community. *Man Child In The Not So Promised Land*. Now, I had something to think about...

CHAPTER ELEVEN

RODNEY KING: JURY TRIAL, FEDERAL BUILDING SECOND INDICTMENT, STACY KOON AND COHORTS

I was in for a rude awakening. The Rodney King trial at the Federal Courthouse in Los Angeles, was taking place. I knew I had to be involved, so I parked my car at the train station lot and caught the Amtrak down to Union Station, and made my way to the Courthouse. For several days I rented a room at one of those flea bag hotels and attended the trial. The crowd was thick and the atmosphere was charged with an unquenchable fire. There were at least 500 people every day, all day. As I began to make friends with several organizations, I looked up one day and there was the new Black Panther Party. Well, well, a new Black Panther Party. What is this all about? I said to myself. I was a part of the old vanguard. Let me go and check them out.

There was also a lady called "The Queen". She was very powerful and seemed to know her way around the community. I never got her real name. It was evident, she was a prominent speaker in the group. The NAACP had representatives there and there were some other radical organizations. For sure the Nation of Islam was also on deck, representing Louis Farrakhan. CBS, NBC and CNN cameras were all over the place and newspaper reporters from around the world too.

Because of my outspokenness, I was in the newspaper several times. One day I got a call from Mama Gloria, saying that Auntie Betty had seen me on the front page of one of the Compton newspapers. I hooked up, with a very astute and likable brother, Stanley 2x. His wife was a Correctional Officer C.R.W. (California Rehabilitation for Women). One day I stood in front of the cameras and began to spout rhetoric. This is right after we had run the Ku Klux Klan away from the Courthouse. This incident became a moment of solidarity among the ranks. Just imagine this, the first jury had found Stacy Koon, and his cohorts not guilty. We had all seen the tape. There was an unbelievable beating, caught on tape. The world had witnessed this atrocity. The City burned and erupted like a volcano whose cosmic energy was long overdue. When you have a society that had been downtrodden for decades when, enough is enough, like a Phoenix they will arise and no longer tolerate the beating and blatant disregard for human life.

There was no way. The jury could not find these fools guilty. Now, it is important for America to listen. If we as a people, had let it go, without outrage, unpunished and unchecked we would have been lost and broken. Finally, your systematic methodology would have reduced us as people to nothingness. As Alprentice (Bunchy) Carter said, and I quote: "A slave that dies of natural death, doesn't balance out the weight of two dead flies." This would have been an end to any Black pride or ones self-worth. The complete degradation of a once proud people. You say, we shouldn't do this, or we shouldn't do that. But dammit we had to do something! Enough was just enough!

When enough pressure is applied to a led pipe it will ultimately explode. In the aftermath, the Federal Government had to come in and indict these racist bigots, Stacy Koon and his cohorts. I was determined to be there, in the Halls of Justice as a watchman. I had to see if America would stand up and live out the true meaning of its Creed. Our eyes were on justice. We were there in a peaceful protest and demonstration. As I scanned around the crowd, there were many different ideologies, as to how we should proceed in the struggle to be free. There were some there, that advocated the ballot. In other words, we would simply vote our way out. Good luck! Some of the others, consisted of the Baby Bullet mentality. Which is to say, will get some guns and fight our way out. Ha! ha!, Good luck! Been there done that! I've come to understand… That we need some heavenly intervention; we need angels. Yes angels! The Bible says, the Angels are ministering spirits, flames of fire sent on behalf of the heirs of salvation. There is no way, that we can defeat this beast on a natural plane. We need supernatural intervention. I'm there personally, as a minister and international evangelist.

But I'm radical to say the least, but I'm not crazy. Now run and tell that.

We were about 500 strong every day. Sometimes there were over 1,000 people. One day while we were there peacefully singing, praying, declaring and decreeing in protest, fighting a corrupt and immoral justice system, low and behold, someone yelled, "The Klan is coming." I could not believe my eyes as we ran to the edge of the building and looked down on the street.

We saw them marching, in full array, about 30 of them. We were outraged to say the least. After all the melee was over there were hoods on the ground, crosses in the street, and Klansmen scattered everywhere. They took a beating and never returned. That's all I have to say about the matter.

I was directed to speak on the radio station KJLH, owned by Stevie Wonder, on a segment called, "The Front Page. The rhetoric "Seize the Time", the story of the Black Panther Party, by Huey Newton, echoed from my mouth with a poetic bliss. These resounding words echo from historical pains of a people's reparations, dignity and culture would one day be realized. When I spoke, my ancestors spoke. When I spoke, Nat Turner spoke. When I spoke, Harriet Tubman spoke. When I spoke, Malcolm X spoke. When I spoke, Martin Luther King spoke. When I spoke, Fredrick Douglas spoke. When I spoke, Marcus Garvey spoke. I spoke for the blood, the sweat, and the tears of my ancestors. As the wind of the Spirit began to capture every perspective ear you could hear that injustice would no longer and could no longer be tolerated in any form. There is still that old adage "*The ballot or the Baby Bullet, no justice, no peace.*" Finally, after weeks and weeks the jury came back guilty. There was jubilation all over the country. Even the city itself, sighed a sigh of relief. One battle at a time while the war rages on.

As a family, we gathered together, and headed to Hoover Street for the Holy Convocation with Apostle F.L. Person. He scheduled me to speak on the rosterum. There must have been about five preachers before me, but it was okay. The Word of God is quick and powerful.

One of the bishops prophesied to me, that day and said, "Son, God is going to give you a Pastor's heart and I see you pastoring soon". Well, I did not want any of that! I've been there at Joy Harvester Church for a few years and being Pastor Raul's armorbearer I noticed that the sheep are real messy. It was a high time at the convocation. I love those apostolic convocations, they are electrifying. God bless Apostle F.L. Person. He is now in Lancaster, CA doing a great work. I hope to see him soon.

I had been receiving death threats at my P.O. Box in Pomona, CA. During the Rodney King trial, I was careful about the information I put on my cards that I gave out. As the letters began to come in, I read things like, "Nigger we'll catch you.", "If you don't like it go back to Africa." and "Burn Nigger burn." I laughed out loud because that slogan was adopted from our slogan, "Burn baby burn", during the Watts riots. It was not funny and I took every threat seriously. I never contacted the police. I still do not trust them. Even being saved by Jesus, not the police in America, I realized there are some good men on the police force, but I do not have time to pick out the good from the bad. I stopped gambling a long time ago.

One day my wife Shawn came home crying. She had lost her job and was very distraught. Because of the fire, we were now cramped in a two- bedroom apartment. The apartment manager said it was a temporary stay. And when another three-bedroom came available he would give it to us. We waited too long and decided to move. This move took us to Sacramento, CA. We landed in a little town called Marysville. There, my oldest sister, Claudia Marshall lives. After much prayer and soul searching, we eventually started a church. It Is funny how God would allow one door to shut, yet open another to fulfill His prophecy. We started the church in the living room of my sister's house. We consecrated the place and began to fast and pray. Soon the living room became too small. We were eventually evicted, for overcrowding. The landlord was nice about it, but said we had to go. One day about a week before our departure, mind you - now with no place to go and little money. One of my new disciples, Vincent Zerameno, came to me and said, "There is this woman that I know and she has two houses that are empty. Both needed to be fixed up. If we do the work, she'll compensate us with several months free rent and buy all the supplies." I said, "Let's go take a look." When we got to the houses, we looked and they were perfect. We signed the needed contracts and went to work.

We turned one of the houses into our Men's Home. It had three bedrooms. One needed a lot of work, the other one needed a fresh coat of paint and landscaping and maybe a few sheets of drywall. The lady's name was Janet. She was a very sweet, kind and obviously generous. The relationship worked well for the both of us. We went into action. One house became our family living space. It had three bedrooms and a huge living room. The other was the Men's house, known as the House of Joseph Christian Men's Training Center. This house also had three bedrooms and a large living room that became our church.

We grew rapidly. In a few months, we were in a storefront building. There we were able to have church in one section, and children's church in another section. We even had a very small office in the back. We began our first non-accredited Bible College there with about 23 students. We named the church, "End Time Harvest Church." One thing for sure, our ministry was all about outreach. We walked out Matthew 25: 35- 39: "For I was an hungered, and ye gave me meat: I was thirsty, and ye gave me drink: I was a stranger, and you took me in: Naked, and ye clothed me: I was sick, and ye visited me: I was in prison, and ye came to me." We began to do Park ministry every week, feeding the homeless, and taking in those that were sick and tired of being sick and tired. They came, the downtrodden, from all walks of life. They came, diamonds in the rough. They came, one after another, those from skid row.

Our Men's Home began to expand and the church was booming. Our choir was second to none. God had blessed us with several keyboard players. On some Sunday's we were able to lend them out to other churches. You see those pieces of coal, lying out there, are really diamonds in the rough. One has to go dig them out and cultivate them and you'll find some of the richest diamonds the world has ever known. I became a "gemologist". Taking rough looking stones and finding emeralds and sapphires. We had some of the "baddest" singers on this side of Heaven. These girls could have won America's Got Talent, Star Search or even Sunday's Best.

There was Lisa, who would sing from her pain. She would have half the church at the altar repenting, weeping and crying. Then Tracy, straight from the crack house, a woman, who had gotten caught up in Street life, could play the keyboard and make the angel's sing. She married Lorenzo Allen, an ex-gangster homeboy of mine. I rescued him out of the same opium den, where I was a former member. But I had turned in my membership card. I was set free and determined to save others.

Then there was Pam. Oh my goodness, this daughter, who would sometimes travel with me to minister in Oakland, Palo Alto, Richmond, and San Francisco. All I can say is, she could sing Heaven down and take the church to a total rapture. Then there was this little angel who was about 16 or 17 years old. She had none of life's pain to sing from. The melodies from Heaven were her forte. She was an unblemished flower, and would bring the church to their feet in jubilation. Her mother was our Choir Director and one of my closest friends. One day Megan asked me, why when Lisa sings, does everyone fall on their knees, crying and weeping in repentance. When I sing they are on their feet in jubilation. I said, "Daughter, Lisa had a very hard life and she is able to sing from her pain which causes the Balm of Gilead to be released by way of the anointing." She was about 17 then, and that was about 17 years ago. By now she should have experienced some bittersweet moments in life. You know, the ups and downs. Megan, Pam, Tracy and Lisa were the best. I speak divine favor over their lives this morning sitting here in Holland, the Netherlands.

As the church began to blossom, we went from one storefront to the next. There were six different businesses in the complex that we were in. Business after business began to close and we began to occupy. We were well known around the community. Our ministry was diversified. There were as many Caucasians as there were African American, with an equal segment of Hispanics. The leadership consisted of, two Caucasian elders, a Hispanic Pastor, a Black Bishop, and the Church Mother was White.

One New Year's Eve, we tore down the wall of the adjoining building and expanded the church. At the stroke of midnight as we closed out one year, we assigned five people to stand in front of the wall with sledge hammers. As the countdown began, ten minutes to midnight, was the cry, five minutes, three minutes, one minute. Happy New Year was the jubilation, of the moment. As five sledgehammers began hammering down the wall to open the room, for the new sanctuary. We had acquired two buildings next door, and the Saints took turns tearing down the wall. We were very fortunate, that within our Men's Home, we had acquired several good carpenters. You must understand, again I say, out there on the broadway, those pieces of coal are diamonds in the rough. That New Year's Eve we completely tore down the wall. Making the three separate buildings one church. Within 30 days, yes, I mean 30 days to the minute the place was transformed to look like Solomon's Temple. We were fortunate with two great Deacons. One worked for a construction site and the other one was a drywaller and a finisher. So, in other words we had five people, that had building skills. What a blessing.

There was also a company out of Sacramento, that was a part of the Christian Business Men's Fellowship. They ended up carpeting our entire church for free. My brother, Jim, James Hilton, owned his own drapery business and donated the draperies for the church, several thousand dollars' worth. The blessings were coming in from everywhere. One day an electrician walked in and saw what was going on and asked if he could help. With his own materials, he transformed the entire lighting system in the church. He did this work and spent thousands of dollars buying the materials. When he finished, he disappeared and we never saw him again.

One of my in-laws, Andre Wharry, led the building campaign, along with Deacon Bradford. This crew was awesome and when I say again, it was like Solomon's Temple. It was indeed inspiring as they finished up the project.

I met Apostle Marlen Lestrick, now deceased, and his beautiful wife, Prophetess Diane Lestrick, and they became sons and daughters of the ministry. One day as the ministry was flourishing, one of the deacons, Mr. Ted Porter blessed the ministry with a cashier's check for $70,000. We then acquired the church van, a twelve seater. Through the blessings of God, we purchased an old abandoned home for the elderly. We quickly transformed this facility into the house of Joseph, Christian Men's Training Center. It had eight bedrooms with a dorm and a huge dining room. There was an adjacent apartment opposite the kitchen with a living room, one-bedroom and bathroom. This house could hold up to 25 men at a time. God was moving and God was moving fast.

Men and women were getting healed and set free. Our deliverance ministry was second to none. There were bikers, ex-Klan members, Crips and members of the Blood Gangs and others. People from every walk of life. One day, Minister Anthony Page came into the office. I was fresh back from Tallahassee and Florida. He was the director of the House of Joseph and came to say, "Apostle do you remember the young man that came to the program and became a born-again biker. He stayed about 11 months and completed the entire program." "Yes" I replied, "Steve. His wife quit him and said she wanted nothing else to do with him and filed a restraining order." Anthony said, "Yes, I counseled them and helped the restoration process and the family came back together. When I saw her and Steve at the Holiday Market, she informed me that her mother had passed away and left her several pieces of property. She told me to tell you there is a ranch that sits on 8.5 acres of land. It has two horses, some goats and a few chickens, along with a five-bedroom house, a barn and a brand-new swimming pool. She thought the best use for the property would be for your organization to help more people." We met and she donated it to the ministry.

The rest is history. I mean a "Quit Claim Deed", he said, as he recounted the story. He said, she began to cry and said how grateful she was to the house of Joseph. To be in love all over again, with the same man, a now born again Christian. She said, "You saved their family." I replied, "Give God the glory!" The ranch was signed over to us and we soon opened the Virtuous Women's Ranch, which was headed up by Pastor Claudia Marshall. Things were moving so fast.

The ministry associated and made a covenant with several churches in the area. There was a Rev. Michael C. Monroe, who soon developed into a Prophet. His church was in the center of town. They had acquired the old Bank of America building. Then there was Pastor

Ruth Catlin, who had been the first in the city to allow me to speak in her pulpit. Her Church services were held in an old Bar. Several years later she bought the property and built a church from the ground up. We became a very tight knit Clergy Association, with the Pastor from the AME Church and Pastor Samuel Thompson, who was a "piece of work." Smile.

There are so many incidents that occurred, at the house of Joseph, that I could write a separate book on some of those events. Let me reflect on one particular incident for just a minute. One day while in Southern California I decided to go to my father in the Lord's church, Apostle Joseph Sims. He had become a strong influence in my life. Having grown up without a father, his kindness was refreshing. He had developed a beautiful 700 seat church, which was in the old shopping center on Sedgwick St. in Riverside, CA. They own the entire strip mall and the beautification was so magnificent. One could never tell it was once a shopping center. The sanctuary had two tunnels which served as an entrance to the pulpit. That was about 6 to 7 feet tall and housed a huge baptismal, which was hidden from view. They also sported a full cafeteria and dining room on the other side of the church. There was a bookstore and several other buildings that were used for different purposes from time to time.

I walked in that morning, unexpectedly and was invited to preach. It seemed that every time I would come, he would have me bring the Word. Not only had favor found me, but I always had Divine Revelation and a Rhema Word from God. When I would finish, I would go and visit some of my old haunts, those drug houses that had been operating for years. One was about 25 miles away in the City of Pomona, CA, which was run by old man, Johnny. As I walked in, I saw Johnny's eyes. Like a vampire who was about to bite another victim while sucking the blood of life from his very soul. He had turned the back house into a drug den. Sometimes there would be up to 30 people at a time smoking the pipe, while others shot smack into their veins and coasted off to Neverland. There were about six couches which circled the interior. With three large dining room tables in the center of the room with chairs around. There were also two bunk beds, a refrigerator and a big screen TV. It was a Junkie's paradise.

As I walked in with a sense of boldness and the confidence of the Hunter; I was no longer the game nor the prey. I came to snatch souls from Satan's grasp. I had become a titanium Christian, no longer to be enticed by the devil's wares. I had come hunting and began to spout, these words: "Is there anybody here, that is sick and tired of being sick and tired, of being sick and tired?" It was the same spot I got Lorenzo and Tracy from two years prior. Lorenzo had become Assistant Director of the Christian Men's Training Center. The House of Joseph. He and his wife, Tracy, who played the keyboard, had been set free and delivered.

I left there that day with Mr. Benjamin Fludd, a.k.a. "Bemo." His deliverance was difficult and after a few challenges, he was totally set free and ended up the running the whole Training Center for over three years. He became a Deacon in the church and took the limousine ride along with 12 other graduates, which included the self-appointed Mayor Brother, Levi Gentry who was rescued from Sacramento. He had been living in a cardboard box, when I found him there in that overgrown field. He stayed with us well over four years. He became an alumni, and lived in the Alumni House across the street from the Center.

About three years later Benjamin became the Director of the Training Center and ran a tight ship. All the while he maintained a job at the industrial cleaners, in downtown Marysville. He had done so well in the program, that one day, about three years later, I said Benjamin, "If I could do anything for you what would be your requests?" He replied, "I've not seen my mama in over 25 years. I would love to see her one more time before she dies." A couple of months later, we drove to New York and the Harlem district. He got his desire. The Bible says if you delight yourself in the Lord, He will give you the desires of your heart. I love to snatch souls from Satan's kingdom. You know I love to preach, but snatching souls is better than preaching! Reflecting back a few years there is another episode, that needs attention. **AND, WHAT HAPPENED WAS…**

As I look back I am astonished at the boldness that had become my forte. I was on the evangelist field in the City of Montclair, CA. One day this old grandmother came to me and said, "Son, I heard your testimony and how you sometimes go into those drug houses and bring people out. My granddaughter is trapped in one of those places. Can you help us?" We found out later, that her granddaughter was being used for prostitution. She had been trapped by getting her drugs on credit. This was a common practice in street life. Here's how the game was played. The dealer would extend an outrageous amount of credit to his prey, who became a victim. No matter how they tried they could never get out of debt. The old saying goes like this, Step into my parlor, said the spider to the fly. I asked the grandmother where was she at? I found out, it was in the City of San Bernardino, up toward the Highland area. One day we drove by and Minister Flot got the address and pointed the place out to me. After careful surveillance, Minister Flot and I drove to the location.

There were about five gang members loitering around in front of the apartment, which happened to be upstairs. I began to pray while putting on my combat boots, along with my Black military fatigues, and a Black beret on my head. I got out of the car and told Minister Flot to leave the car running as he waited. Then I walked boldly up the stairs, passing the gang members without a word. I knocked once on the door and then opened it. There was one thing I understood above everything and that was this; I would have to move very fast. I knocked once, opened it and walked in like I owned the place. As I walked inside I yelled, Sarah! Sarah! At the top of my voice. There was a subtle reply and the next thing I knew a good- looking Black girl came walking out of the back with a startled look on her face. I quickly said, "Are you Sarah?" She said, "Yes." I said, "Your Grandmother Lois, sent me to get you." By this time two young gang members walked out of the kitchen, as one shouted, "Hey man what do you want?" I quickly snatched Sarah up and placed her over my shoulder and began to walk out the house. I knew if I hesitated just one second all would be lost. They yelled, "Wait a minute, what the hell are you doing?" I kept walking as they followed.

I made my way down the stairs to the car. They were in hot pursuit and had awakened from their confusion. I threw Sarah in the back seat and then jumped in the front and said "drive." We were gone, like a "chicken through the corn", yeah man!" We got ghost. We left the City of San Bernardino and drove to Montclair. I called my wife, Shawn, on the phone and said, "Guess who's coming to dinner." I took Sarah to my wife Shawn, knowing she could no longer stay in San Bernardino. I knew the gang members would be looking for her there. If they found her, all my labor would have been in vain. She stayed with us for several months and soon got her child back.

She joined Joy Harvester Church with Pastor Raul. Her sister also attended. A year later she was married and doing well. To God be the glory! That was a close call. "Not by might nor by power, but by my Spirit, saith the Lord." Yes, I was led by the Spirit of God according to Romans 8:14. I'll say to the Sons of Sceva, you cannot make this kind of move unless you are Spirit led. Holla if you hear me!

"There Is A Moment Of Reflection"

Often times, as I think about past events, I laugh out loud to myself. It seems, I have enough memories for a lifetime. When I was on the evangelist field in the city of Pomona, I can remember, that we formed a coalition. I will give a big thumbs up, to Pastor Ricky Porter of the Presbyterian Church. The Mann family and Sister Mann, a school teacher in the Pomona area, and a powerful woman who owned a carpet business on Gary Boulevard with her husband. They were also benefactors to the Kingdom of God. Then there was Stanley 2X, a Muslim minister. We began to dialogue as we mapped out strategy pertaining to the repairing of the breaches that existed in our community. We outlined a few directives that would bring awareness, pride and culture to Black people. One year they put together a Black male celebration. I had been invited to be the guest speaker. They already had a keynote speaker; whose name was Dr. IV Muhammad. I believe he was the Overseer of the Nation of Islam, in California, at that time. He seemed to be a very gracious man and well spoken. This was indeed an opportunity of a lifetime. I brought together some of the old guard from the Black Panther Party.

In the evening service I spoke about the Valley of Dry Bones from Ezekiel 37. The Holy Spirit was there and the fire erupted as words began to flow out of my mouth. I expounded on the question, which was asked to Ezekiel, from God. Can these bones live? I saw Ezekiel scratching his head in ambiguity. But from the depths of my soul, I shouted yes! These bones can live. I began to prophesy to the audience. The prostitute can live. The Crips can live. The Bloods can live. The drug addict can live. The thief, and the robber, they can all live.

The house erupted. Now, being the guest speaker, I was allowed 30 minutes, while Dr. Avi Muhammad being the keynote speaker, was given one hour. After all was said and done, Dr. Avi came to me and said, "Young minister, today you were the keynote speaker." His words of congratulations were warm and gracious. I was in jubilation! Imagine this Muslim telling me, a Christian Evangelist, that I out spoke him and that I, instead of him, had given the keynote address. He then asked, if I will come to Los Angeles, to a special meeting they were having at the Bonaventure Hotel downtown. I was a dedicated Christian, and knew Jesus was the Christ, the Son of the living God. But, I was intrigued by the love and respect they showed me.

Two weeks later Stanley 2X picked me up and we drove to down town Los Angeles, for that special meeting. The Bonaventure Hotel sits in the middle of downtown Los Angeles. The hotel is luxurious and extravagant to say the least. The meeting consisted of 30 to 40 people. The famous football player, Mr. Jim Brown, who was the founder of I.C.A.P., was seated at the table. Also, Ice Cube and a few other celebrities. Along with some well- known preachers from the Los Angeles area. As I was being seated, I heard a familiar voice say, "Well, Rev. Michael Sterling and what are you doing here?" It was a reformed O.G. Pimp named Johnny Cool Daddy Harris, out of Riverside, CA who had a church on the East side. I was very happy to see him. After the meeting, he invited me to preach at his church several weeks later. Also, for a season, Stanley 2X would pick me up, and escort me to different parts of Los Angles to preach on Sunday to a house full of Bloods, from the notorious street gang.

The next week like clockwork, he would pick me up and he would escort me to South Central. This was the Crip's territory. I would put on the whole Amour of God, as we headed to 113th and Grape St. This was right in the middle of the Projects. I would preach, the Kingdom message and found out how Universal it was. Jesus, Paul and Peter preached the Kingdom message. You know! "Seek first the Kingdom of God and His righteousness and all these things shall be added unto you." The Kingdom of God is not in word, but in power and demonstration. The Kingdom of God comes not with an observation, the Kingdom of God is within you. Unless a man be born again, he cannot see the Kingdom of God. Unless a man be born of water and the spirit, he cannot enter into the Kingdom of God. The Kingdom of God is not in meat nor drink, but righteousness, peace and joy in the Holy Ghost. I could go on and on! Thy Kingdom come!

We must teach our children to understand, when they pray, to pray, "Thy kingdom come, thy will be done in Earth, as it is in Heaven." We are on the earth and we are calling for the power of God to come inside of us. You see, the Bible also says, "But we have this treasure hidden in earthen vessels, that the excellency of the Power may be of God and not of us." It has always been about bringing us into heirship with dominion and power. I could go on and on, expounding on the Kingdom concept, which includes, ruling and reigning.

I was reflecting for a brief moment, nostalgically on the early years, as an International Evangelist. When I think on the Kingdom message, I'm inspired to say that Jesus, the Christ, spoke on the Kingdom of God and the Kingdom of Heaven. Which are synonymous, yet one is the total rule of God by Himself, and the other is a co-rulership with mankind. I began to understand the revelation of the Kingdom through Bishop Earl Paulk, now deceased. Chapel Hill Harvester Church, and The Cathedral of the Holy Spirit in Decatur, Georgia. I remember while in Liberia, West Africa with Dr. Cindy Trimm, Apostle McDonnell Jaa and a team of 12 were sent there to hold a conference. It was on Tubman Boulevard at Bishop Bella's Church. This was before Dr. Miles Monroe had gotten the Kingdom message. This was a time when the Kingdom message was not popular.

An author named, Hal Lindsey, had written a book called "1999." It was supposed to be on eschatology. But it was far off the mark. He came against Bishop Earl Paulk, who was a pioneer of the Kingdom message, and a General in the faith, who later fell on his own sword. Hal Lindsey was in total error with nothing but logos and no Rhema. I remember we were on Tubman Boulevard, down the street from John F. Kennedy Hospital at Pastor Bella's church in Liberia, West Africa. Dr. Cindy Trimm had preached a message on the Kingdom, for about three hours straight, without taking a breath nor a drink of water. She was dynamic, to say the least. At that time, I thought I was the baddest kid on the block, with the insight to understand the Kingdom. The next day as we were sitting in the conference, I asked her where she received such revelation about the Kingdom. Her answer did not surprise me. She replied, "I sat under Bishop Earl Paulk for several years."

The Cathedral Of The Holy Spirit

Bishop Earl Paulk & The Fall Of An Empire....

Looking back...It was 1989 when I first arrived at Chapel Hill Harvester Church. I was the one with the video camera, and totally out of my depth. I also acted as Armor Bearer for Pastor Raul Genera, of Joy Harvester Church. He left the Association of Power of God Ministries and became a networking partner of Chapel Hill Harvester Church. I remember Pastor Craig Turley of Redlands, California and Pastor Jim, who both had ministries in the fellowship, and met us in Atlanta. The Three of us came to Chapel Hill for the national convention. I got to come because I was a good Armor Bearer. Later they would find out I was the worst video tech ever! (Smile!) "And we know that "All things work together for good to them who love the Lord and those who are called according to His purpose." Romans 8:28.

There were three sessions throughout the day. They were very intense and each lasted about 90 minutes. I made sure I paid close attention because the Kingdom message was being expounded upon daily. Having come from the Baptist Church, I had never heard this revelation, nor did I understand the difference between the logos or the rhema of the word. I took exact notes during the daytime and compared everything to the King James Version at night. It was accurate to say the least. I remember that John Avanzini was there and talked on Biblical economics like nobody's business. One of the other major headliners that year was John Osteen, his son Joel Osteen, now has the largest church in America.

Those were exciting days for a young man who had no aspirations of becoming a preacher. I was just thankful to be in the door. You may not understand what I mean, but my friends from the neighborhood know exactly what I'm talking about. I was a gangster, thief, and a robber who dabbled in street life from con games to pimping and pandering. I was a cold hustler dope fiend and a real Mac Daddy. Yes, I was glad just to be in the door. Thank God for mercy and grace. If it had not been for the Lord on my side and his precious blood, where would I be? And, thank God for Mama Bessie's prayers.

I remember walking behind Chapel Hill Harvester Church, which sat about 2,500 people. In the back of it, I eyed the skeleton of the newly erected Cathedral of the Holy Spirit. As we strolled through the massive structure, I was in awe. It was completed the following year and I visited often. Pastor Bobby and Mona Brewer came to San Bernardino, CA and spoke several times at our church. He and Pastor Raul, became good friends. Pastor Bobby was also a real estate agent, who donated hundreds of thousands of dollars to Chapel Hill, Bishop Earl Paulk and the ministry. In the scheme of things, as we look over what had happened to him was unfair to say the least. He was a good man and the truth would make its way into life's drama several years later.

There was another man I met, Dr. Kirby Clemens who was the number one man under Bishop Earl Paulk. He became a mentor and a friend. I would dine at his house, located in a small suburb in the back of the Cathedral. It was awesome real estate. I remember the first day as we drove around through the security across the bridge to those gorgeous houses that were built for the Pastors and leadership of the Cathedral. There were about 30 houses, exclusively for the leadership. The ministry was awesome in appearance but behind it laid an uncompromising demon that would cause it all to crumble one day.

The ministry in Marysville, California was going well and after a couple of years of pastoring along with my wife, Shawn and Claudia Marshall, my sister I decided I needed a covering and began to make my trek to Decatur, Georgia and Chapel Hill Harvester Church the Cathedral of the Holy Spirit, Bishop Earl Paulk. The Bible says, that he that is led by the Spirit of God, they are the sons of God." When I decided to go to Chapel Hill, I left town with very little funds and made it all the way to Dallas, Texas. I knew I would make it because I had divine favor on my side and favor is fair especially when it's on your side! I was at Dallas Airport and decided to spend the night there. In the morning, I'd hitchhike the rest of the way to Atlanta. But, at last I ran into a couple that owned one of the kiosk booths there at the Airport. They invited me to their church that night and put me up after the service. The next day they paid for my ticket to Atlanta. I cannot, for the life of me remember their names, but God, I ask you to bless them beyond compare.

When I arrived in Atlanta, I had enough money for a flea bag hotel. I pulled out Dr. Clemens tattered business card and called him. He immediately answered the phone. "Dr. Clemens, it's me," I said. "I came to Chapel Hill several years ago, with Pastor Raul Genera and Pastor Jim. Do you remember them?" Immediately I could hear him chuckle and he said "Yes." I explained that I started a church in Northern California two years ago and God sent me to Atlanta for counseling and covering. I was a little nervous as I waited for his reply. You see I was out of money and "stuck like Chuck!" If his response was nonchalant or negative, I would have to come to the conclusion that I was being led by the wrong spirit. Silence filled the air as I waited for his reply. He laughed and said, "Welcome to Atlanta." It was a Saturday night in 1992. He instructed me to bring my suitcase to the Cathedral and leave it at Charlotte Lemon's office in the center of Chapel Hill. He said she would be expecting me and to leave my belongings there Sunday morning and come to the service. He would meet me afterward.

I was ecstatic to say the least because he welcomed me with open arms. Bishop Paulk preached a message I would never forget, about the 11th hour church. Bishop Kirby Clemens found me immediately. We went to the office and picked up my belongings after the service. He drove me past his dental office and across the street to an adjacent new development of tract homes. It was just 10 minutes walking distance from the Cathedral.

As he pulled into the driveway he said, "This is it." He unlocked the door as we walked into a fully furnished three-bedroom house. I noticed all the furnishings were brand-new. He showed me the master bedroom with a king size bed and Jacuzzi. "My God", I said to myself, "Is this heaven?" As I set my belongings down, he motioned for me to follow. He opened the side-by-side freezer and it was fully loaded. He said, "I hope you can cook, this is for you." I laughed and replied, "I know how to make skillet sandwiches that taste like steak!" He smiled and escorted me to the walk-in garage. There were some keys hanging on the wall and as we walked in he handed them to me. He said, "Son, this Toyota truck is at your disposal while you are here."

He looked at me and smiled one of the warmest and most endearing smiles I had ever seen. He said, "Well, I'm going to have Charlotte make a few appointments for you. One with Pastor James Powell in our legal department and with Pastor Bill Harman." He said, "Good night" and briskly walked to the door, "I'll see you at church", he stated, "About 6 p.m. tomorrow night. Is there anything else you need?", as he paused before exiting the door. I said, "No", as tears filled my eyes in a grateful salute to God and His Kingdom.

I was overwhelmed to say the least. There was no doubt about it this was too good to be true. I came by faith and faith showed up, as evidence of the things hoped for. In real time now, that's faith in action! As he walked out the door, I sat down in the big chair in the living room and cried. I was humbled, their love and kindness was overwhelming. It was a joyous cry and I hadn't cried in a very long time.

As the day was fading into night I sat there in unbelief. Suddenly I remembered the freezer full of food. I sprang from the chair immediately and quietly made my way into the kitchen. I opened the refrigerator which was also full of food and grabbed a sirloin steak, with some Birdseye vegetables and Irish potatoes. Yes, steak, tatas, and matas! Well, for the layman who does not understand Ebonics. I will have a baked potato with all the trimmings, a steak well done, with vegetables and a glass of iced tea. Wow, this was good!

I stayed there in Georgia for about a month soaking up the kingdom and its atmosphere. I made friends quickly. One day as I was walking through the Christian mall, I heard a voice say, "Hey California, come here and let me take a good look at you." It was Bishop Earl Paulk, founder and visionary of Chapel Hill Harvester Church. He shook my hand and held it for a long time while assuring me if there was anything I needed just to let him know. As I reflected on the moment of that encounter, it was safe and secure. I spent several days with Pastor James Powell of the Legal Defense Forum. He helped me revise my ministry paperwork and assured me I was set and ready to file.

Earlier that week, I played hooky one evening and drove down to College Park and was able to sit in on one of Dr. Creflo Dollar services. His message was on the power of faith. I went by Bishop Eddie Long's Church and saw they were erecting a new sanctuary at that time. I remember that while in Decatur, Georgia, I actually met a man named Monty. Monty was a character to say the least. Monty was out of "Chi-town", but had convinced everyone in Stone Mountain, where he bought a home, that he was an African Prince from Kenya. And he flew the Kenya flag along with the American flag on a pole in front of his house. His Mercedes had a Kenyan flag flying on each side, like a diplomat. He had convinced me when I first met him that he was indeed an African Prince. This went over well until I was invited to his house for dinner and saw his family pictures on the piano. There was one particular picture of him in a tuxedo, standing with the Prom Queen, sporting an Afro. I said, "Monty what part of the game is this?" He dropped his accent and laughed and we laughed for hours.

The "African prince", Monty and I became very close friends. He began to help me understand that in America, Africans that came from Africa to this country were treated better than the African-Americans who were the siblings of slaves. I remember back in the day-day, my Step Daddy, Bobby Hilton, taught me a con game called, "The Jamaican bomb." Well, that's another story for another time.

It seemed the month at Chapel Hill went by too fast. I was sad to be leaving Georgia. As I reflected on the time spent, I was grateful. On the last day, Dr. Kirby, now Bishop Kirby, dropped me off at the airport with several thousand dollars' worth of books and materials. I was indeed satisfied and I had become a networking partner with Chapel Hill Harvester Church. I would never regret it, regardless of how the ministry had fallen. Millions of dollars' worth of kingdom expression had been devastated by human error and failure. I would come back to Chapel Hill often because they were my covering in ministry.

The understanding of the Kingdom message was imparted into my soul. The word of God simply says in Luke 19:13; "And he called his ten servants and delivered them ten pounds and said unto them occupy until I come." The word occupy means to take possession and control of a place, as by military, conquest, or invasion. For example, the German army occupied Poland. Another example is when Gen. MacArthur's troops were commanded to occupy Normandy.

We the church have failed to occupy local banks, schools, governmental offices, commerce, sports media, the military, and so on and so forth. We are being systematically driven out of society by the forces of darkness. We were mandated to occupy until He comes. The Bible tells us that the whole world is waiting for the manifestation of the Sons of God. The Bible also reports in Psalm 110:1-3; "The LORD said, unto my Lord, Sit thou at my right hand, until I make thine enemies thy footstool. The LORD shall send the rod of thy strength out of Zion: rule thou in the midst of thine enemies. Thy people shall be willing in the day of thy power, in the beauties of holiness from the womb of the morning: thou has the dew of thy youth."

The church has failed in this Kingdom mandate because of false teaching. This false teaching has harmed the church and its Kingdom Citizens with a "flyaway mentality", called "The Rapture"! This word "rapture" is not even found in the Bible and has been mistranslated. I want you, the reader, to examine this. I just explained occupy. Now look at occupy versus rapture; one says to take over until Jesus comes, and the other says, were going to escape the tribulations and flyaway. That is indeed a mistranslation and a misnomer.

Men and women of God, unpack your bags and get ready for war. Spiritual warfare where the kingdoms of this world shall become the kingdoms of our Lord in Christ, and we shall rule and reign forever with Christ Jesus. "The meek shall inherit the earth", that's the Scripture we need to stand on. Moving right along...

As the plane landed back in Sacramento, I was excited to be home with all the networking information, along with my corporation papers. As I have told you in previous pages how the ministry began to expand and how over the next couple of years we had acquired several pieces of property, and developed the 32-bed facility for men, called

The House of Joseph Men's Training Center. The Virtuous Women's Ranch, was on the 8 ½ acres given to us. and Pastor Claudia Marshall was the director and had the task of transforming women's lives.

We were truly blessed in our years in California and I praise our Heavenly Father for His faithfulness.

CHAPTER TWELVE

"Ali Bouvier" Muhammad Ali 1942 - June 2016

I woke up this morning here in Holland, the Netherlands, and received the sad news that one of my heroes died last night. As I sit here, I have so many emotions and tears are falling out of my eyes as I reflect on the character of Muhammad Ali. All I can say is, "Ali Bouvier, Ali Bouvier." For those who do not know Muhammad Ali, in the latter part of his life, he received the Medal of Freedom Award from President George Bush. He also lit the Olympic torch prior to his death.

As I reflect on his life, it was not about his four wives or his nine children. It was what I saw, as a young Black man, a David fighting a Goliath. To whit; the United States Armed Forces, by refusing to go to Vietnam as a conscientious objector, he made a stand and was willing to go to jail for his beliefs. It did me, as a Black man, proud to see him stand up and refuse to fight a people that had never done us any harm. I also refused to be drafted, but in a different way. **AND WHAT HAPPENED WAS....**

One day I called my two best friends, Jerome Davis a.k.a. Drack and Irvell Morgan. "Hey man, I just got my draft notice. I'm not going to fight in anyone's war." Drack replied, "I got mine a few weeks ago and I'm not going either." He said, "Say Homie, let's get big Hank." "I got a plan", I said. When we got together we mapped out strategies and decided to go down to the recruiter's office.

As we walked into the Draft Office, I spoke up immediately, "We are here to see the recruiter," I yelled. A stocky looking peckerwood Sargeant came from the back office. "Do you have your draft notices?" he said. I held up mine and he quickly snatched it out of my hand while retrieving Drack's and Irvell's. As he began to walk away, I shouted, "I am a member of the Black Panther Party and our 10-point platform and program says in point number six, "We want all Black men to be exempt from military service." I said, "Man listen here, if you send me to Vietnam, it will be my duty as a revolutionary to disrupt, and dismantle all U.S. military equipment and do everything in my power to defeat my enemy. You issue enough injustice down on our streets. You beat us down, send us to your prisons, while robbing us of our civil liberties and human rights here in America. America has not stood up for me. Why should I stand up for America?" The Sergeant turned beet red and marked our papers "4F" and demanded that we get out of the office immediately! We never heard from them again.

We laughed and howled all the way back to the neighborhood, never knowing that we were marked for life. Ali did it as a national hero. He was the Champion of the world. A Black Muslim, and now in America everyone has something good to say about him. I say, "No America, the truth is you were wrong in Vietnam. Ali and the rest of us were right. Many conscientious objectors ran to Canada. Others burned their draft card. All across the streets of America, Blacks, Whites, Hispanics and other nationalities refused to go. At that time, most of America's white folks hated Muhammad Ali. After he was reinstated and the Supreme Court overturned his conviction, everyone got on his bandwagon. He did not beat America down with it. He was very gracious when he and George Foreman fought in Africa. He became untouchable as a world figure. He is and always will be my hero, written by a Christian who loves Jesus. Note, I was almost a Black Muslim myself. One day Ron Al-Amin talked me into going to the Mosque. I attended for a few weeks, went through the ritual of the washing, and the prayers. Then I heard that at the end of your life, they will bring out the scales and weigh your good deeds against the bad. Well, that was the end of that for me. My bad deeds were too numerous. I needed the Blood of Jesus which washes all my sins away.

Yeah, and oh by the way, that 7,000 Virgin myth for martyrs, that they tell. Well, if you would like to buy the Golden Gate Bridge, I got the deed, just give me a call and I will sell that to you.

The End Time Harvest Church which we founded in Marysville, CA was expanding. We started out with one storefront and we ended up with five buildings in the shopping center across from the Holiday Market. The Men's Training Center was filled to capacity and there was also the Alumni House across the street for Men who graduated from the program, but stayed on. They were either going to college or working jobs.

By this time, we had graduated several groups of women from the Ranch and acquired the transition home for women and children, a block from the church. We were evangelizing and God was blessing. I visited Nigeria and adopted a spiritual son, Dr. Fred Okamami. We were overseeing 23 churches in Nigeria at that time and had a work going on in Nairobi, Kenya with Bishop Hillary Abugu.

Both men had come to the United States as our special guests and we treated them well. On my second trip to Nigeria, I took one of my spiritual daughters with me, a Pastor Regina Lindsay of Jubilee Ministries. She had fallen in love with an African Prince whose father was a Chief and a man of great influence. She had fallen so hard, that she refused to come home with me. It was a disastrous situation to say the least. And it caused irreparable damage to Dr. Fred's and our relationship. But at last, I got her home to her children and family.

While visiting Chapel Hill Harvester Church along with Pastor Regina and Minister Nicole, it was during one of the international conventions. The delegates had arrived from all over the world and it was a high time. It must've been about 2008. I was in the Christian Mall sitting at a table, watching people with Down Syndrome (DS) having the time of their lives. They were communicating and laughing, just like ordinary people. As I was reflecting on memories of my past encounters with people who had DS. It seemed that many of them were angry and frustrated because they were unable communicate their thoughts and ideas properly. This group seemed unencumbered and were indeed at peace. You know that peace that surpasses all understanding.

It was astonishing as I took in the pleasing atmosphere that was created by the Holy Spirit, there at Chapel Hill. I want to reiterate, for all the Saints reading my life story, when the men and women of God come together, in unity, there is a power in prayer that is creative. This brings about healing, miracles, signs and wonders. The prayer fortress that was erected around Chapel Hill Harvester Church caused even those with Down Syndrome to be at peace.

I remember one day while I was in the vast church parking lot, I was walking along as a woman drove up and got out of her car and started dancing. I stopped dead in my tracks, as she continued dancing and giving God the praise. As she was winding down, I inquired, "Is everything okay?" She replied, "It is now!", as she began to shout hallelujah, hallelujah and hallelujah some more. She said, "Son it's all right now, and further stated, "I knew if I could just make it to the church parking lot and breathe, it would be okay." She asked, "Are you going to the morning session, Mr. California?" She grabbed my arm as we started walking towards the entrance of the Cathedral. It is a shame how a dynamic ministry, that sat over 7,000 people, with a Christian mall, a college, and a nursery could have fallen; leaving in its wake the faithful, the tried, and the true.

T.D JAKES

It was the year 2000 when TD Jakes and Pastor Marvin Winans, Bishop Clarence McClendon and several other headliners attended the convention at Chapel Hill. I remember it just like it was yesterday. I had just gotten in from Nigeria, West Africa and was sporting a beautiful African outfit that was designed for Chiefs. I came to the Cathedral early, because I knew the place was going to be packed. I was sitting in the center section about the sixth row. Bishop TD Jakes was in high gear. This is when the Potter's House was not yet finished, but due to open soon.

On the stage, off to my right, sat Bishop Earl Paulk, his wife and his brother Pastor Donald Paulk, Clarice Paulk his wife, and Dr. Kirby Clements, while the other special guests sat on the other side, along with Pastor Dan Roades, Pastor Bobby Brewer and several other predominant Pastors of the Cathedral staff. At the end of Bishop

Jake's message, he called for 10 people to come up to the stage with an offering. If I remember correctly, he called for a $10,000 seed. Not only did 10 people come up with a $10,000 seed, but it must've been several hundred. The people just would not stop coming with that $10,000 seed. I looked over towards Bishop Paulk, who had turned beet red and literally walked out.

Afterward it was Bishop Jake's turn to speak to the audience. He said, "Young man in the beautiful African outfit. He was talking to me. I want you to come up here." As I looked around, he said, "Yes I'm talking to you." I rose to my feet and approached the stage. He said, "I do not know if it's a nation, a country, or a ministry, but I see masses and masses of people being blessed all up under your ministry." He continued to use the word mega and prayed for me for about five minutes.

You must understand there were over 7,000 people in attendance. The church was packed. He prophesied over me and only me. I still believe the prophesy was true, delayed, but not denied. I believe that we can alter, hamper and delay our own destiny by the choices we make. The worst thing we can do in a ministry is to get a divorce. The people will almost forgive anything if you just come clean and genuinely repent, but a divorce will almost always split the church in half and cause irreparable damage. We must understand that most ministries cannot and do not recover from this broken covenant. I do not care if the wife was a double witch and the man, a constant professional or vice versa. If the ministry even survives, it has lost the essence of Ephesians 5:32, which states: "This is a great mystery: but I speak concerning Christ and the church." I now speak from the experience of a hardhead and a softer behind. Thank God for mercy! In Romans 8:28, "God will indeed turn a bad situation around for your good if you truly love the Lord and are called according to his purpose."

I am not talking about one who decides to be a preacher and just went according to his own volition. You must be called and chosen. This is the criteria for success in the fivefold ministry. I went back and forth to Chapel Hill attending seminars and special events. I saw the church go from 70% Caucasian and 30% African-American to 70% African-American and 30% Caucasian. Everything was okay until those white teenage girls started dating those Black jocks.

As we look deep into our society, we find the hidden truth of man's tolerance and intolerance one towards another. This is evident, even in the halls of our integrated churches. I can remember a while back, there was a great controversy throughout the word of faith movement. Several power houses such as Fred Price, Kenneth Hagan, Sr. and Kenneth Hagan, Jr. had become caught up in the hidden deep bias and racist sentiments lodged deep within our society. I had the occasion to hear the tape where Kenneth Hagan, Jr. had said openly that he did not want his daughter to marry a Black man. Dr. Fred Price of Crenshaw Christian Center, had a love and admiration for Dr. Kenneth Hagan, Sr. that was unparalleled and had spent thousands of dollars supporting the ministries. When he heard the tape of Kenneth Hagan, Jr. he was devastated and hurt. He could not believe the underlying racism that still existed even within the fellowship.

We as Americans must begin to understand the truth and the truth needs to be told and discussed openly. The fact is this, there is some immoral and inhuman treatment that has been done to our people, who were slaves, and it had become big business in America. There were great abolitionist, and freedom fighters that helped turn the tide of man's inhumanity to man. But, in the underlying dredges of our society, there still lies the evil, maniacal, white supremacist who really believes they've been sent by God, to rule the world. And they are the chosen people. If we were to investigate further they even believed that inbreeding with other nationality is against the laws of their culture and their race as a whole. They will sit at your dinner table exchange money, goods and services with you in a Phileo type of love. But when it comes to the mixing of the races this is when their tolerance ends.

In retrospect, as we take a look at those young unencumbered White and Black children who began to live out the dream of Martin Luther King, Jr., through socializing, falling in love, and intermingling, the subterranean alarm deep within the human cavity of white supremacy went off as the alarm was sounded. White flight became the order of the day. As if the south had been resurrected and those southern right-wing Christian brothers and sisters began to separate. This hatred and bias is inbred in our society and we must come to grips with it. I believe that in the next hundred years, that the percentage rate of this behavior should be down to about 1-2%. Oh! by the way where is my forty acres and my mule!

In 1997, I remember there was a devastating flood in the city of Marysville and everyone was evacuated to higher ground. Some folks fled to Beale Air Force Base while others took shelter at Sutter Buttes. Right before the city-wide evacuation about half of our church family assembled at the sanctuary to prepare.

Meanwhile, our men's home, House of Joseph, helped with sandbagging the levees. The rain was coming down in torrents and many homes were lost already. The men at the Training Center worked for hours. Our young pastor, Vincent Zeromino was being transformed into a modern day Jeremiah and began to point us up to the Church of the Nazarene in the Hall Wood Community located at 2825 State Hwy. 20, Marysville CA. We had been there several times for the hallelujah festival in which our choir sang every year. When Pastor Vincent called the Hall Wood office, they were packing up and leaving the church, even though they were on higher ground above the levees.

We made an agreement that we would come and use the facility, the gym, kitchen, and four classrooms as a Red Cross emergency center. The rain was coming down harder and harder and the people were in a state of desperation as they exited the city. There was plenty of food and a playground and most of our children thought we were on holiday. The truth of the matter was if the levy had broken in a certain section, the city of Marysville could have been lost forever. We were over 100 people and by the third day we were running out of supplies.

Our emergency teams stood on the highway with flashlights and lanterns, flagging the people down who were evacuating. We supplied water and sack lunches as many continued on their way. Others would stay. I had been trained as a Chaplain in the early days of my ministry and quickly began to impart ethics and concerns to the makeshift staff. Things were going well until a young deacon in training, began to panic and started hollering, "This is the end of the world." Things did look bad, and as I said, the food was running out and the storm was not letting up. We had been given a report by the Highway Patrol that a man had been shot trying to sneak back into the city and breaking into houses. Everyone was on edge, but this man was out of control.

Then others began to cry and I began to see the spirit of panic sweep through the room. All of a sudden, before I knew it, I reached across the table and slapped the young man. I want to say his name, but let's call him Mr. V. I slapped Mr. V as hard as I could. I had seen it done on television and in the movies, that when someone begins to panic during a disaster, just slap them and things will begin to calm down. So, I did and everyone was in shock! You could have heard a pin drop. That young man, Mr. V, put on a show. "Oh! my back", he said, "Oh! My back", he cried, "Somebody call the police. I'm pressing charges and you're going to jail." Two days later the storm was over and the levees had held. Some of the people who saw me slap Mr. V, never came back to the church again. I saw Mr. V two days later stumbling down the street drunk, with a bottle of wine, smoking a cigarette. I just laughed and said to myself, "Save the drama for yo mama."

The House of Joseph Men's Training Center had an ongoing contract with the Human Resource Development Center, where we housed and transported several of their clients to various redevelopment facilities. We also supplied room and board for these clients. The contract lasted about two years. Our training was intense and many men graduated with honors. People were coming in from all over the country: Harlem, New Jersey, Los Angeles, Denver, Colorado, San Bernardino. They came from all walks of life, men and women who were being transformed and restored with new morals and work ethics. They received training on how to live in a lost and dying world. We had a 12-step program whereas our clients would never say, "My name is John and I'm an alcoholic, after five years of sobriety. No, death and life is in the power of the tongue! Our people would confess: Hello, my name is John and I'm totally transformed from my dependency on drugs and alcohol. I am totally and forever set free." Our success ratio was between 88 and 90%. That's fabulous! Some of our clients still send me gifts of thanks and appreciation.

We developed a work program, House of Joseph Handyman Service. Where we would send out two Vans to various locations to work. Pastor Vincent and his crew would go out and survey the neighborhood and find those homes that consisted of the elderly, on fixed incomes. We would paint, roof, and repair these homes at little or no cost at all, with the cooperation of Ace Hardware in Yuba City who donated much of the materials and some at cost. The men would fixup homes for free. By the time they were finished, we would have acquired 2 to 3 paying jobs on the same street.

Every Saturday morning the House of Joseph would have a car wash at the 711 store on the corner of Highway 70 and Colusa Boulevard. For five years we had a car wash there and we were blessed. Our evangelistic team would minister to the people, as we washed their cars for any donation. It was funny, as I watched sometimes, some people gave as little as $.50 while others gave $100. It was mandated that we would wash every car with a spirit of excellence. I was amazed at the talented people that God had sent us. They may have fallen through the cracks of life's despair, but many were diamonds in the rough.

Some of those men and women were professionals, carpenters, painters, plumbers, tree trimmers, mechanics, artists, musicians, hairdressers, secretaries, brick layers and those that could cut and lay tile. All of them were Jewels that have fallen prey to drugs, broken marriages, prison, jail, homelessness and despair. We would make a big to do once a year for graduation after one of the clients had completed an 11-month program. They would take the limousine ride to the banquet hall.

We had five paparazzo's out in front when that limousine door opened and that ex-drug addict stepped out on the carpet along with that ex- prostitute and walked the red carpet into the banquet hall. Some of these people had never completed anything in their life. Some had never graduated and now it was their time. Our ministry was fulfilling, Matthew 25:35-36 which says, "Where were you when I was hungry?" You see there's a great misnomer in Christendom. While the Bible says to do good to all men and especially to those in the household of faith, there are many wounded soldiers who love the Lord Jesus Christ, but have been wounded and betrayed by the church.

Why do we leave our wounded lying on the floor of despair. We must do a better job. It is incumbent on the church to evangelize and set the captive free. All over the world, darkness is covering the earth and gross darkness the people. Just recently a man walked into a place in Florida and killed 50 people from the LGBT community. Once again, some of those people could have been changed. Now they're doomed to face judgment in an abominable state.

I'm glad I did not get killed in my mess, like the Apostle Paul, Saul of Tarsus. We may not have been a part of the LGBT community, but Saul killed Christians and God turned his life around. I have done some things that I regret, but I thank God I got the chance to be redeemed, born again and transformed by the renewing of my mind. It's too bad that the evangelists keep recycling Christians. I remember reading in the Bible, "Go ye out to the highways and byways and compel them to come in".

Poetry in Motion

"For God so loved the world that He gave His only son... to give us another chance in following the martyred One. He gave His life so graciously, and shed His blood that day, upon the very cross our Lord, did pass away. The greatest shepherd who ever lived, the keeper of the flock, always on the lookout, to keep us from the jaggedrocks. I remember as a boy, I always wondered why, Jesus never came, to dry my tear stained eyes. Why this man was a cripple, and this one could not walk, another born blind, and another could not talk. Why there was rape and murder, and madness everywhere; did my holy Savior, did he even care. They said he was coming back, to judge this cruel cruel world. Oh why, oh why, great Shepherd, have you yet not came. Don't you know the hunger. Don't you know the pain. One day when I was hitching, upon the highway road, a gentle man did stop, and asked me did I know. About a man named Jesus, who died so long ago. With a smile I answered yes, and told him of my mind, and about that very question,

that troubled me from time to time. If Jesus loved us oh so much, why has he yet not come? Does he know the hunger? Does he know the pain? This is what he said, and I remember it very well, for this has been my comforter, to deal with this crazy world. He said, all the true, true Christians are written in the book of life, but all have yet not crossed, into the path of light. Now Jesus being the shepherd of the Christian flock, will never shut the gate, while one sheep is in the rocks. Now the moral of the story is you may be the last, and if you give your life to Christ Jesus the book would close real fast. Holla if you hear me!"

Romans 10:9; If thou shalt confess with thy mouth the Lord Jesus and shall believe in thy heart that God has raised him from the dead thou shall be saved." There's no other prerequisite for salvation. Many men have placed a lot of religious dogma on salvation. This is erroneous and a false doctrine. The Bible really says "If thou would confess with thy mouth and believe with thou heart the Lord Jesus thou shall be saved." Listen! There's no other conditions for salvation. Now, to walk in power and authority one must be born again. There's another level of ministry understanding that must be applied. But for salvation it simply confess and believe!!!

The Church - Marysville, California

The air was sweet and crisp as a new day dawned upon the horizon. Life was good and End Time Harvest Church was flourishing. It seemed that God's favor was all around us and the community had come to understand, we were taking men and women off the street and leading them to the abundant life. The Bible says, "Beloved I wish above all things that thou would prosper and be in good health even as thy soul prospers, (3rd John 1:2). All is well in "Hooterville", I mean Marysville, CA. It would be the very last conference I would attend at Chapel Hill Harvester Church Cathedral of the Holy Spirit with Bishop Earl Paulk.

I had flown down to the conference in Atlanta and met with Bishop Kirby Clements one of my mentors. He had invited me to dine at his house with several other convention pastors. I had been there about two days when I got the call from my son Rascheed. He said, "Dad the police are everywhere and the NBC news camera and trucks are sitting in front of the transition home. The police came to the house on Val Drive." I replied, "What's going on son?" He said, "Do you remember the young man that came to church with Shanea one time. He was real short and looked like a teenager?"

I could not recall the young man he was talking about but I continued to listen. He said, "Well anyway, he's on television on the 10 Most Wanted List TV show and the police are saying that you brought him up here and he's staying at the Men's Training Center. And could possibly be one of your sons." "What the hell" I replied, "I don't even know who you're talking about and let alone he sure is not one of my sons and has not been a part of the House of Joseph or the ministry."

"I know dad", Rascheed replied, "But this young man is wanted for murder in Hemet, California and he killed a young teenage white boy at a party the other night. Listen Dad, what I've been told so far, this guy, whose nickname is "Snap", I believe that's what they called him. He was engaged to some girl in Hemet, some 600 miles away and got into an altercation. He shot and killed the father of the girl he was engaged to and he's been on the run for several months. They say he's a part of the House of Joseph Christian Men's Training Center.

The talk is people in the community are saying they knew something was going to happen. You keep bringing those gang members up here from Los Angeles." "What the hell," I replied. "Dad I'm just telling you what's going on. You need to get home ASAP. Things have gotten crazy. Listen while I tell you the worst part", Rascheed said. "This guy named Snap was only about 5 foot three and no facial hair. He looked like he was 16 or 17 years old. He used to ride Timothy's bike around the town and hang out with the teenagers. He fit right in with them. It was his disguise even though he was 23 years old. So, what happened was, he went to a house party for teenagers only. So, while he was there, one of those white kids had confronted him and called him a bunch of Niggers. Adrian, Pastor Vincent's son, you know mother Shirley's grandson was standing right next to the young white boy who was about 17 years old, and all of a sudden this guy snapped, pulled out a gun and shot and killed him point blank. Daddy, he was

DOA. The whole town is tripping and they're holding you responsible. This happened Saturday night and on Sunday morning there was not one white person in the church. "Wow", I said "that's about 30%." "It's bad" Rascheed replied, "You need to come home."

Three days later I arrived back in Marysville from Atlanta. The air was thick and toxic, the very atmosphere had been subdued by hatred and the devil called "racism" filled the air. I knew that Satan once again had caused this division. I immediately went down to the Marysville Police Department to check in and find out what was going on. After being there a couple hours and being interviewed like I was a suspect, I read them the riot act and assured them I did not know this young man. Surely he had never been a part of our ministry even though he may have visited our church at one time or another.

Everywhere I went throughout the town, it seems that those who had once smiled, now frowned and shook their heads in disgust. Looks of hatred now replaced warm and gentle favor. You, the reader, must realize there is one thing about a small town like Marysville. News travels fast and opinions are often generated by the few. On my third day back, I began to realize the whole town had turned against us for something we were not responsible for. The devil had served us a major blow. Our carwashes that would generate an average of $800-$1200 a week, were stopped by code enforcement. We were told it was causing too much soap suds and that was affecting the Yuba Sutter River. We had been doing these carwashes for over 10 years. What a difference a day makes. Also, our youth department who had been selling candy and doing quite well and that too had been stopped. We were told now they need a permit.

I think the kicker was when someone planted 10 pounds of methamphetamine in the side storage of an RV that had been donated to the ministry. This RV was parked on the side of the alumni house and I would spend the night there from time to time. It was across the street from The House of Joseph. At least once a week when the house was full, I would spend the night there for a couple of days and do counseling at the training center which was in Olivehurst, CA, about 10 miles from the church in Marysville.

In the set up, I could clearly see the devil's strategy to destroy me and the ministry. The set up was like this: I would be sleeping in the trailer and about 4 or 5 a.m. the police would make a raid. I would be sleep and awakened by the powers that be, the next day. I can see it plainly. The newspaper would report a picture of me coming out the trailer handcuffed in my boxers or underwear and place me in front of those drugs. It would have read, "so-called pastor caught with 10 pounds of methamphetamine." If God had not intervened I would still be imprisoned today!

When The Enemy Comes In Like A Flood!

One thing we must realize and understand is that our enemy is Satan. He is always trying to assassinate the character of God's people. He does this through trickery, fraud, lies and innuendos. The Bible says in Matthew 11:12, "The kingdom of heaven suffers violence but the violent take it by force." We know there are great opposing forces of darkness, whose agenda is to destroy the people of God. We must stand up and violently fight against the forces of darkness. It's a shame that through these lies and innuendos, many of our people that have supported the ministries, were often defeated by these falsehoods. We must realize that some of the same people who are applauding you today might turn against you the next day.

I couldn't imagine that some of the people that knew us would be heard saying, "I knew something was going on." "They had too much money and every time we looked up, they were traveling to Africa and buying property. We wondered how did they get that 8 ½ acre ranch and all those vans too. "Oh, by the way! What about that beautiful house on Val Drive, right in the middle of the suburbs?" The fact is this! "God will supply all of our needs according to his riches in glory by Christ Jesus." Our ministry has always been based upon faith, and we walk by faith and not by sight. See, God said not so. Before this plot was to take place, God had already set in motion, His plan that we would not be caught in Satan's trap and his deception. **NOW, WHAT HAPPENED WAS...**

One of the men from the House of Joseph was doing some painting at the hamburger stand across the street and was told there might be some paintbrushes and rollers in one of the storage cabinets on the side of the RV. He found the methamphetamines that morning and reported it. Wow! I was slated to spend the night in that RV that night. The Bible says, "Many are the afflictions of the righteous, but the Lord delivers them out of them all. (Psalm 34:19) To God be the glory!

My son was accosted continually. They had been stopped on the streets and harassed by the police on several occasions. One of my members who was warm and very pleasant over the years, came up to me and said, "Apostle Sterling, If you would just stop bringing those gang members up here from Los Angeles everything would be fine." I replied to her, "We are commissioned to save the lost at any cost. Our commission is go ye therefore into the highways and byways teaching all nations and baptizing them in the name of the Father, the Son, and the Holy Ghost. We must never allow the enemy to stop us from doing what God has told us to do.

We had another church in Sacramento. It was called the Church of All Nations, which we launched right in the midst of all that drama. Psalms 110 says, "Rule thou in the mist of thy enemies" and Psalms 23:5, says paraphrasing, "You prepared a table before me in the presence of my enemies." So, we went on the offense and launched the Church of All Nations in Sacramento. The staff consisted of some seasoned ministers, unlike the Marysville Church, which was purely grassroots. This church was comprised of some seasoned ministers and there was Apostle Wilma Brooks, a prayer warrior extraordinaire. She had been ostracized from the Church of God where she had ministered for many years. All because of a religious zealot who would not allow women to take pastoral roles in the church and relegated them no further than that of a missionary.

There was also my newly acquired spiritual son and daughter in the ministry: Apostle Marlen and Prophetess Diane Lestrick. They were truly a dynamic duo. Prophetess Diane, had started preaching at the age of 16 and flowed in the prophetic like it was nobody's business. She was a seasoned veteran and her husband, who was slated to be my successor, had become edifying in the Kingdom message and was walking the word out with power and demonstration. I was with him on his death bed as he began his journey home. I remember his wife Diane had left the hospital room that morning, having spent the night with him. While I was there, he lifted his right hand up in the air and waved goodbye with a great big smile on his face. I just cried. He had not only become a son, but a friend.

Then there was an Indian couple, Pastor Sat Vender and Josephine Sandu who were millionaires and owned a shopping mall with about 20 units and also five other properties. Pastor Sat Vender was a great man of faith, who also had obtained the gift of faith, which was far different from the measure of faith. We went to India several times and during one of the Crusades they spent over $50,000 for a revival that was held in Pinjabi, India, next to the Pakistan border. Let me take a minute to testify about the India experience.

We had arrived in New Delhi in the latter part of March 2008. My natural mother had died that same week. I think it was March 19. I had spent some time with her at the hospital right before her exit into eternity. Our team consisted of about 12 ministers. They had rented two vans for our 16 day missionary journey. We rested in New Delhi and headed for a city called Morso.

The next day, he reached one of the networking churches, which had about 700 people. On the first night of the revival, about 2,000 people showed up. I was blessed to be the keynote speaker every night. On the first evening that I was slated to preach with an interpreter, the church was charged with excitement. Most of the people that came out were non- believers, who only came out for the fishes and the loaves and to be entertained by us, whom they considered to be those crazy Christians. This particular night, they were in for a rude awakening. **AND WHAT HAPPENED WAS...**

I had been preaching for about 30 minutes, when some man lifted two blind girls up on the stage on my left side. I did not see it happen because I was facing the other way and was in the mist of preaching heaven down. All of a sudden, Pastor Josephine and Sister Peggy began to tap me on my shoulder and cried out, "These two young girls are blind." I turned to look at them and believe me as I looked into their eyes I saw white balls with no pupils. I immediately laid hands on one and said, "In the name of Jesus be healed!," and I did the same to the next girl. I turned away quickly and went right on preaching heaven down. All of a sudden in the back of me I heard people screaming and yelling, "Apostle!, Apostle!", as I turned back around the team along with the people were in pandemonium. They were crying and jumping and praising God. You see the two girls had received their sight and began to tell them the color of their dresses. When these types of miracles occur, salvation becomes easy. There must have been over 1,000 people that got saved that night because of power and demonstration.

We were just getting started and after two days there, we left for Punjabi, where we were expecting between 30,000 and 50,000 people. In all actuality, it was about 30,000 to 40,000 people that showed up every night. As we arrived at the Grand Hotel in Punjabi, it was a very luxurious place with about 20 marble stairs that ascended into this grand structure. We were treated like kings. You see I've been to Africa and Mexico and slept on the floors doing missionary work. I've also slept in palaces as I learn how to abound and to be abased. I was content no matter what the journey had allowed. It was truly about the work. It was a long trip from New Delhi to Punjabi. We rode for hours and arrived about midnight. I was escorted to my room and fell fast asleep only to be awakened at 5 a.m. by a voice in panic. Brother Ronnie informed me that the Police Commissioner and several officers had informed Pastor Sean and Josephine that they were going to shut down the meeting because of possible rioting. I dressed quickly and descended down the stairs into the main lobby. As I approached Pastor Sean, Sat Vender pulled me to the side and explained the situation. I then greeted the Commissioner who was a well-groomed, stocky young man with a ready smile.

I was introduced as, "The Overseer." I listened intently as the Commissioner showed us three different newspapers that was written in the Punjabi language. The headlines read that these Christians have come to town to destroy our culture. It was a call to arms for the people to rise up and protest and run the Christian missionaries out of town. There was some serious threats to our safety, so "to take it by force" became, "Be wise as serpents gentle as doves." We began to take on a more serious attitude. We understand the Scripture says, "The Kingdom of Heaven suffers violence". Again, there is a violent opposition to us going forward. We had already hired a security team of about 50 people from a local agency. The Commissioner began to say, "This will not do" and he could not allow the crusade to go further. He also stated that he could not jeopardize American lives. After several hours of closed negotiations, we hired 50 additional security guards. The Commissioner had vowed to escort us to and from the event with his military police, which were armed with military AK-47 rifles.

The next evening as we left from the hotel headed to the venue, which had been prepared by a local company, I couldn't contain my excitement. They built a 6-foot stage, about 50 yards long, with huge generators to light up an area the size of a football field. As we drove off in the night, I felt like I was in an Indiana Jones movie. The streets were narrow, dark and ominous. We had become very quiet as our caravan began moving towards the makeshift stadium. The Commissioner's Jeep led the way, along with his four armed men, as the convoy, which now consisted of five vehicles, two vans, a military truck with about 10 men and another Jeep behind us. I watched closely to see if some of the distraught citizens would start throwing bottles or even firebombs from the rooftops. Yes, this heightened expectation of the meeting and the people, came from everywhere. I began to pray and I knew I had to be in top form for this evening's message. I started casting down every negative thought that would try to invade the kingdom of my mind, knowing that God had not given me the spirit of fear, but of power and love and a sound mind. We arrived at the stadium safely and I could hear Pastor Eric praying and exhorting the people. As we parked the cars, I could hear the choir, that consisted of about 50 women, which we could hear from a distance. It was a refreshing sound as we were escorted to the platform. All of a sudden I started to dance a two step as the spirit began to serge throughout my entire being. Yes, it was going to be a fantastic night!

Two vehicles drove up as our team was being seated. Eight men got out of the two cars all dressed in the elite traditional Indian garments. We came to find out later, that the head man was one of the leading Shaman's who was running for election. Even though they opposed us, they asked our host, Pastor Eric, if the head man could sit on the stage with us. I pondered the situation and when I observed them, I realized that they understood that they could never bring together a crowd as large as had assembled there for the crusade. It was politics that had won out and to my surprise on the next night a group of Gurus had shown up, who also wanted to speak and sit on the platform. They were not allowed to speak, but their seating was arranged and they were accommodated.

They escorted me to the stage to bring forth the message. The spirit took me into a prophetic mode and I began to declare and decree over the country; over the city; over the nation. Several lives were blessed by a prophetic word as well. God was good, as I began to hit the mark, thousands of people were saved and gave their life to Christ Jesus. There were several healings. One man had thrown down his crutches and walked home freely. Many miraculous signs and wonders had been done at the crusade. However, I could not stop my mind from drifting, as I thought about Mama Gloria's death and the family gathering together at the church, that I had founded in San Bernardino. They were celebrating Mama Gloria's home going, while I was halfway around the world. I knew some of them, my brothers and sisters, would never forgive me for not eulogizing Mama as they had expected. What a price to pay for the high calling that was on my life. **Moving right along…**

The crusade was successful and it was one of the most exciting ministerial events of my life. God allowed me to minister to over 40,000 people and thousands had come to the saving knowledge of Jesus. As the plane landed in Singapore, we were blessed to layover for about 18 hours; where we enjoyed the exquisite food of the region, served on banana leaves. It was, I believe, one of the cleanest cities I had ever seen.

A Long Road Well Traveled

The Kingdom of God Apostolic and Prophetic Ministries International now has branches all over the world. We have affiliates in Nigeria with Dr. Fred Okanami who had become a son, that represented 23 branches. Nigeria was the first African nation I had visited. When I touched the deep rich soil of the Motherland, it was an awe-inspiring experience. Between the Yoruba and the Igbo people, in the southern region, we were celebrated like long- lost children who had found their way home.

I remember being taken to one of the King's palaces for an introduction. He was a charming young Muslim of about 23 years, who talked to me through an interpreter. As we entered the palace, we walked down a long hallway. I looked around and observed that there was about 30 Chiefs sitting on one side, dressed in the traditional African regalia, and on the opposite side, there sat about 20 Kings. As I approached the throne, I stopped and carefully followed the directions of my host and son, Dr. Fred Okamami. Then all of a sudden, a loud stirring voice erupted from the throne. "American man. What do you want in my country?", was the question. Immediately, I replied, "You called me, "American man", but I am a son of the soil who has come home. My ancestors came from this continent. Some were sold by warring tribes, and others were captured along the shore." I continued to say, "I do not know if my ancestors were from Togo, Ghana, South Africa, Kenya, Ethiopia, or even here from Nigeria. But I am a son of the soil." The place erupted with a pounding of the staffs on the floor of the assembly. The king went on to state, "Young man, as long as you are in the country, you are a special guest. Welcome home," he smiled.

Dr. Fred looked at me in amazement as these words thundered from the very depths of my soul. The songs of my ancestors seemed to echo throughout my being as I began to imagine their cries in the cotton fields as they sang, Kum By Ya My Lord. They dreamed dreams long ago of once again being emancipated on the shores of this vibrant continent. It was like Kunta Kente being told, he was now Toby and because of his refusal to be Toby, he was whipped repeatedly and ultimately his foot was cut off. He finally surrendered and said, "I am Toby", as he fell unconsciously into oblivion.

As we traveled throughout Lagos, Warri, the Plateau's of Jos and Edo State, Nigeria I was asked to preach at Pastor Academy's church. And when I did I appeared on nationwide television throughout the region. I vividly remember standing on the bridge one day above the Niger River, contemplating the goodness of God as tears of joy, and pain simultaneously dropped into the flowing river of my homeland.

Back in America things were going well. We had placed Pastor Sat Vender and his wife, Josephine Sandu over the Sacramento church. The prototype of our vision was now being manifested in practicality. The Sacramento Church of All Nations, consisted of Apostle Wilma Brooks and Apostle Marlin Lestrick. There were two Apostles, the Prophetess Diane Lestrick, two Evangelists, Josephine and Janet, and David Duke as the Master Teacher. The leadership was dynamic and second to none.

Those of you who have embraced the Kingdom of God, its concepts and formula, must now walk it out in practicality. The fivefold ministry with its Kingdom ideology will turn the church upside down. Those sectarian houses of worship, which we now see are so far away from the pattern of God and its blueprint, are subject to fall. The Apostle Paul writes in 1ˢᵗ Corinthians, Chapter 3; "As the wise master builder we must be careful how we build there upon". We have chosen to follow the letter to the best of our ability with the rhema word and revelation. We must take this understanding into different cities and establish governmental authority. The Bishops are surrogate fathers who must surrender to Apostolic authority.

While in Ohio, we installed a Bishop under Apostle Christopher Hal. Then in Riverside, CA, we installed two Bishops under Apostle Joseph Sims, my father in the Lord. In Sacramento, we installed Bishop Claudia Marshall under yours truly, Apostle Michael P. Sterling. In Liberia, West Africa we installed, Bishop Emanuel Sesay. In Los Angeles, county we installed Bishop Terry Redmond, another son of mine.

It's time for the church to come into divine order according to the Word of God. There has been a paradigm shift with a new wine and a new wine skin. 1ˢᵗ Corinthians 12:28 states, "And God hath set some in the church, first apostles, secondarily prophets, thirdly teachers, after that miracles, then gifts of healings, helps, governments, diversities of tongues". My question to you, the reader, is if these are the set men in the church where are the pastors and evangelist? Where are the bishops, and elders? I tell you they are there, right in front of your eyes. But to see it you must have a regional mindset. Ephesus was a region. Crete was a region. California is a region. Nigeria is a region. Liberia is a region.

If you look carefully at the New Testament Letters, you will see that Timothy, who was a son under Apostle Paul, was installed as a Bishop over the churches in Ephesus. And Titus, who was also a son was installed as a Bishop over the Isle of Crete. Note: The New Strong's Exhaustive Concordance of The Bible, page 113:

BISHOP

> If a man desire the office of a bishop ... 1Timothy 3:1
>
> A bishop then must be blameless, the ... 1Timothy 3:1-2
>
> ordained the first bishop of the... 2Ti s
>
> For a bishop must be blameless, as the...Titus 1:7
>
> Ordained the first bishop of the...Titus
>
> The Shepherd and Bishop of our souls...1Peter 2:25

This has been my life story. The coming of age of Michael P. Sterling. Nothing is fabricated, exaggerated or embellished for entertainment purposes. It's all true, and it yet continues. Believe it or not this is Part 1, and I'm living out Part 2.

AND WHAT HAPPENED WAS...

RESOURCES

By Dr. Michael Paul Sterling, Apostle of God Founder & Visionary – Kingdom of God Apostolic & Prophetic Ministries International

- •Upon This Rock: Revival of the Five-Fold Ministry $20.00
- •Five-Fold Ministry Workbook $20
- •School of the Prophets Workbook $20.00
- •School of the Apostles Workbook $20.00
- •Christian Counseling Workbook $20.00
- •Basic Theology New Testament Survey $20.00

Telephone Number: 951-675-7201

Email Us at: Apostle.Sterling11@gmail.com

Visit Our Website: www.kogapmi5fold.com

PHOTO ARCHIVES
OF MICHAEL PAUL
STERLING

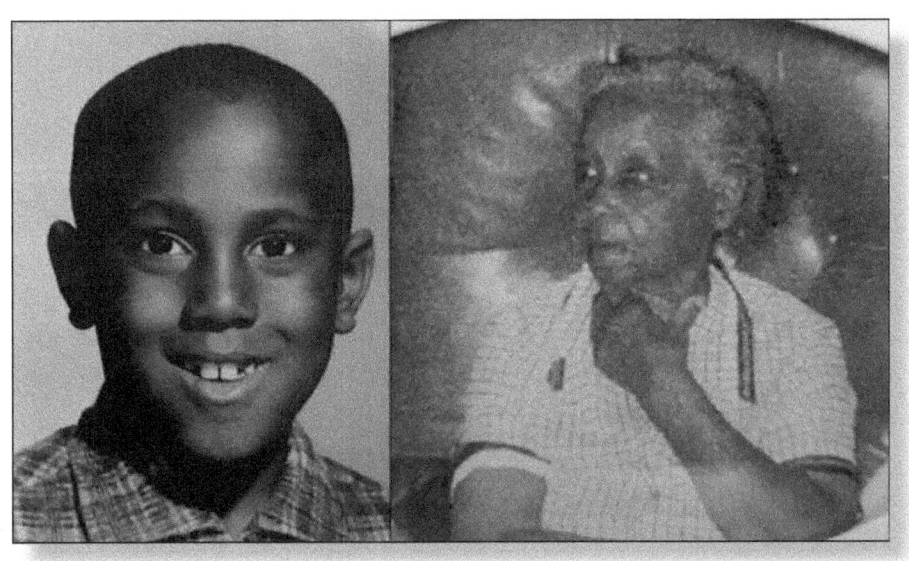

Michael Paul Sterling Age 5, Bessie Parthenia McDowell Michael's
Prayer Warrior & Intercessor

Bishop Claudia Marshall & Apostle Marlin Lestrick RIP &
Apostle Sterling Apostle Sterling

Kingdom of God Bible College Graduation

Bishop Emanuel Seasay & Prophetess Jane Brown
(Liberia, West Africa)

Bishop Emanuel Seasay

Kingdom of God Apostolic & Prophetic Ministries International

Mother of Zion Banquet

Apostle Sterling Christian Academy Liberia – West Africa
Overseer, Bishop Emanual Seasay

www.ingramcontent.com/pod-product-compliance
Lightning Source LLC
Chambersburg PA
CBHW051143120626
46547CB00012B/927